Death and Inheritance:

The Islamic Way

A Handbook of Rules Pertaining to the deceased

Being a Translation of

AHKAM-E-MAYYIT

By

Dr. Muhammad Abdul Hai 'Arifi

Translated by

Professor Muhammad Shameem

KITAB BHAVAN

New Delhi-2 [India]

KITAB BHAVAN
Publishers, Exporters & Importers
1784, Kalan Mahal, Darya Ganj
New Delhi - 110 002 [India]

Phones : *3274686, 3263383*
Telex : *31-63106 ALI IN*
Fax : *91-11-3263383*

ISBN 81-7151-200-3

First Print in India 1995

Fonts : Bookman — 11pt.

Laser Typesetting at:
Laser Track
1784, Kalan Mahal, Darya Ganj
New Delhi-110 002 [India]

Published by:
Nusrat Ali Nasri for Kitab Bhavan
1784, Kalan Mahal, Darya Ganj
New Delhi - 110 002 [India]

Printed in India at:
Seema Offset Press
Chooriwalan,
Delhi - 110 006 [India]

AHKAM-E-MAYYIT

by

Dr. Muhammad Abdul Hai 'Arifi
Written in Conjunction with

Maulana Muhammad Yusuf Ludhianawi
Madarsah Islamiyya Arabiyyah Binnoriah
New Town, Karachi

Maulana Subhan Mahmood Sahib
Shaikhul-Hadith
Jamia Darul-Uloom Karachi.

Mufti Abdul Rauf Sukkhurwi
Naib Mufti, Jamia Darul-Uloom, Karachi.

Muhammad Rafi Usmani
President Darul-Uloom Karachi

Translated by
Muhammad Shameem

TRANSLATOR'S NOTE

The author has himself answered a large number of possible questions that may arise in varying situations. However, should there be other problems peculiar to an area which need juristic solution, one may write to Maulana Mufti Muhammad Rafi Usmani.

The present translation was made at the instance of Hadrat Maulana Muhammad Taqi Usmani and was completed under his generous guidance. All credit for whatever good is found in the rendering goes to him, may Allah make his presence among us widely beneficial. As for errors, they are mine. May Allah forgive me for my shortcomings and accept my humble effort in His way. May Allah also bless the readers of this English version of *Ahkam-i-Mayyit* with a born - again view of life, particularly those of them who elect to suggest improvements in its presentation.

Finally, I do not wish to be ungrateful to my family, Shamail and Sadeem and their mother, who made it possible for me to devote my time to this and similar other works in the way of Allah. I pray for them - may Allah grant them the best of *Dunya* and *Akhirah*.

What could I have done unless Allah had enabled me to do it?

Muhammad Shameem

INTRODUCTION

DEATH AND INHERITANCE: THE ISLAMIC WAY is the English version of *Ahkam-e-Mayyit* originally written in Urdu by Dr. Abdul Hai 'Arifi رحمة الله عليه, highly revered spiritual master in this part of the world and an authorized deputy of the great Maulana Ashraf Ali of Thana, India. This is an indispensable handbook of rules and regulations governing important aspects of death among Muslims. The purpose is to bring basic information on what has to be done in the light of the teachings of the Holy Prophet صلى الله عليه وسلم when death approaches near, which it takes place and all that follows in its wake. Since Muslims who are unaware of the correct conduct in this respect are likely to remain deprived of rewards from Allah.

For Brother Muhammad Shameem who has prepared the present English version this has been an exercise in love and sacrifice. He has set aside an earlier translation he had already completed from the second unrevised edition during his stay abroad. Since his return, he has done it all over, again to bring the subject out in its most authentic form. May Allah bless him for his effort in the way of Allah and make it beneficial for Muslims who read English in many parts of the world. ***Amin.***

Muhammad Taqi Usmani

Contents

CHAPTER I

On Sickness, Medical Treatmnent and Visiting the Sick

Sayings and Prayers of the Holy Prophet ﷺ

Every Disease has a Cure

Sayyidna Jabir, may Allah be pleased with him, narrates that the Holy Prophet صلى الله عليه وسلم said:

عن جابر رضى الله عنه أن رسول الله صلى الله عليه وسلم قال: إن لكلّ داء دواء، فإذا أصيب دواء الداء برئ بإذن الله،

"For every disease, there is a cure. When medicine matches the disease, the patient gets cured by the will of Allah."

Sayyidna Abi Al-Darda', may Allah be pleased with him, reports that the Holy Prophet صلى الله عليه وسلم said:

عن أبى الدرداء رضى الله عنه أن رسول الله صلى الله عليه وسلم قال:

إن الله أنزلَ الداء والدواء، وجعل لكل داء دواء، فتداووا، ولا تداوَوا بحرام.

"Allah Almighty sent down the disease and the cure both. And then, He made for every disease a (matching) cure. So, seek medical treatment, but not by what is forbidden."

Medical Treatment: Concern and Caution

When indisposed, the Holy Prophet صلى الله عليه وسلم

would himself take medicine and ask people to do the same. He said:

يا عباد اللّه! تداووا، فإنّ اللّه لم يضع داء إلا وضع له شفاءً، إلا داءً واحداً،
قالوا: يا رسول اللّه! وما هو؟ قال: الهرم. (ترمذی)

"O servants of Allah, seek medical treatment in sickness for Allah did not create a disease unless He created a cure for it - except, one disease. People asked, 'O Messenger of Allah, what is that?' He said: "Extreme old age."

The Holy Prophet صلی اللّه علیه وسلم directed the sick to consult a professionally expert physician for the treatment of their disease and instructed them to follow prescribed regimen.

He prohibited the use of unlawful (haram) things even as medicine. He said that Allah Almighty has placed no cure for us in what is forbidden.

He said:
"Collect the blessings of your health before sickness overtakes you and pick the fruits of your life before you die."

The good counsel above means that health and life should be regarded as a wonderful opportunity. The best policy is to let these be harnessed in the pursuit of what is good and right. Otherwise, nothing can be accomplished in sickness or in death.

ATTITUDE TO DEATH

Remember Frequently, Welcome Ultimately

Sayyidna Abu Hurayrah رضی اللّه عنه narrates that the Holy Prophet صلی اللّه علیه وسلم said:

عن أبى هريرة رضى الله عنه قال: قال رسول الله ﷺ: أكثروا ذكر هاذم اللذات الموت . (رواه الترمذى)

"Frequently revive the remembrance of that terminator of enjoyments - the death."

Sayyidna 'Abdullah ibn 'Umar رضى الله عنه narrates that the Holy Prophet صلى الله عليه وسلم said:

«تحفة المؤمن الموت» (شعب الإيمان للبيهقى)

"Death is a gift for the true Muslim."

Wishing and Praying for Death is Forbidden

Sayyidna Anas رضى الله عنه has narrated that the Holy Prophet صلى الله عليه وسلم said:

"Let none of you wish for death because of some pain or harm that befalls him. Then, should one become totally unable to do anything about it, only then he should say: "O Allah, keep me alive as long as life is good for me and take me away when death is better for me."

The reward of deeds during sickness is Like what it was in health

As reported by Sayyidna Abu Musa al-Ash'ari رضى الله عنه the Holy Prophet صلى الله عليه وسلم said:

عن أبى موسى قال: «إذا مرض العبد أو سافر كتب له بمثل ما كان يعمل مقيماً».

"When a servant of Allah becomes sick, or goes on travel (and becomes, because of this sickness or travel, unable to carry out his usual acts of worship and remembrance of Allah) his deeds are recorded as if he was continuing to do what he did when at home and in health."

Suffering can bring higher ranks with Allah

Narrted Muhammad ibn Khalid As-Sulamiyy from his father, and he from his grandfather, that the Holy Prophet صلى الله عليه وسلم said:

عن محمد بن خالد السلميّ عن أبيه عن جده قال: قال رسول الله صلى الله عليه وسلم «إن العبد إذا سبقت له من الله منزلة لم يبلغها بعمله ابتلاه الله فى جسده أو ماله أو فى ولده ثم صبّره على ذلك حتى يبلّغه المنزلة التى سبقت له من الله » (أبو داود)

"When a high rank from Allah stands ordained for the servant, something he can never achieve by his deed, Allah puts him to suffering through his body or his belongings or through his children, after which, He enables him to be patient over all that until when he is raised to the high station which had already been determined for him by Allah."

Sayyidna Abu Sa'eed al-Khudri رضى الله عنه reports that the Holy Prophet صلى الله عليه وسلم said:

عن أبى سعيد عن النبى صلى الله عليه وسلم قال «ما يصيب المسلم من نصب ولا وصب ولا همّ ولا حزن ولا أذى ولا غم حتى الشوكة يشاكها إلا كفّر الله بها من خطاياه» (رواه البخارى و مسلم)

"Whatever of sickness or distress or anxiety or grief or pain or sorrow afflicts a true Muslim - even the pinch of a thorn - through these Allah effaces some af his sins."

Prayers in Sickness

One who recites the following *du'a (prayer)* forty times while sick, will reccive the reward equivalent to that of a *shaheed* (martyr in the way of Allah) if he dies; and if he gets cured of his disease, all his sins will be forgiven:

لاَ إِلٰهَ إِلا أَنتَ سُبْحَانَكَ إِنِّي كُنْتُ مِنَ الظَّالِمِيْنَ

There is no god but Thee. Pure art Thou. I am (but) one of the unjust.

Should one make the following *du'a*, and die, the fire of Hell will not touch him:

لا إلهَ إلا الله الله أكبر. لا إلهَ إلا الله وحده لا شريكَ له، لا إلهَ إلا الله
له الملك وله الحمد، لا إلهَ إلا الله ولا حول ولا قوة إلا بالله

"There is no god but Allah: Allah is great. There is no god but Allah: He is One - for Him there is no partner. There is no god but Allah: For Him, all power and for Him, all praise. There is no god but Allah: And there is no power and there is no strength but with Allah."

During the days of sickness, one may wish to recite the following *du'a* in all sincerity and with true spiritual longing:

اللّٰهم ارزقنى شهادة فى سبيلك، واجعل موتى ببلد رسولك.

"O Allah, bless me with martyrdom in Thy way and let my death be in the city of Thy Messenger."

VISITING THE SICK

Merits and Rewards

The Holy Prophet صلی اللہ علیہ وسلم is reported to have said that a Muslim who visits another Muslim during his sickness in the hours of the morning has seventy thousand angels praying for him right through the evening and if he makes that visit in the hours of the evening, seventy thousand angels pray for him right through the morning.

It was blessed practice of the Holy Prophet صلی اللہ علیہ وسلم that he would make it a point to visit those indisposed among his Companions.

Sayyidna Thawban رضی اللہ عنہ narrates that the Holy Prophet صلی اللہ علیہ وسلم said:

> "When a true believer visits his brother-in-faith, he is, in a way, in the garden of Paradise until his return."

Ummul-Mu'mineen Umm Salma رضی اللہ عنہا reports that the Holy Prophet صلی اللہ علیہ وسلم has said:

> "When you visit a sick person, or someone else on his death-bed, say what is good, for the angels say *'Amin'* (Amen) after what you say."

Sayyidna 'Umar رضی اللہ عنہ reports that the Holy Prophet صلی اللہ علیہ وسلم said:

> "When you go to visit a sick person, ask him to pray for you, for his prayer is like the prayer of angels."

Giving Comfort and Showing Concern

Sayyidna Abu Sa'eed al-Khudri رضى الله عنه reports that the Holy Prophet صلى الله عليه وسلم said:

> "When you visit a sick person, make him feel good about his age (that is, talk to him ahout the years ahead of him, about things that give him hope in lile). This will not cancel something that has to be, but it will please him inside his heart for sure. And this is what a visit is all about."

The blessed Companion, Sayyidna 'Abdullah ibn 'Abbas رضى الله عنه says:

> "While visiting the sick, avoiding a loud presence and staying briefly are also part of the *Sunnah*"

Fixing a day or time for visiting the sick was not part of the good way of the Holy Prophet صلى الله عليه وسلم Instead, he would go to visit the sick during the day or the night (as needed).

While making one of such visits, the Holy Prophet صلى الله عليه وسلم would go near the sick person, sit by the head of the bed and ask him how he was and how he felt.

There were occasions when he would place his blessed hand on the forehead of the sick person, then, gently moving it over his chest andf abdomen he would pray: "O Allah, help h'm get well". They were other times when he would tell the sick not to worry and that everything will, *Insha Allah*, come out right, adding once in a while the remark that their sickness will become a *Kaffarah*, an expiation - the cleanser of sins.

The Breathing of Benediction and the Prayer for the Speedy Recovery of a Sick Person

It has been reported that the Holy Prophet صلى الله عليه وسلم used to repeat the words of his prayer for the sick person three times, exactly as he did for his Companion, Sayyidna Sa'd رضى الله عنه Praying for him, he said:

"O Allah, help, Sa'd get well."

"O Allah, help, Sa'd get well."

"O Allah, help, Sa'd get well."

There were times when he would place his right hand on the forehead of the sick person or on the spot that was hurting him and say:

اللهم أذهب البأس ربَّ الناس، اشف أنت الشافى، لا شفاء إلا شفاؤك شفاءً لا يغادر سقما

"O Allah, remove pain. O Lord of men, heal - for Thou art the Healer. There is no healing except Thy healing - perfect healing that leaves no trace of disease."

Also reported from him is the following prayer:

اللهم اشفه اللهم عافِه

"O Allah, deliver him from sickness, O Allah, keep him safe and sound."

As an alternate, the visitor to the sick person may recite the following prophetic prayer seven times:

أسأل الله العظيم ربَّ العرش العظيم، أن يشفيك

"I pray to Allah, the great, the Lord of the Throne,

may He deliver you from sickness and bless you with health."

Anyone who visits a sick person, not yet destined to die, and recites this prayer, Allah Almighty will certainly remove that disease from the patient.

Sayyidna 'Uthman ibn Abi al-'Aas رضى الله عنه narrates that he complained of pain in a certain part of his body before the Holy Prophet صلى الله عليه وسلم who asked him to place his hand on the spot where he was hurting and say, *Bismillah,* three times and then say the following prayer seven times:

أعوذ بعزّة الله وقدرته من شرما أجد وأحاذر

"I seek refuge in the great might of Allah, and His powerful reach against the evil I face and dread."

Sayyidna 'Uthman رضى الله عنه said that he did just that and Allah Almighty removed that pain from him. As narrated by Sayyidna 'Abdullah ibn 'Abbas رضى الله عنه the Holy Prophet صلى الله عليه وسلم recited the following prayer and entrusted his grandsons, Sayyidna Hasan and Husain رضى الله عنه to the ultimate protection of Allah Almighty:

أعيذ بكلمات الله لتامّة من شركل شيطان وهامّة ومن كل عين لامّة

"I give you under the protection of the most perfect words of Allah against the evil of every Satan and every hurting creature and against every evil eye."

And he said: "Your patriarch, Ibrahim used to breathe benediction on his sons, Isma'il and Ishaq, by reciting these words."

For anyone suffering from a wound or abscess or

some other ailment, he would breathe his benediction on him while resting his forefinger pointed on the ground and reciting the following prayer:

بسم الله تربة أرضنا بريقة بعضنا يشفى سقيمنا باذن ربنا

> "I begin with the name of Allah. This dust of our land mingled with saliva from some of us is there to cure our sick people by the leave of our Lord."

following which he would move that finger over the ailing spot.

Ummul-Mu'mineen Sayyidah 'A'ishah رضى الله عنها narrates that the Holy Prophet صلى الله عليه وسلم when he himself got indisposed, used to seek the benediction of Allah's words by reciting the *Mu'awwidhat,* that is, the last three verses of the Holy Qur'an, being the Surahs Al-Ikhlas, Al-Falaq and An-Naas. After having recited these Surahs of Protection, he would blow his breath on the palms of his hands and then move them gently over his body.

Later when the Holy Prophet صلى الله عليه وسلم was afflicted with the disease that took away his blessed life, Sayyidah 'Aishah رضى الله عنها, says that she used to recite these very Surahs, through which he used to seek benediction, following which she would hold his hand and help him move it over his body.

Note: The three Surahs mentioned above are:

سورة الاخلاص

Suratul-Ikhlas

قُل هُوَ اللّٰهُ أحَدٌ. اَللّٰهُ الصَّمَدُ لَمْ يَلِدْ وَلَمْ يُولَدْ. وَلَمْ يَكُنْ لَهُ كُفُوًا أحد

In the name of Allah

The All-Merciful, The Very-Merciful.

Say: 'He is Allah, One, Allah, the Independent, Who has not begotten, and has not been begotten, and equal to Him is not any one.'

سورة الفلق

Suratul-Falaq

قُلْ اَعُـوذُ بِرَبِّ الفَلَقِ . مِنْ شَـرِّ مَـا خَلَقَ . وَمِنْ شَـرِّ غَـاسِقٍ اِذَا وَقَـبَ . وَمِنْ
شَرِّالنَّفّٰثٰتِ فِى العُقَدِ . وَمِنْ شَرِّ حَاسِدٍ اِذَا حَسَدَ .

In the name of Allah

The All-Merciful, The Very-Merciful.

Say: 'I take refuge with the Lord of the Daybreak from the evil of what He has created, from the evil of darkness when it gathers; from the evil of the women who blow on knots, from the evil of an envier when he envies.'

سورة الناس

Suratun-Naas

قُلْ أَعُوذُ بِرَبِّ النَّاسِ . مَلِكِ النَّاسِ . إِلٰهِ النَّاسِ . مِنْ شَرِّ الْوَسْوَاسِ الْخَنَّاسِ . الَّذِي يُوَسْوِسُ فِي صُدُورِ النَّاسِ . مِنَ الْجِنَّةِ وَالنَّاسِ .

In the name of Allah

The All-Merciful, The Very-Merciful.

Say: 'I take refuge with the Lord of men, The King of men, the Allah of men, from the evil of the slinking whisperer who whispers in the breasts of Jinn and men.'

After having recited these, one should gently blow his breath on the palms of his hands and move them over one's body from the head down to the feet. This should be done three times.

CHAPTER II

The Time of Death

When signs of death start showing up

The blessed Companion, Sayyidna Abu Sa'id al-Khudri رضى الله عنه narrates that the Holy Prophet ﷺ said:

«لقّنوا موتاكم : لا إله إلاّ الله»

"Prompt the dying among you to say: La Ilaha Illallah: (I declare that) There is no god but Allah."

(Sahih Muslim)

The blessed Companion, Sayyidna Ma'qil ibn Yasar رضى الله عنه narrates that the Holy Prophet ﷺ said:

«إقرءوها عند موتاكم، يعنى (يٰس)»

"Recite it near the dying among you, that is, Yasin."

(Musnad Ahmad, Sunnan Abu Dawood, Ibn Majah).

In the agony of death

Turn the face of the dying person towards the Qiblah. Let him or her make the following prayer:

اَللّٰهُمَّ اغْفِرْلِىْ وَارْحَمْنِىْ وَاَلْحِقْنِىْ بِالرَّفِيْقِ الْاَ عْلٰى

"O Allah, forgive me and have mercy on me and have me join higher companions".

(Tirmidhi)

Rulings:

1. Soon after the signs of death become obvious, make the dying person lie on his back with the Qiblah on his right. Turn the face slightly towards the Qiblah, raise the head a little by placing a pillow or some other head-rest, in which case also, the dying person will be considered as facing the Qiblah. (Thanwi, Travellers to the Other World)

But, leave the dying person as is, if he feels uncomfortable while being made to face the Qiblah. One should sit down close by and let someone say loudly:

اَشْهَدُ اَنْ لاَّ اِلٰهَ اِلاَّ اللّٰهُ وَحْدَهٗ لاَ شَرِيْكَ لَهٗ وَاَشْهَدُ اَنَّ مُحَمَّدًا عَبْدُهٗ وَرَسُوْلُهٗ

"Ashhadu alla ilaha illallahu wahdahu la sharika lahu wa ashhadu anna Muhammadan 'abduhu wa rasuluh."

"I bear witness that there is no god but Allah. He is one - there is no partner in Him; and I bear witness that Muhammad is His servant and His messenger."

Given his condition, do not ask him to recite the *kalimah,* for that is a time of great trial - who knows what he might say under stress.

(Bahishti Zewar)

2. After the dying person has recited the *kalimah* once, leave it at that. Do not try to make him say the *kalimah* non-stop in an effort to see that he breathes his last while reciting it. For,the purpose is simply to make sure that the last words he says should be the *kalimah.* It is not at all necessary that the recitation of the *kalimah* continues right through the last breath.

However, should he return to the mundane, to the ordinary concerns of life, start reciting the *kalimalh.* When he, taking the cue, recites it, then stop and be silent.

3. When breath loses its momentum and starts heaving faster and legs sag down unable to stay up and the nose-top turns aside and the temples collapse inwards, take these signs to be the certain knock of death. At this time, start reciting the *kalimah* in a raised voice.

(Bahishti Zewar)

4. Reciting the *Surah Yasin* lightens the hardship of death. Recite it sitting on the side of his head, or anywhere else near the body, or ask someone else to do it.

5. At a time such as this, say nothing which diverts his attention to the concerns of worldly life, for this is the time to leave the mortal world and the inevitable time to be present in the majestic Court of Allah Almighty. Do and say what makes his heart turn away from the concerns of the mortal world and makes it tilt towards the thoughts of his Creator, for it is here that the well-being of the dying lies. At a time like this, bringing his children and family members before him, or anyone else he loved most, or to remind him of things or people in a nostalgic manner causing the dying person to be swamped in the thoughts of loves lost, is a terrible thing to do to him. It is not nice that he says farewell to his life in the world so bound by its fond memories.

(Bahishti Zewar)

6. If, at the time of death, some unfortunate remark bordering on *kufr* (the denial of Faith) escapes

the lips of the dying person, feel or say nothing about it. Instead, take it to be a slip of his reason under the stress of approaching death. When man loses his reason, what he does stands forgiven. Keep praying that Allah Almighty forgives him.

(Bahishti Zewar)

7. When death comes, all concerned say:

اِنَّا لِلّٰهِ وَاِنَّا اِلَيْهِ رَاجِعُوْنَ ،

"Surely, to Allah we belong and to Him we are to return."

and make the following prayer:

اَللّٰهُمَّ اْجُرْنِى فِىْ مُصِيْبَتِىْ وَاخْلُفْ لِىْ خَيْرًا مِّنْهَا ، (ترمذی)

"O Allah, help me in my distress and replace it for me with what is better."

(Tirmidhi)

8. When death is final, take a strip of cloth, wide enough to pass under the chin, bring it on to the head, tie a knot, then close the eyes gently and pray:

«بِسْمِ اللّٰهِ وَعَلٰى مِلَّةِ رَسُوْلِ اللّٰهِ، اَللّٰهُمَّ يَسِّرْ عَلَيْهِ اَمْرَهُ وَ سَهِّلْ عَلَيْهِ مَا بَعْدَهُ وَاَسْعِدْهُ بِلِقَائِكَ وَ اجْعَلْ مَا خَرَجَ اِلَيْهِ خَيْرًا مِّمَّا خَرَجَ عَنْهُ

"I begin with the name of Allah while being faithful to the religion of His Messenger. O Allah, make his matter easy on him and let equally easy be what he shall face after that and make him the blessed beholder of Thy sighting, and make that to which he has departed better than what he has departed from."

(al-Durr al-Mukhtar)

9. Then, straighten hands and feet, bring toes of the feet close together and tie them with a strip of cloth. Then, throw a sheet over the dead body and place it on a cot or a flat wooden bunk—do not leave lying on the ground. It is advisable to place some weight on the stomach lest it inflates. Anyone needing cleaning up through shower, or a woman in menstruation or parturition, should not be allowed near the dead body.

(al-Durr al-Mukhtar Musafiran-i-Akhirat & Bahishiti Zewar)

Now, inform relatives and friends of the deceased so that they all can participate in the funeral prayers for him.

10. Some incense, if available, (such as oblibanum *[luban]* or frankincense) may be placed near the deceased.

11. Reciting the Holy Qur'an near the deceased, before washing of the body, is not correct.

(Bahishti Zewar)

12. All funeral arrangements including the shrouding of the dead body, have to be made very quickly. Start with locating a grave-site and the preparation of the grave. Collect everything needed for the stages of washing, shrouding, funeral and interment, a list of which follows later on.

13. If a person dies on a Friday, it is better to make all arrangements and bury the deceased before the *Jumu'ah* Congregational *Salah*. Holding on to the prepared body with the thought that there will be a lot of participants in the *Janazah Salah* after *Jumu'ah* is *makruh*.

(Shami, Bahishti Gauhar)

Rulings for Special Situations

A) FOR ONE WHO DIES IN A STATE OF *IHRAM*

For anyone who dies in a state of *Ihram,* while on a Hajj or 'Umrah visit, the arrangements for his funeral, washing and shrouding would be done like all others because his *Ihram* ends with death. Therefore, covering the head and using perfume will remain valid for him as is done for all Muslims.

(Fath al-Mulhim. p. 441, v.3 Shami, p 803, v.1)

B) FOR ONE WHO DIES AT SEA

If a person dies on a ship or boat at sea and land be far enough to cause the dead body being spoiled, then it is necessary that washing of the body, shrouding and the *salah* of *janazah* (prayer for the deceased) be carried out immediately, following which the body should be wrapped and tied nicely in the shroud and lowered into the waters with added weight, stone or iron, so that it sinks down.

In case the waterfront is not that far and there is no danger of the dead body being spoiled, perform the *salah* of *janazah,* keep the body and bury it on the land when you reach there.

(Bahishti Gauhar and 'Alamgiri)

C) WASHING AND SHROUDING: HOW TO HANDLE A DEAD DISBELIEVER

Upto this point, all rulings relate to the dead body of a Muslim. If the deceased be a *kafir* (disbeliever) and his corpse has to be disposed of, or if, from among the relatives of a Muslim deceased, there happens to be a *kafir,* then the rulings governing such situations are being given below:

1. If the dead man be an apostate *(murtadd)*, that is a Muslim who turned *kafir* and died a *kafir*, in which case, there will be no washing, shrouding and *janazah salah* for him. He will not be given a funeral the way Muslims do, nor any effort will be made to deliver his dead body to his *kafir* clan. Instead his dead body should be buried straight away.

(al-Durr al-Mukhtar and Shami)

2. For a *kafir* who is not an apostate but happened to be a *kafir* all along and died in the same state, it is better that his corpse be left for his cohorts, if one is available, so that he can bury or dispose of the corpse at his discretion. If there be no relative of the diseased from among his cohorts, then, it is certainly not obligatory on his Muslim relatives to take care of his washing, shrouding and burial, however, the minimum permissible for them is that they should avoid following the Muslim way of preparing and burying the deceased as shown by the Holy Prophet صلى الله عليه وسلم and, instead of that, they should wash the dead body, wrap it up in some cloth and bury him without observing the rules provided for the burial of the dead body of a Muslim.

(al-Durr al-Mukhar and Shami)

3. If all relatives of a Muslim deceased happen to be *kafir*, his funeral and shrouding, his *salah* of *janazah* and burial are *fard 'al-Kifayah* on Muslims, that is, if some Muslims discharge this obligation, others will be absolved of it. As such, the dead body of the person under reference should not be handed over to *kafir* relatives. The *kafir* relatives do not have the right to even wash the dead body.

(al-Durr al-Mukhtar and Shami)

4. When burying a Muslim, his kafir relative should not be allowed to enter the grave.

(al-Durr al-Mukhtar and Shami)

5. If a Muslim male dies at a place where another Muslim male is not available, nor his wife who could wash his dead body, instead, there be a situation of compulsion. Under this dilemma, Muslim women should explain the method of washing the dead body to some *kafir* male because it is not permissible for a woman, other than the wife, to wash a male dead body. The *kafir* male, therefore, will wash the dead body following which Muslim women can offer the *salah* of *janazah* for the deceased.

(Shami, p. 833, v. 1)

Let there be no mourning and wailing over the dead body of a Muslim

Sayyidna 'Abdullah ibn 'Umar رضى الله عنه narrates that the blessed Companion, Sayyidna Sa'd ibn 'Ubadah رضى الله عنه was once very sick and the Holy Prophet صلى الله عليه وسلم came to visit him along with some of his Companions. When he came in, he found his condition very grave as there was a crowd of anxious people round him. May be he was dismayed or simply anxious when he asked, 'Passed away?' People said, 'No, not yet.' Seeing him in this condition, the Holy Prophet صلى الله عليه وسلم was in tears. When people saw him in that state, they too started weeping. He said:

> 'Listen to me, O people, and listen well. Allah Almighty certainly does not apprehend the weeping eye and the hurting heart, for a servant of Allah has no control over these.' Then, pointing to the tongue, he added, 'But, a mistake made

by this, (that is, on intentional mourning and wailing,) He punishes; and on reciting انّا لله وانّا اليه راجعون (*Inna lillahi wa inna ilaihi raji'un.* To Allah we belong and to Him we are to return), and on raising hands of prayer and on seeking of His forgiveness, He bestows His mercy.'

(Sahih al-Bukhari and Sahih Muslim)

Ummul-Mu'mineen, Sayyidah Umm Salma رضى الله عنها narrates that the Holy Prophet صلى الله عليه وسلم came to the house at the time of her husband, Abu Salma's death. His eyes were left open. He closed them and said: 'When the spirit is taken out of the body, sight goes with it, therefore, eyes should better be closed after death.' Hearing this from him, members of the berieved family broke into loud wailing and, under the stress of their sorrow, words started escaping their mouths, words that were, in effect, curses against their own persons; whereupon, he said, 'When you make a prayer, pray for what is good for you. This is because angels say *Amin* (Amen) after what you say.' Then, he prayed in the words translated below:

"O Allah, forgive Abu Salma. Raise his rank among Thy servants who have been gifted with guidance from Thee. And, in his place, let Thee alone be the guardian of those he has lelt behind. And O Lord of the Worlds, forgive us, and him, and make his grave wide and lighted."

(Sahih Muslim)

Weeping for the Deceased is Permissible

The Holy Prophet صلى الله عليه وسلم has declared that saying انّا لله وانّا اليه راجعون, (*Inna lillahi wa inna ilaihi raji 'un:* To Allah we belong and to him we are to return), and being content with the Divine will are part of his way.

Eyes in tears and the heart in pain should not stop one from following this way. This is the reason why he was, among the entire creation of Allah, the most content with Allah's will and the most-devoting to His praise, yet, so it was that he wept with tears when his dear son, Ibrahim died. Despite this love and paternal attachment and the great sense of loss that shook him, his heart was full of gratitude for Allah, all set to say yes to His Will and Decree, and his words spelt nothing but the remembrance of his Lord and nothing but the glorification of His name.

(Zad al-Ma'ad)

Kissing the Deceased

After the deceased has been given the required *Ghusl* (bath, washing), it is permissible to kiss the deceased under intense desire to express one's love or personal devotion as it was with the Holy Prophet صلى الله عليه وسلم when he kissed Sayyidna 'Uthman ibn Maz'un رضى الله عنه and wept. Very similar to this, the noble Companion, Sayyidna Abu Bakr As-Siddiq رضى الله عنه kissed the forehead of the Holy Prophet صلى الله عليه وسلم after his departure from this mortal world.

(Zad al-Ma'ad)

All Funeral Arrangements Should be Swift

Sayyidna Hasin ibn Wahwah رضى الله عنه narrates that the Messenger of Allah صلى الله عليه وسلم came to visit Sayyidna Talha ibn Bara' رضى الله عنه when he was sick. Seeing his condition very grave, he said to other people around, 'I feel the time of his death has just about come. If it does come to pass, I should be informed and funeral arrangements be made with dispatch, for it is apropriate that the dead body of a Muslim should be left to stay amidst his family members for long.'

(Sunnan Abi Dawud)

Sayyidna 'Abdullah ibn 'Umar رضى الله عنه narrates that he heard the Holy Prophet صلى الله عليه وسلم saying:

'When one of your men dies, do not keep him in the house for long. Make haste in taking him to the grave and in burying him'.

(Baihaqi, Shu'abul-lman)

Who pays for the Funeral and Shrouding?

Preparing the deceased for his or her last journey involves expenses. These include *ghusl* (the required bathing of the body), incense, *kafan* (shroud), *janazah* (the funeral bier with prepared and shrouded body) and *dafn* (the burial, interment). Details as to who pays for these are given below:

1. If the deceased has left behind cash or assests in his possession and it is enough to cover payment foı these services, then this will be paid from the inheritance of the deceased.

(Shami)

But, should someone pay for all these expenses out of his free will, then, this too is perfectly all right. The person doing this could be an inheriter of the deceased, or a total stranger, it does not matter. However, it is necessary that he should be sane and adult.

2. The payment of all funeral arrangements for the deceased who left nothing behind is the responsibility of the person on whom it was necessary

to pay for the maintenance cost *(nafaqah)* of the deceased during his life-time. If the maintenance cost of the deceased, during his life-time, was jointly obligated, Shari'ah-wise, on more than one individual (such as inheritors etc.), the payment of funeral expenses will also be jointly obligated on them. In other words, all inheritors should be asked to contribute in accordance with their shares in the inheritance of the deceased, that is, in case this deceased person had died leaving behind some assests of value, then, the person who was to inherit more from the assests would have been the one to pay more in that ratio; and the person who was to receive less from the assets would have been the one to pay less for the funeral costs in that ratio.

(Shami, p, 810, v.1 and Mufidul-Warithin, p. 36)

3. If the deceased be a married woman, the expenses on her funeral arrangements will be the responsibility of her husband, irrespective of the fact that the woman has, or has not, left any inheritance.

(al-Durr al-Mukhtar, Shami, Imdadul-Fatawa)

4. If the deceased left no assets behind and there is no one alive on whom it would have been obligatory to pay for his maintenance, then, it is the bounden duty of an Islamic government to pay for the funeral expenses from the *Baitul-Mal* (Public Treasury).

In case the government too fails to discharge this obligation, then, the crucial responsibility falls on all such Muslims who come to know about such a deceased person and it is they who should share the funeral expenses on the deceased as *fard 'alalkifayah* (an obligation, if discharged by some, will absolve others). If none of those, who have come to know of the incident of such death, do so, all of them will incur the sin of abandoning an obligation.

5. If someone, in the absence of the inheritors of the deceased, and without permission from them or the government, spends on his own to take care of the funeral expenses hoping that he will be ultimately reimbursed by the inheritors later on, then, he faces two situations. If, later on, the inheritors pay him back willingly, then, there is no problem and things work out fine. But, should he think of forcing them to pay back what he had spent, then, he cannot do this, because this was a favour he himself elected to do and the inheritors are not responsible for it.

(Shami)

6. The rules governing the funeral arrangements given here relate to expenses which are allowed by the Shari'ah of Islam, the details of which appear later. There are a lot of customs ignorant people have invented on their own. No expenses on these come under the orbit of standard rules. Anyone who spends extra will be solely responsible for all such extra expenses.

(Shami)

Ruling:

It should be remembered well that the obligation of paying *zakah* is not liquidated by using *zakah* funds to cover the funeral expenses on someone deceased, even if the person deceased be a pauper, because to make a correct and valid payment of *zakah*, it is necessary that the amount be given to some needy person making sure that it has gone in his possession as its owner. As far as a dead person is concerned, 'it' cannot become the owner of something, or for that matter, possess it.

However, if *zakah* is given to a needy person, delivered in his possession as its owner without any condition, the needy person may, on his own accord and pleasure, spend it on the funeral arrangements for someone. In this case, such a needy person will receive the reward for having taken care of a funeral and the *zakah* payer's *zakah* will stand 'paid' as due.

FUNERAL AND SHROUDING

A Complete List of Things Needed

The detailed method of giving *Ghusl* and *Kafan* to the deceased, the *Janazah* and *Dafn* along with necessary ruling will appear later as required, but there are things needed in this whole procedure, a list of which is being presented here for convenience so that these can be assembled at one time saving the trouble of running for them haphazardly. Being a simple procedure, things available in the house, provided that they are clean, can be used without having to order new ones from the market. Most of what is needed is available readily through non-profit welfare bodies which supply cloth for shrouding, make arrangements for burial and provide transport for the *janazah*. As said earlier, the use of these articles will be explained later at their appropriate place.

THINGS NEEDED FOR *GHUSL*

1. **Water containers for bathing the body.**
   As needed (even if used).

2. **A water pot with nozzle, or jug with pout.**
   As need (even if used).

3. **Wooden plank or platform board.**
   One (usually available in mosques; or some other

improvised board in which the dead body could be placed and bathed.)

4. **Clod of earth, or solidified chalk to dry up urine drops.**
   Three or five.

5. **Leaves of the *jujube* tree, *ber* or *kunar*, *Zizyphus Jujuba.***
   Two handful (ignore if nor available).

6. ***Luban,*** an aromatic gum or resin from trees, specially Boswellia *Carteri* used as incense, also called white benzoin frankincense.)
   -About 210 grains.

7. **'*Itr*, (perfume, fragrance, essence extracted from flowers, wood etc.)**
   -About 50 grains.

8. **Cotton**
   -About two ounces.

9. ***Gul Khairu,*** (Mallow-flower or the *Gilli* flower from the *Malva* or Mustard family. Common in the U.S.A. as the running or *dwarf* Mallow with yellowish flowers. Also the known stock of wallflower or the rocket. Used as organic cleanser and available in the East at apothecary stores.)
   - About four ounces (If not available, bath soap is sufficient).

10. **Camphor, *Kafur***
    - About 100 grains.

11. **Under-Wrap (a garment worn round the loins, usually cotton.)**
    — Two (If not available within the house, a cloth-piece, 1¼ yards long and about a yard wide is

sufficient for one under-wrap. This measurement applies both for a man or a woman. For two under-wraps, you may thus procure 2½ yards of cloth length with its width not being less than stated above.

12. Gloves

— Two Common latex gloves, if readily available, may be used. If not, stitch up two bags from some coarse and clean cloth, large enough to easily fit the hands, upto the wrist or the fore-arm, of the person bathing the dead body. These bags will be used as gloves. For one bag, a piece of cloth measuring 6/16 of a yard long and 3/16 wide is sufficient.

CLOTH FOR SHROUDING *(Kafan)*

13. Cotton Yardage

— For the whole shroud of a male: Yard-wide white cloth, about ten yards. For a female: 21 1/2 yards white cloth. This includes the necessary sheet-spread or *purdah* covering on the bier. Shroud cloth used for children is the same as used for adults with the difference that these use lesser yardage. So, decrease order for shroud cloth in accordance with the particular need.

OTHER FUNERAL NEEDS

14. *Janazah* Carrier

— The Bier, usually a four-legged cot. Commonly available in mosques, or with funeral service places. If not available, a simple and clean home cot is sufficient.

15. A Cradle top (for women only)

— This is a simple device placed on top of the

Janazah (bier which resembles the top of a grave, oblong and protruding upwards. This is there to place a sheet securely on to observe *purdah* for the female deceased. Known as the *Gahwarah* (Cradle) in some eastern countries, this is also readily available in mosques or funeral service places. If not available, light and thin bamboo sticks, or a tree branch may be placed on the *Janazah* and this may be covered up with a sheet

(Musafiran-i-Akhirat)

16. The Covering sheet for *janazah* - one — This is a sheet thrown over the *Janazah*. Generally available in mosques and with funeral service places. If this is not placed on the *Janazah* of a man, it makes no difference, therefore, it is not permissible to buy such a sheet from out of the inheritance of the deceased man.

However, a sheet is necessary for the *Janazah* of a woman so that she remains covered. If there is no sheet available in the house, a sheet which can be used to cover the *Janazah* of the woman should be purchased from out the inheritance of the woman, taken out after arrival at the gravesite, brought back and placed along with her inheritance at her home.

(Islah ar-Rusum, p. 170 bi Ziadat al-Idah)

This is the reason why this sheet has not been counted in the total cloth yardage needed for the shroud of a man. As for the shroud of a woman, the total of 21½ yards long and 2 yards wide sheet for the sake of convenience, otherwise, this too is not part of the *kafan* (shroud). As such, it is not necessary that it be in the same colour as the *kafan*.

(shroud)

CHAPTER III

غسل و كفن

Bathing and Shrouding

The Reward of Bathing and Shrouding the Deceased:

The Holy Prophet صلى الله عليه وسلم has said that the person who bathes the body of the deceased is as cleansed of sins as a newborn child; and the person who dresses the deceased in a shroud will be dressed with the apparel of Paradise by Allah Almighty.

Who Bathes the Deceased?

To begin with, the closest relatives of the deceased have the primary right to bathe the deceased. It is better that they do it themselves; making sure that a female deceased is bathed by a close female relative, for doing so is the last service rendered for someone dear.

(al-Durr al-Mukhtar)

The deceased can be bathed by another person as well, but bathing of the male deceased is done by a male and that of the female by a female who knows necessary rules, and is religiously observing.

(Shami)

Bathing for the deceased can be arranged by paying wages to someone, but the person who bathes the body of the deceased on wages deserves no spiritual rewards, although the taking of wages for this purpose is permissible.

(Bahishti Gauhar)

If a man dies and there be no man around to bathe the deceased, it will not be permissible for any woman, except his wife, to give that bath. This condition will hold even if the women present were *mahram* of the deceased, that is, women in the prohibited category. If the wife of the deceased is not there, women present should give *tayammum* to the deceased and skip the bath. But, should the women giving *tayammum* be non-*mahram*, that is, not in the prohibited category for the deceased, they should not touch the dead body with bare hands, instead, they should wear gloves on their hands and then give the *tayammum*.

(Bahishti Zewar).

When a husband dies, it is correct for his wife to see his face, to bathe and shroud him; but, when a wife dies, it is not correct for her husband to bathe her or to touch her body. However, seeing is correct. Also permissible is touching over the cloth, and the raising and carrying of *janazah* (bier)

(Bahishti Zewar, Musafiran-i-Akhirat).

If a boy dies, and he still be minor and non-pubert, women too can bathe his body as can men; and should a girl die, and she still be minor and non-pubert, men too can bathe her body as can women.

However, if the minor boy or girl have grown into a passionprone age, men will bathe the body of the boy and women that of the girl.

('Alamgiri).

It is better that the person bathing the deceased should be with *wudu.* (ablution).

A person in the state of *janabah* (major impurity requiring a bath) or a woman in menstruation or childbed should not give a bath to the deceased, for the bath given by those in such a state is *makrooh* (reprehensible).

(Shami, Bashishti Zewar)

Some instructions for those who bathe the body of the deceased

1. The body of the deceased is to be bathed in accordance with instructions appearing later.

2. The list of things needed for bathing should be collected and placed at hand's reach.

3. To start with bathing, prepare hot water adding, Jujube leaves. When water becomes lukewarm, use it for bathing If jujube leaves are not available, this plain lukewarm water is sufficient.

(Bahishti Zewar)

4. Do not bathe the body with water which is too hot.

(Bahishti Zewar).

5. Pots and pans available in the house can be used for bathing, even if they are already in use. It is unnecessary to order new ones for this purpose.

(Bahishti Zewar)

6. The place selected to bathe the body should not be such as would hold water which spills down in the process of bathing, otherwise it would cause inconvenience to those moving around.

(Bahishti Zewar)

7. The place where the bath is being given should

be shut out of public sight with a curtain or purdah.

8. Do not comb the hair of the deceased and do not pare nails or cut hair from anywhere. Let these remain as they are.

(Musafiran-i-Akhirat)

9. If those bathing the deceased see some defect, they should not mention this to anybody. If, God forbid, death has caused the face to be deformed or turn blue, they should not speak about this as well making sure that the word does not go round through them, for all this is impermissible.

(Bahishti Zewar)

10. However, should they see some good sign, such as a glow or smile on the face, making it known is allowed.

(Shami)

11. The rules governing the bathing of those dying in accidents or other unusual circumstances such as drowning, burning, *jihad,* killing, accident, abortion or still-birth have been dealt with in a separate section which will appear later on.

12. If, in absence of water, someone deceased has been given a *tayammum,* but later on when water becomes available the body of the deceased should be given the regular bath.

(Bahishti Gauhar)

Bathing the Deceased: Details of the Method

Treat the wooden plank or flat board being used for bathing the deceased with smoke from burning incense *luban* or *olibanum)* three, five or seven times. Make the deceased lie on it in a way that the Qiblah comes to be on his or her right. If the situation does not permit or there be some difficulty in doing so, let the body lie on any side possible.

(Musafiran-i-Akhirat)

After this, tear or cut clothes on the body of the deceased and, by placing a sheet-wrap on the area of the body known as *satr,* that which must be concealed, remove the clothes working under the sheet-wrap. This wrap should be of coarse cloth good enough to cover the area from the navel to the calf of the leg so that the body underneath does not show through once it is wet.

Ruling:

It is not permissible to see the body from the navel to the calf of the leg. Touching this area even with hands is also not permissible. When giving *istinja* (purification after offices of nature) to the deceased and in bathing the body, gloves should be worn for this particular area or, in absence of gloves, a cloth piece should he wrapped on hands. This is because the area that cannot be touched even with hands during one's life-time cannot be touched with hands without gloves even after death. It was not permissible there and it is not permissible here. Do not even cast a glance on it.

(Bahishti Zewar)

Before starting the bath, put gloves on your left hand and give *istinja* to the deceased using three or five lumps of earth (or chalk cubes or sticks), then, purify by washing clean with water. When you give *wudu* (ablution), skip gargling and wetting the nasal opening with water, and washing of the fore-arm.

Instead, wet a flock of cotton, pass it on the lips, teeth and gums and throw it away. Do this three times. In the same way, clean the two openings of the nostril with another wet flock of cotton. However, if death has occurred in a state of *janabah* (requiring a bath for purification), or if a woman has died in a state of menstruation or child-bed, it is then necessary to put water in the mouth and the nostrils. The water thus put can be soaked out with a piece of cloth.

Now place cotton in the nostrils, the mouth and the ears so that water does not go in there while giving *wudu* (ablution) and *ghusl* (bath) to the deceased. After that, wash face, then hands upto the elbows, then give *mash* of the head (passing of wet hands over the head) and finish by washing both feet three times.

After you have given the *wudu* (ablution), wash the head (for men include the beard) with *Gul-Khairu* (gilliflower) or *khatmi* (marsh-mallow, *althea officinalis*) or oil-cake from sesame or mustard seed or flour from gram or chick-peas (all organic cleansers) or with plain soap, the purpose being to rub it clean.

Now let the body lie on its left side, pour lukewarm water boiled in jujube leaves on the right side three times from the head down to the feet just enough to trickle down to the left side. While bathing, keep reciting غفرانك يا رحمٰن (We seek Your forgiveness, O *Rahman*, the All-Merciful). Then, make the body lie on the right side and repeat the procedure by pouring water on the left side now up, from the head down to the feet, three times, just enough to trickle down all the way to the right side.

After that, by supporting the body of the deceased, bring it in a posture just about close to that of sitting and start to gently rub and press the abdomen from the top in a downward motion. If excrement (urine or stool) comes out, cotton-clean and wash off. You do not have to repeat *wudu* (ablution) and *ghusl* (bath) for the excretion of this impurity does not affect the *wudu* or *ghusl* of the deceased adversely.

Taking the next step, make the body lie on its left side and pour camphor-mixed water abundantly enough on the right side now on top, three times from the head down to the feet so that the left side underneath gets sufficiently wet. Then, wear another glove, dry off the body with a piece of cloth and change the under-wrap.

After this, lay out the shroud clothes on top and under on the cot in a way explained under the section, 'The Sunnah Method of Shrouding' appearing a little later. Once this is done, lift the body of the deceased slowly and gently from the bathing board and place it in a lying position over the shroud. Take out the cotton placed in the nostril openings, ears and the mouth.

(Fatawa-e-Hindiya, al-Durr al-Mukhtar, Musafiran-i-Akhirt and Bahishti Zewar).

Ruling:

The method of bathing mentioned above is *Sunnah*, but in case someone does not bathe the deceased in this manner three times, instead, washes the whole body only once, the obligation does stand discharged.

(Bahishti Zewar)

If water rains on the body of the deceased, or the body gets wet in any other way, this getting wet of the body cannot replace the need for a formal *ghusl* or bathing. Bathing the deceased still remains obligatory. Similarly, for someone who dies by drowning, it is necessary that the body should be bathed once it has been taken out of the water. This is because bathing the deceased is obligatory on the living and they have done nothing personally in any of the situations mentioned above. However, if the body of the deceased, while being taken out of the water, is moved in the water with the intention of giving *ghusl*, the obligation of bathing the body of the deceased will stand discharged.

(Bahishti Zewar)

Taking a Shower after bathing the Deceased

For a person who bathes the body of the deceased it is desirable *(Musthabb)* that he himself takes a bath once he has finished doing it.

(Shami)

According to a narration from the blessed Companion, Sayyidna Abu Hurayrah, رضی الله عنه the Holy Prophet صلى الله عليه وسلم said:

"The person who bathes the deceased should himself take a bath."

(Ibn Majah)

In other *ahadith*, the statement appears with the addition that the person who carries the *janazah* of the deceased should make his *wudu* (ablution).

Bathing and Shrouding the Deceased: Some *Ahadith*

The Holy Prophet صلى الله عليه وسلم said:

"The person who bathes the deceased is cleansed

of sins as if he were a child just born out of the womb of his mother and he who throws a shroud on the deceased would be dressed in the apparel of Paradise by Allah Almighty."

The Mother of the Faithful, Sayyidah 'A'ishah رضی اللہ عنہا says that the Holy Prophet صلی اللہ علیہ وسلم was shrouded with three cloth sheets from Yemen. Of these three pieces of cloth, none was a (sewn) shirt or turban (*'amamah*).

(Bukhari & Muslim)

Sayyidna Ibn 'Abbas رضی اللہ عنہ narrates that the Holy Prophet صلی اللہ علیہ وسلم said:

"You should wear white clothes. They are good for you. And, in these (whites) you should shroud your dead."

(Abi Dawood, Jami' Tirmidhi and Sunnan Ibn Majah)

On *Kafn*: Rules about the Shroud

1. Just as bathing the deceased is *Fard al-Kifayah* so are giving of the *kafn* (shrouding), performing the *salah* of *janazah* and the burial *(dafn)*. All these done for the deceased are known, in the terminology of the Shari'ah of Islam, as *Fard 'al al-Kifayah* that is, an obligation which, if performed by some, absolves others.

2. If the *kafn* cloth is available in the house and is clean and free of any possible impurities, there is no harm in using it for shrouding the deceased.

(Bahishti Zewar)

3. The cloth used for shrouding should be of

the normal standard used by the deceased during his life-time. Any ceremoniousness in this connection is wasteful and redundant.

(Bahishti Zewar)

4. White cloth is the best *Kafn* material for men and women both. New or old makes no difference; it is just the same for the purpose.

(al-Durr al-Mukhtar and Imdadul-Fatawa)

5. For the *Kafn* of men, cloth in pure silk or cloth coloured in saffron or in bastard saffron *('usfur:* safflower) is *makrooh* (reprehensible). For women, however, it is permissible.

(al-Durr al-Mukhtar)

6. Keeping *kafn* cloth ready for use in anticipation of one's death is not *makrooh* (reprehensible) but keeping a grave ready in advance of one's death is.

(Bahishti Gauhar)

7. For that matter, there is no harrn in giving a *Kafn* soaked in the sacred water of the well of *Zamzam* as a source of *barakah:* In fact, it is.

(lmdad al-Fatawa including notes)

8. It is not correct to place inside the *Kafn* or in the grave an *'Ahd Namah* (a written testament of obedience to God) or the genealogical tree *(shajarah* شجره an ascending list of saintly predecessors or some revered elders), or the verses of the Holy Qur'an or some prayer. Similarly, it is not correct to write the *kalimah,* the essential declaration of Islamic faith, or its likes, or some prayer written with camphor or ink, on the *kafn* or on the chest of the deceased.

(Bahishti Zewar)

9. For the *kafn*, the lining of the Cover of the Holy Ka'bah, or the used cloth of a man of Allah is better than the new and unwashed cloth. If large enough, use it as the shirt-piece of standard *kafn;* if small, it can be patched up in the regular *kafn*-shirt.

(Imdadul-Fatawa vol 1. p.,488)

10. It is not correct to place a piece of the top black Cover of the Holy Ka'bah, which has the *Kalimah* or the verses of the Holy Qur'an written into it through textural embroidery, inside the *kafn* or into the grave.

(Imdadul-Fatawa & Shami)

If the Cover of the Holy Ka'bah is made of pure silk, using it as part of a man's shroud is, for all intents and purposes, impermissible - even if it carries no writing; for shrouding the deceased in a cloth the wearing of which was not permissible for him during his life-time is also not permissible for him after death. It should be noted that wearing cloth from pure silk, while being impermissible for men, is perrnissible for women.

(al-Durr al-Mukhtar)

11. There is a custom at some places that survivors of a dead young girl or a newly-wed bride would place a red sheet or a scarf with ceremonious gold or silver applique work. This is not permissible.

(Radd al-Mukhtar & Imdadul-Fatawa)

12. If, for some reason, the grave housing the deceased opens up, or the corpse surfaces out, and has no *kafn on* it, then it becomes necessary to put it is in a *kafn* according to the practice of the Holy Prophet صلى الله عليه وسلم The condition is that the corpse should

have not decomposed or disintegrated. If that be the case it sufficient to wrap it up in some cloth; the giving of *masnun kafn* is not required.

(Bahishti Gauhar)

Note:

As indicated earlier, appearing later shall be special rules governing the bathing, shrouding, *janazah salah* and burial of those who die by drowning or burning in fire, or in fighting against infidels, or those killed for no fault of theirs, or those shred to pieces in some accident, or those who die through abortion or still-birth.

Ahadith:

According to another narration of Sayyidna Ibn 'Abbas رضی الله عنه the Holy Prophet صلی الله علیه وسلم said:

"You should wear white clothes. They are good for you. And, in these (whites) you should shroud your dead."

(Sunnan Abi Dawood, Jami Tirmidhi and Sunan Ibn Majah)

Sayyidna 'Ali Murtada رضی الله عنه narrates that the Holy Prophet صلی الله علیه وسلم said:

"Do not use expensive *kafn* (shroud), for it wears off soon enough (this being the fate of the shroud, what really does the deceased get out of an expensive one?)

(Sunan Abi Dawood)

The Shroud of a Man

The number of clothes given in the *kafn* of a man is three. These, according to the practice of the Holy Prophet صلى الله عليه وسلم are as follows:

1. ***Izar***: loin cloth, under-wrap
   - From the head to the feet.
2. ***Lifafah***: Enveloping or winding sheet
   - A quarter-yard longer than *Izar*.
3. ***Qamis***: Shroud tunic without sleeves and without gussets, that is, triangular pieces added to enlarge the body garment. Shroud-dress.[1]
   - From the neck down to the feet.

The shroud of a woman

The number of clothes required in the *kafn* of a woman is five. These, according to the practice of the Holy Prophet صلى الله عليه وسلم are as follows:

1. ***Izar***: loin cloth, under-wrap
   - From the head down to the feet, same as men.
2. ***Lifafah***: Enveloping or winding sheet
   - A quarter-yard longer than the *Izar*, same as men.
3. ***Qamis***: Shroud-tunic without sleeves and without gussets, that is, triangular pieces added to enlarge, the body garment.

---

1. Not too difficult to visualize these days since it happens to be the latest fad among young people in the West who feel comfortable in an outsize *camise*, anglicized of Arabic *qamis* through the Latin, *Qamisia*. Common with mendicants, dervishes and *faqirs* in parts of the East, the long and loose garment is known as *Kafni* which literally translates as the shroud-dress showing a certain usually un-noticed affinity with the ultimate end of things in life. MS.

- From the neck down to the feet, same as men.

4. **Chest-Wrap:** It is better to have it cover the area from the arm-pits to the thighs. Should it cover as far as the navel, that too will be correct. It should be wide enough so that it can be tied up.
5. **Scarf: *Khimar***, *sarbund, orhni* or *dupatta:* veil or scarf to cover head and face.
   - Three fore-hand lengths about 1 1/2 yards

In short, the first three clothes used in the *kafn* of a woman are exactly the same as those used in the *kafn* of a man. However, the last two, that is, the chest-wrap and the scarf, are extra and particular for women.

(Bahishti Zewar)

Rulings:

1. Shrouding men in three clothes, and women in five, is *masnun*, that is, as in the practice of the Holy Prophet صلى الله عليه وسلم. But, should it be that a man was shrouded in two clothes, that is, the *Izar* and *Lifafah*, and a woman in three clothes, that is, the *Izar, Lifafah* and Scarf, that too will be correct being sufficient enough.

Shrouding the deceased in less than this is *makrooh* (reprehensible). Despite its being bad practice, allowance has been made for situations of extreme helplessness, in which case, even less will be correct.

(Bahishti Zewar)

Note:

Details about the measurement and preparation of *kafn* clothes and the method of shrouding the deceased in them appear immediately after the following section.

The Shroud of Children: Rulings:

1. If a minor boy or girl dies before attaining the age of puberty but having reached close to it, it is a Sunnah to give the boy three clothes for his *kafn* and the girl, five. If the girl is given three instead of five and the boy two instead of three, that too will be sufficient. In other words, the rule that governs an adult man or woman is the rule that governs a miner boy and girl. For an adult man or woman the rule is 'emphatic' while it is simply 'better' for minors.

(Bahishti Zewar & Shami)

2. For a boy or girl who dies very young, much earlier than their age of adulthood, it is better that the boy be given three clothes like men and the girl, five clothes like women, as their *kafn*. If the boy is given only one and the girl only two clothes for their *kafn*, that too is correct. The *salah* of *janazah* and the burial will be carried out as usual.

(Bahishti Zewar & 'Alamgiri)

3. For a child who was born alive yet died shortly after or immediately after birth, the rule is that he will be bathed and shrouded as usual, and a *janazah salah* will be offered following which he will be buried. Besides this, he should be given a name.

(Bahishti Zewar)

4. For a child born dead from the womb of his mother without having exhibited any sign of life at the time of birth, the rule is that he should be given the usual bath, but not the formal *kafn* as required. Instead, wrap him in one piece of cloth and bury. The *salah* of *janazah* will not be offered on him, however, he should be given some name.

(Bahishti Zewar)

5. In a case of abortion while the physical parts of the body such as the hands, the feet, the mouth, nose etc. have not yet formed, the rule is that he should not be bathed or shrouded. None of these have to be done. Instead, the fetus should be wrapped in some cloth and buried in a hole dug in for this purpose. Should it be that some parts of the body of the child were formed, the rule governing his case will be the same as that of a child born dead, that is, he should be given a name and a bath - but no shroud and no *salah* of *janaza* - and a burial after wrapping in a piece of cloth.

(Bahishti Zewar)

6. In the case of a child whose head comes first at the time of birth showing sign of life, yet he dies later, he will be covered by the rule governing the birth of a dead child. However, should it be that a larger part of him comes out and he dies after that, he would be taken to have been born alive. If he comes out head first and comes out as far as the chest, it would be assumed that a larger part of him has come out; and if he is born feet first, the other way round, and comes out as far as the navel, it will be assumed that a larger part of him hascome out.[1]

The Method of Measurement and Preparation of the *Kafn* (Shroud)

The method of measuring and preparing the shroud for men is as follows:

Take a strip of wood[2] equal to the body length of

---

1. فلو خرج راسه وهو يصيح، ثم مات، لم يرث ولم يصلّ عليه، مالم يخرج اكثر بدنه حيًا، وحدّ الاكثر من قبل الرُجل سرته، ومن قبل الراس صدره . (ردالمحتار)

2. The purpose is to measure. If a measuring tape used by tailors and housewives is ready at hand, feel free to use it for measurements. (Rafi Usmani).

the deceased. Mark it parallel to the shoulder. Take a thread, place it horizontally on the chest and pass it round the contour of the body so that the two ends of this thread reach[1] the ribs on both sides. Now break the thread and keep it with you. Then, take a piece of cloth the width of which should be equal to this thread, or close enough. If the width falls shorter, add a patch and make it that wide. Tear out a sheet equal to the full length of the strip of wood you are using as a convenient measure. This is known as *'Izar'* or loin cloth.

Similarly, tear out another sheet which should be of the same width but quarter of a yard longer than the Izar. This is known as the *Lifafah* or enveloping or winding sheet-wrap.

Now take a cloth length, the width of which should be equal to the body width of the deceased, and tear it off the length of the marked measuring stick. Align both ends of the cloth length, then make an opening in the middle, big enough to slip through the head onto the shoulders. This is known as *Qamis* or shroud-tunic.

The *Kafn* for Women

As stated a little earlier, *kafn* clothes for women are the same as men - even the method of their preparation is identical. However, women have two extra clothes - the Chest-Wrap and the Scarf. The Chest-Wrap extends from under the arm-pits down upto the thighs and is as wide as the thread measure mentioned above. The Scarf is a little less than a quarter of a yard longer than half of *Izar* and is three-quarter yard wide.

---

1. That is, the end on the left comes over the right rib and the end on the right comes over the left rib.

(Rafi Usmani)

Things Connected with the *Kafn*

The *masnun kafn* (as given by the Holy Prophet صلى الله عليه وسلم is no more than what has been stated above. However, there are some clothes that serve as adjuncts to the *kafn*. These include two under-wraps for bathing, two hand gloves and a cradle sheet-cover for the *janazah* of a woman. Details of these items have already appeared under the list of things needed for the funeral and shrouding.

Given below is a cumulative list of *kafn* clothes for adult males for the sake of convenience:

No	Name	Length	Width	Estimated Measure	Remarks
1	Izar	21/2 yards	11/4-1 1/2 yards	Head to feet	1 1/2 times from cloth which is a yard wide, or a little
2	Lifafah	2 3/4 yards	as above	Quarter yard longer than the Izar	Same as above
3	Qamis	2 1/2- 2 3/4 yds.	1 yd	Quarter yard longer than the Izar	Same as above
4	Chest-Wrap	2 yds.	1 1/4 yds.	From under the arm-pits to the thigh	Tied to cover this.
5	Scarf	1 1/2 yds.	3/4 yd.	As far as it goes	Thrown on the head and the hair; not wrapped.

Note:

A man's *kafn* takes, in accordance with the practice of the Holy Prophet صلى الله عليه وسلم , approximately ten yards of cloth the width of which is one yard. For a woman, including the sheet to cover the cradle of her bier, it comes to 21 1/2 yards. The under-wraps needed for bathing and the cloth to make improvised gloves (if regular gloves are not available) are not included in this count. The *Kafn* for a child takes cloth-yardage appropriate to his or her size in forms stated earlier.

Extra Cloth-Materials

There are some cloth-materials people have taken to be necessary along with the standard *kafn* although they are excluded from the *masnun kafn*, that is, from the *kafn* approved under the practice of the Holy Prophet صلى الله عليه وسلم . Therefore, buying these from the inheri-tance of the deceased which is common to all inheritors - may be some of them are minors or some of them are absent on the occasion - amounts to a misuse of property without the permission of rightful owners. To begin with, these things are not needed. In fact, this is a case of 'making what is not necessary as something necessary'. As such, to be bound with it is *bid'ah*, that is, an act of padding up on to the established religion something that does not belong to it. However, if these are made available without any self-imposed restriction and to satisfy some expedient circumstances and if an adult buys it from his own personal pocket, then, there is no harm in doing so. As far as the sheet needed to cover the cradle of a woman's bier agains public view is concerned, that is necessary, details about which have appeared earlier under the list of things needed for funeral.

The extra cloth-materials are as follows:

1. PRAYER SPREAD: This cloth piece measuring about 1 1/4 yard in length and a yard or a little less in width is simply a product of custom. Just as those who are offering the *salah* of *janazah* need no mat or floor-spread to do that, so is the position of the Imam leading the *salah;* he needs no prayer mat either.

2. SASH or GIRDLE: This cloth piece is 1 1/2 yard long and a little less than one yard wide and is used to lower the body of the deceased into the grave (by passing the sash under the waist of the deceased and holding on to the two ends standing accross the grave to help the lowering of the body into the grave evenly).

3. BED SPREAD: Length: 2 1/2 yards, width: 1 1/4 yard. This is a sheet spread on the cot.

4. A WOMAN'S MANTLE: This 2x 1/2 yards cloth peice is for women. Those who can afford give away 4 to 7 of such peices to the poor and needy.

5. LARGE SHEET: This sheet measuring 3 x 1 3/4 yards is used to cover up the *janazah* of a man and is sufficient to cover the cot or bier. Although not necessary for men, this sheet is necessary for women. It is used to cover the cradle of the *janazah* of a woman, but this is, as far as the rule goes, outside the *kafn* requisite. It is for this reason that this sheet does not have to be necessarily of the same colour as the *kafn*. Since the purpose is purdah, any cloth is sufficient. Details on this have already appeared under the list of things needed for the funeral.

The Process of Shrouding

After the deceased has been bathed, lay out a cot and treat the *kafn* with smoke from burning incense (like *luban*) three or five or seven times. Then, spread out the *kafn* on the cot and lift the deceased up to lie on it. Take out the cotton from the nose, ears and the mouth which was placed there while bathing the body. Since the method of laying out the *kafn* and shrouding the deceased in it is somewhat different for men and women, details for each of the two are being given separately.

The Method of Shrouding a Man

To put a man in his *kafn*, first spread out the *Lifafah* on the cot, then lay out the *Izar* on top of it. Then, lay out the lower half of the *Qamis* gathering up the remaining top half and placing it neatly on the farthest head of the cot. Now lift the body of the deceased, slowly and gently, from the bathing board and lay him down on the *kafn* already spread out. Now hold the top half of the *Qamis* you had gathered up and placed on the head-side of the cot and flip it back towards, the head of the deceased seeing that the opening already made in the *Qamis* goes over the head and onto the neck like a cape. Ungather and push it farther down to the legs. When you have dressed the deceased with *Qamis* in this manner, take out the under-wrap which was placed on the.body of the deceased while bathing. Anoint the head and the beard with perfume (*'Itr* or its like). Please remember that the male body is not annointed with saffron. Just, rub camphor on the forehead, the nose, both palms, both knees and both feet (which are parts of the human anatomy one uses to perform his *sajdah,* the prostration for Allah).

Finally, fold the left edge of the *Izar* following it up by folding the right edge, over the body of the deceased, that is, the left edge stays under and the right edge over. Now fold the *Lifafah* in the same manner so that the left edge stays under and the right edge stays over. Now take a strip of cloth and tie up the *kafn* on the side of the head and the feet. Also, take another strip of cloth, a little larger, pass it on in the middle under the waist of the deceased, bring it up and tie so that it does not open up because of movement or wind.

The Method of Shrouding a Woman

For a woman, first lay out the *Lifafah,* then the Chest-Wrap and then the *Izar* on top of it following it up by laying out the lower half of the *Qamis*, gathering up the remaining top-half and placing it neatly on the farthest head of the cot. Now lift the body of the deceased, slowly and gently from the bathing board and lay her down on the *kafn* already spread out. Now hold the top-half of the *Qamis* you had gathered up and placed on the side of the head and flip it back towards the head of the deceased seeing that the opening already made in the *Qamis* goes over the head and onto the neck like a cape. Ungather and push it farther down to the legs. When you have dressed the deceased with the *Qamis* in this manner, take out the under-wrap which was placed on the body of the deceased following the bathing. Anoint the head with perfume ('*Itr* or its like). For women, saffron may also be used. After that, rub camphor on the forehead, the nose, both palms, both knees and both feet. Then part the hair in two portions and leave them resting on the chest over the *Qamis* in a way that one portion goes on the right and the other on the left. Then place the Scarf over the head and on the hair without braiding or winding them.

Finally, fold the *Izar* over the body of the deceased in a way that the left edge comes to rest under the right edge. The Scarf will thus go inside the fold. After that, bring the Chest-Wrap from under the arm-pits over to the chest as far as the knees and tie up the right and the left ends together. Now fold the *Lifafah* in the same manner so that the left edge stays under and the right edge stays over. Now take a strip of cloth and tie up the *kafn* on the side of the head and the feet. Also, take a longer strip of cloth, pass it on in the middle under the waist of the deceased, bring it up and tie so that it does not open up while being moved.

(Bahishti Zewar & Musafiran-i-Akhirat)

If you follow this method, the Chest-Wrap will be over the *Izar* and inside the *Lifafah*. But, should the Chest-Wrap be tied over the *Qamis* earlier than the *Izar*, it will still be permissible. Even if it is tied over all clothes, that is, over the *Lifafah*, that too will be correct.

(Bahishti Zewar & Musafiran-i-Akhirat)

Rulings:

1. Some people dab the *kafn* with *'Itr* perfume. They would even tuck perfume-soaked swabs into the ear-wall niches. All this is sheer ignorance. The rule is: Do what the Shari'ah tells you to do and do no more.

(Bahishti Zewar)

2. The sheet thrown over the *janazah* is not part of the standard *kafn*. For men, it is not even necessary. But, should someone throw his sheet-wrap over the *janazah* and take it away at the grave-site, then, there is nothing wrong with it.

(Musafiran-i-Akhirat)

Although it is necessary to cover the *janazah* of a woman with a sheet for the sake of shielding it from public view, yet this is not included in the standard *kafn*. As such, this need not be of the same colour as the *kafn.* Since purdah is the purpose, any cloth is sufficient. In fact, should someone throw his own sheetwrap on the cradle of the *janazah* and take it away after having reached the grave-site, this too will be good enough.

(Musafiran-i-Akhirat & Bahishti Zewar)

3. If a cradle is readily available, it should be placed over the *jananazah* and a sheet thrown over it. Otherwise, place thin bamboo sticks or a branch of some green tree and cover it with a sheet so that the *janazah* remains shielded from public view.

4. Prepare the *janazah* following the method given above and say farewell to your dear traveller bound for his ultimate journey to the Hereafter. Bid him the best on his way to *salatul-janazah* with patience, forbearance and dignity. If you want someone to have a last look at the face of the deceased, do so. But this being an unusual time of life, there are women who start crying loudly or mouring plaintively or come out of the house negligent of their purdah-less demeanour in public. Staying away personally from doing such things and making an effort that other do not fall into this error is necessary. If this is not done, the great reward of patience will be all gone and instead, the ill consequences of such deeds, in the Hereafter, will become one's fate.

THINGS LEFT OVER AFTER THE FUNERAL

Rulings:

1. If, out of the things collected for bathing, shrouding and burying the deceased, some cloth material is left unused, it is not permissible to give it to someone casually or summarily or to throw it away as waste. The position taken here has supporting

details, for instance, if this cloth was taken from the inheritance of the deceased, then it is obligatory to put it back as part of the inheritance so that the things left over at the funeral get included in the distribution of inheritance according to the Shari'ah. And should it be that the funeral materials were given by some individual on his own, then the things left over should be returned to him.

('Alamgiriah)

2. If a contribution was made to take care of the funeral of some heirless poor person, it is necessary that things or money left should be returned to contributors. If the contributors cannot be traced, these should be spent over the funeral of a similar person. Otherwise, let these be given as *sadaqah* (charity) to the poor and needy.

(al-Durr al-Mukhtar & Shami)

On Raising the *Janazah:*
Sayings of the Holy Prophet صلى الله عليه وسلم

Sayyidna Abu Hurairah رضى الله عنه narrates that the Holy Prophet صلى الله عليه وسلم said:

> 'Anyone who accompanies the janazah of a Muslim, with the quality of *Iman* (faith) and the intention of *thawab* (Allah's reward), and stays with the *janazah* right through the time it takes to offer the *salah* (prayer) for the *janazah* and its burial, he will return with two karats of *thawab*- each karat being equal to the Mount of Uhud. Anyone who returns after offering the *salatul-janaaza* only - without waiting to be present as a participant in the burial - he will return with one (similar) karat of *thawab*.'

(Sahih al-Bukhari, Sahih Muslim)

Sayyidna Abu Hurayrah رضی اللہ عنہ narrates that the Holy Prophet صلی اللہ علیہ وسلم said:

> "Take the *janazah* briskly. If he is good, good awaits him where you will take him soon enough; and if, it is otherwise, it is a bad burden which you will unburden off your shoulders (without loss of time).'

(Sahih al-Bukhari, Sahih Muslim)

It appears in *hadith* that one who raises and carries the *janazah* cot (the bier) from all four sides (that is, carries it on his shoulders shifting from one to all four corners of the cot), forty of his major sins will be pardoned.

(Bahishti Zewar from Ibn Asakir)

Rulings:

1. If the deceased be a neighbour or a relative or someone known for righteousness and piety, accompanying his *janazah* is more merit-worthy than offering a voluntary *salah*.

('Alamgiri)

2. If need be, the *janazah* can be raised and carried on payment of wages.

('Alamgiri)

3. The act of women going with the *janazah* is, in the terminology of the Shari'ah, *Makrooh al-Tahrimi* (that is, reprehensible in the degree of forbiddance).

(Bahishti Gauhar)

The Method of carrying the *janazah* as taught by the Holy Prophet صلی اللہ علیہ وسلم

Rulings:

1. If the deceased be an infant or a little older, people should carry the *janazah* hand to hand. In other words, one person lifts the body on his forearms, then the other person takes it from him. Carry the *janazah* changing hands like this.

(Bahishti Gauhar)

If the deceased be an adult (man or woman), carry only after having laid the body on a cot or some similar bier.The side that holds the head stays in front. All four legs of the cot are lifted by four different men. Raise the cot, which holds the deceased, with your hands and then make it rest on your shoulders. Lifting without using hands, like one would haul boxes and bags, is reprehensible *(makrooh)*. Similarly, carrying the deceased on one's back is also *makrooh*. Also, carrying the deceased on a beast of burden or carriage etc. is *makrooh*, if this be without a valid excuse. In case, such excuse is there, it is permissible without any element of reprehensibility *(karahat*, the state of being *makrooh)*; for instance, the graveyard could be far away.

(Bahishti Gauhar with marginal notes)

2. Lifting and carrying the *janazah* in a way that one man holds it by the wood or metal frame in the front and another in the back is also *makrooh*. This would give the impression of hauling some heavy baggage. However, should there be a situation of compulsion, it does not matter; for instance, the passage way be so narrow that four men cannot walk by it lifting the *janazah* in accordance with *Sunnah*.

('Alamgiri)

3. The desirable *(mustahabb)* method of raising the *janazah* is that you should first place the front cot-leg on the right of the deceased on your right shoulder and walk at least ten steps; then, place the back cot-leg of the same side on your right shoulder and walk at least ten steps; then, move over to the front again and place the front cot-leg on the left side of the deceased on your left shoulder; then, falling back, place the rear cot-leg on the same left side of the deceased on your left shoulder and, on each of the two shoulderings, walk at least ten steps so that you would be walking a total of forty steps after having shouldered the *janazah* at four leg-points and walked ten steps each. The noble *Hadith* speaks highly about the merit of lending your shoulder to the *janazah* of the deceased for at least forty steps.

(Bahishti Gauhar, al-Durr al-Mukhtar, Shami)

4. Taking the *janazah* briskly is an act of *sunnah*, but not so briskly that the body gets unsettled and stirred.

(Bahishti Gauhar)

5. Accompanying the *janazah* on foot is desirable *(Mastahabb)*. If riding, follow behind the *janazah*.

6. It is *mustahabb* (desirable) that those who accompany the *janazah* walk behind it, although walking in front of the *janazah* is also permissible. However, should one walk too far ahead of the *janazah* or everybody was to move in front of the *janazah*, that will be *makrooh* (reprehensible). Similarly, riding in front of the *janazah* on any vehicle or conveyance is also *makrooh* (reprehensible).

(Bahishti Gauhar)

7. Those going with the *janazah* should not walk on its right and left.

('Alamgiri)

8. Praying to Allah or repeating words in His remembrance loudly *(du'a* and *dhikr)* by people with the *janazah* is *makrooh* (reprehensible).

(Bahishti Gauhar from Al-Bahr Ar-Ra'iq)

9. People not with the *janazah* but sitting somewhere without any intention to go along with the *janazah* should not stand up at the sight of the *janazah.*

(Bahisti Gauhar from Al-Maraqi Al-Falah)

10. For those going with the *janazah*, it is *makrooh* (reprehensible) to sit down before the *janazah* is taken off the shoulders and placed on the burial site. However, should there be some need to sit down, there is no harm in doing so.

(Bahishti Gauhar)

11. Anyone with the *janazah* should not come back without offering the *salatul-janazah* (the prayer for the deceased). If necessary, he should inform the relatives of the deceased and excuse himself while no such seeking of permission is needed after the burial.

('Alamgiri)

Ahadith:

The Holy Prophet صلى الله عليه وسلم used to walk with the *janazah.*

(Tirmidhi).

He would not sit until the *janazah* was taken off

the shoulders and put down. He said:

إذا أتيتم الجنازة فلا تجلسوا حتّى توضع

"When you come with the *janazah*, do not sit until it is put down."

In another narration, it appears:

"Do not sit until it is laid down in the grave."

(Madarijun-Nubuwwah)

When he accompanied a *janazah*, he walked. He said: "I do not ride when angels walk."

After having finished (with the burial), sometimes he walked while at others he would ride back.

(Zad al-Ma'ad)

The Holy Prophet صلى الله عليه وسلم when he walked with a *janazah*, used to keep silent with his noble heart feeling the aftermath of death.

(Ibn Sa'd)

CHAPTER IV

Salatul-Janazah

The Prayer for the Deceased

Offering the *salah* of *janazah* (the prayer for the deceased) is *Fard 'alal-Kifayah* (an obligation which, if performed by some, would absolve others). In other words, if no one offers the *janazah salah* over the deceased, all those who knew would be sinners, and if, only one person has offered the *salah*, the *Fard Kifayah* will stand discharged because a *jama'ah* or congregation is neither a condition *(shart)* nor an obligatory necessity *(wajib)* for the *salah* of *janazah*. Details will appear later.

(Shami)

Rulings:

1. If some one dies on a Friday morning, it is better to take care of the bathing, shrouding, *janazah salah* and burial, positively if possible, before *jumu'ah salah* (Friday Congregational Prayer). Holding on to the *janazah* with the exclusive thought that there will be a big attendance in the *jumu'ah salah* is *makrooh* (reprehensible).

(Shami. Bahishti Gauhar)

2. If the *janazah* arrives at a time when the *jama'ah* (congregation) for the *Fard* (Obligatory) *Salah* (prayer) (of *jumu'ah* or non-*jumu'ah*) is ready, first perform the *Fard* and *Sunnah*, then offer the *salah* of *janazah*.

(al-Durr al-Mukhtar, Shami)

3. If the *janazah* has arrived at the time of the *salah* of *'Idul-Fitr* (the post-Ramadan thanksgiving congregational prayer usually performed in the open), first offer your *salah* of *'Idul-Fitr,* then listen to the *khutbah* (sermon) which follows it, then perform the *salah* of *janazah.*

(Imdadul-Fatawa p. 505, Vol. 1)

4. In case the deceased has made a will that the *salatul-janazah* for him should be led by a particular person, this will is not valid. According to the rules of the Shari'ah, acting in accordance with this will is not necessary. A list of those entitled by the Shari'ah to lead the *salah* of *janazah* will appear a little later. These are the ones who should be requested to lead the prayer as Imam. However, if they themselves were to make someone else lead the prayer as Imam, there is no problem there.

(Maraqi al-Falah p. 324)

The Time of the *Janazah Salah*

Unlike the five daily prayers the timings for which are fixed, no such particular time for the *janazah salah* is either necessary, or is a condition.

(Shami, Bahishti Gauhar)

Rulings:

1. As commonly known, offering *Sunnah* and *Nafl,* after the *Fajr salah* and before sunrise, and after the *'Asr salah* before the sun turns pale, is prohibited, but offering the *salatul-janazah* is correct during these timings as well without any element of reprehensibility *(karahat)*

('Alamgiri, Shami, Imdadul-Fatawa)

2. The *salah* of *janazah* too, like others, is not permissible at *tulu‘* (sunrise), *zawal* (noon) and *ghurub* (sunset).

Tulu‘, the rising of the sun, as envisaged in the Shari‘ah, begins with the appearance of the top arc of the sun and continues up to the time until the sun rises full and high on the horizon, that is, until eyes could be set on it. The time of *ghurub* begins when the light of the sun pales down, that is, when eyes begin to set on it,. and continues up to the time the whole sun disappears from the horizon.

(Shami, p. 341, 344, v. 1; ‘Alamgiri. p.52, v.1; Bahishti Zewar)

3. Offering *salatul-janazah* at the three timings cited above is not permissible in a situation when the *janazah* has arrived earlier than these timings. If the *janazah* arrives exactly at these particular timings, that is, *tulu‘ zawal* or *ghurub*, offering the *salah* over it is permissible even at those times.

(‘Alamgiri, al-Durr al-Mukhtar, Shami)

Summary

The *salah* of *janazah* is permissible without any element of reprehensibility (*karahat*) at all times except three, that is, *tulu’ zawal* and *ghurub*. In a particular situation, however, when the *janazah* arrives exactly during these timings, the *salah* of *janazah* is permissible during these three as well.

Conditions under which *Salatul-Janazah* becomes obligatory *(Fard)*

The conditions that make the *salah* of *janazah* obligalory are the same as other *salats*. These are:

Ability, Adulthood and Islam. However, in the *salah* of *janazah*, there is an additional condition, that is, one should be aware of the death of that person. So, one who does not know about it shall stand excused *suo-jure*. The *salah* of *janazah* will not be obligatory on him.

(Bahishti Gauhar)

Conditions that make *Salatul-Janazah* correct

There are two types of conditions that make *salatul-janazah* correct

(A) The first type of conditions are the same as should be found in all performers of *salah* necessarily. These are the same as govern other *salats* - that is, *Taharah* (the state of prescribed cleanliness), *Satr 'Aurah* (the covering of body parts that must be covered), facing the Qiblah and making an intention *(niyyah)*.

However, should one apprehend that he will miss the *janazah salah, tayammum* is permissible. For instance, if the *janazah salah* is in progress and there be the danger that the *salah* will be over by the time the *wudu* is made, one should make *tayammum* and join in offering the *salah* - even though water for *wudu* be available. This is contrary to what is done is other *salats* wherein *tayammum* is not permissible when water for *wudu* is available even if there be the danger of missing the *salah* in congregation.

(Bahishti Gauhar)

Offering *Salah* with shoes on

Some people offer the *janazah salah* these days with shoes on. For them it is necessary that the place where they are standing and the shoes they are wearing should both be clean, otherwise, their *salah* will not be valid.

(Bahishti Gauhar)

And in case, one takes his feet out of the shoes and stands on them, only the top of the shoe touching the feet must be clean, irrespective of the condition of the sole which may be unclean. Furthermore, given this situation, there is no harm even if the standing ground too is unclean.

(Bahishti Gauhar, Imdadul-Ahkam)

Conditions which must necessarily be found in the deceased

(B) The second type of conditions concern the deceased. These are six in number.

FIRST CONDITION: The deceased must be a Muslim. So, *salah* for a disbeliever or apostate *(kafir)* and *(murtadd)* is not correct. *Salah* over the *janazah* of a Muslim, even though a sinner and an innovator in religion, is correct. This excludes all those who are killed while fighting in rebellion against the rightfully-ruling Muslim authority, or while committing highway robbery, or while fighting under tribal, national, provincial or linguistic prejudice - *Salatul-Janazah* will not be offered on them. However, if they are killed after the fight, or were to die their own death after the fight, the *salah* of their *janazah* will be offered.

(Bahishti Gauhar, al-Durr al-Mukhtar, Shami)

Similarly, the *salatul-janazah* for a person who killed his father or mother and is killed in retaliation will not be offered.

(Bahishti Gauhar)

The correct position in respect of the one who has committed suicide is that he will be bathed and *salatul-janazah* too will be offered for him.

(Bahishti Gauhar)

Ruling:

'Mayyit' or 'deceased' means a person who died after having been born alive, or the major portion of his or her body may have come out of the womb of the mother in a state of being alive. If born dead, or died before its major portion could come out, the *janazah salah* for it is not correct.

(Bahishti Zewar, Bahishti Gauhar)

SECOND CONDITION: The body and the shroud of the deceased should have been cleansed and purified from all impurities,[1] real or constructive.

However, if real impurity was excreted from the body of the deceased after it has been shrouded and which makes the body or the shroud overly filthy, it does not matter. The *salah* of *janazah* will be correct. Washing off is not required.

(Bahishti Gauhar)

Ruling:

1. If no purificatory measure has been taken to

---

1. In the language of Islamic Fiqh, impurities find precise descriptions. Filth or impurity or *najasat* is known as *'An-Najasah'* which is of two kinds. The first is knows as *Najasah-Haqiqah* (real impurity). It has two sub-divisions: Heavy (*mughallazah*) such as, urine, stool, blood and carcass, and Light (*mukhaffafah*). The other kind of *Najasah* is known as *Hukmiyyah*, which means that the Shari'ah has associated it with impurity and has prescribed relevant rules governing these. For example, a major occurrence of such impurity requires a bath while a minor one would require a *wudu* (ablution). We may call the later, canonical or legal or constructive.

cleanse the deceased from a ruled impurity, that is, the deceased has not been given a bath, or has not been given a *tayammum* in the event giving a bath was not possible, the *salah* of *janazah* over such a deceased person will not be correct. But, given the condition that it is just not possible to formally purify the body of the deceased, for example, the body has been buried without a bath or *tayammum* and the grave has been filled with earth, in which case, subject to the body not having been disintegrated, the *salah* of *janazah* for the deceased will be offered on his grave as is.

If *salah* has been offered on a deceased person without his having been given a bath or *tayammum* and has been buried in that state and then comes the post-burial realization that the deceased was not given a bath, the *salah* of *janazah* should be repeated on his grave before such time that the corpse has not disintegrated. This is because the first *salah* was not correct. Now, that the *ghusl* or required bath is no more possible, the *salah* will become valid.

(Bahishti Gauhar)

2. If a Muslim has been buried without offering *salah* of *janazah* that prayer for him will be performed at his grave subject to the condition that the corpse is not likely to have disintegrated. When there appears to be a strong likelihood that the corpse would have disintegrated by that time, the prayer should not be offered. How long does it take for the corpse to be decomposed and disintegrated? Such period differs from place to place and cannot be fixed universally. This position is the most sound. However, some Muslim jurists suggest a period of three days, some ten and still others, a month.

(Bahishti Gauhar)

3. If the body of the deceased lies on a clean cot, wooden platform, mattress or comforter, the place underneath these need not be clean. This is not part of the condition. The *salah* of *janazah* thus offered will be correct without any shade of doubt. In case the very cot or platform is unclean or the deceased has been placed on unclean ground without any cot or platform, it has to be decided whether the condition that the place holding the deceased should be clean is valid and operative under these circumstances. There is a difference of opinion in this matter. According to some Muslim jurists, the situation is governed by the condition which means that the placing of the body of the deceased on an unclean cot or platform or on unclean ground will render the *salah* of *janazah* incorrect. There are others who do not regard this as a condition and according to them the *salah* thus offered would be considered as correct.

(Bahishti Gauhar)

THIRD CONDITION: The cover-worthy part of the body of the deceased should be necessarily covered. If the body of the deceased is naked, *salatul-janazah* over it will not be correct.

(Bahishti Gauhar)

FOURTH CONDITION: The deceased should be ahead and in front of those offering the *salah*. If the body of the deceased is behind those offering the *salah*, that *salah* is not correct.

(Bahishti Gauhar)

FIFTH CONDITION: The body of the deceased or whatever is holding it should be placed on the ground. If the body of the deceased is being held by people on their hands, or it has been placed on a vehicle or beast of burden and the *salah* of *janazah* is offered in that very stance, then, it will not be correct unless there be a valid excuse.

(Bahishti Gauhar & Shami p. 813, v. 1)

SIXTH CONDITION: The body of the deceased should be physically present there. If the body of the deceased is not there, the *salah* for it will not be correct.

The obligatory components *(Fara'id)* of *Salatul-Janazah*

In *Salatul-Janazah* two things are *fard:*

1. Saying *Allahu-Akbar* four times. Here, each *takbir* (saying of *Allahu-Akbar)* is supposed to stand for one *raka'ah.* In other words, the way the *raka'ah* is necessary in other *salats,* each of the *takbirs* is necessary in *salatul-Janazah.*

(Bahishti Gauhar)

If the Imam of the *Salatul-Janazah* calls more than four *takbirs,* the Hanafiyyah in the congregation may not follow these additional *Takbirs.* They should stand observing silence. When the Imam turns for *salam,* they too should follow and turn for *Salam.* In the event, the extra *takbirs* are not heard directly as called by the Imam, instead, are heard as relayed loudly by a *mukabbir* (one appointed to relay the calls of the Imam from the back rows), the followers in the congregation should follow the call of the *mukabbir* and consider each *Takbir* as *Tahrimah,* that is, a *takbir* or saying of *'Allahu-Akbar',* which is an obligatory act in the beginning of *salah.* This will be under the assumption that the first four *takbirs* relayed by the *mukabbir* earlier may have been miscalled and the Imam may have actually called the *Takbir al-Tahrima,* (the first one in the beginning of the *salah,* at that very time).

(al-Durr al-Mukhtar, Shami)

2. *Qiyam*, that is, offering the *salatul-janazah* in a standing position. This is very much like *fard* and *wajib salats* where *qiyam* (standing) is obligatory (*fard*) and abandoning it without a valid excuse is not permissible. So, the *salah* of *janazah* too cannot be performed validly by sitting without excuse.

(Bahishti Gauhar)

Ruling:

There is no *adhan* (the initial call for prayer), *iqamah* (the later call for the congregation to stand up for *salah* the *qira'ah* (recitation from the Holy Qur'an), ruku' (the bending posilion), *sajdah*[1] (prostration) and *qa'dah* (sitting position) in this *salah*.

(Bahishti Gauhar)

The Sunnah components in *Salatul-Janazah*

The following three things are acts of *Sunnah* in the *janazah salah:*

1. Praising Allah *(hamd)*

2. Reciting *Darud*, the invoking of Allah's blessings for the noble Prophet صلى الله عليه وسلم

3. Praying, for the deceased.

---

1. Done with feet standing erect on fingers turned towards the Qiblah, knees going first on the floor, then the palms of the hands with fingers naturally close together and facing the Qiblah, then the nose top and then the forehead, which has nothing in common, in form, purpose or philosophy, with ways of prostration known in animist cultures, cults, even in religions.

Jama'ah or congregation is not a condition in this salah. As such, even if one person was to perform the *salah* of *janazah*, the given obligation will stand discharged, whether the person offering the *salah* be a man or woman, adult or minor. If the *salah* of *janazah* is not performed by anyone, then everyone will end up being sinners.

(Bahishti Gauhar, Shami)

4. However, the larger the congregation, the better it is, for the *janazah salah* is a prayer for the deceased. When Muslims get together and pray before Allah for something, the act has a mysterious effectiveness. It opens the doors of Divine acceptance of prayers and makes Allah's mercy descend upon those who turn to Him. But, delaying the *janazah salah* in the hope of having a larger congregation is *makrooh* (reprehensible).

(Bahishti Gauhar)

The Method of *Salatul-janazah*:

According to the practice of the Holy Prophet صلى الله عليه وسلم the desired method of offering *salatul-janazah* is as follows:

The body of the deceased is placed in front of the Imam who leads the prayer. The Imam stands in line with the chest of the deceased, everyone in the congregation makes the following intention (*niyyah*):

نَوَيْتُ اَنْ اُصَلِّىَ صَلٰوةَ الْجَنَازَةِ لِلّٰهِ تَعَالٰى وَدُعَاءً لِّلْمَيِّتِ،

"I intend to offer the *salah* of *janazah* in devotion to Allah Almighty and in prayer for the deceascd".

After having made this intention, raise both hands

up to the ears as is done is *takbir al-tahrima,* the first call of *Allahu-Akbar* in the beginning of usual prayers, say *Allahu-Akbar* once and fold your hands over the navel as you do in usual prayers.

Recite *Thana'* : ثناء

سُبْحَانَكَ اللّٰهُمَّ وَبِحَمْدِكَ وَتَبَارَكَ اسْمُكَ وَتَعَالٰى جَدُّكَ وَلَا إِلٰهَ غَيْرُكَ

after that say *Allahu-Akbar* once again but do not raise your hands up to the ears this time, then recite the *darud*, preferably the same as recited in usual prayers. Then say *Allahu-Akbar* once again, not raising your hands this time as well. As soon as this *takbir* is over, pray for the deceased. If the deceased is an adult, male or female, recite the following prayer:

اَللّٰهُمَّ اغْفِرْلِحَيِّنَا وَمَيِّتِنَا وَشَاهِدِنَا وَغَائِبِنَا وَصَغِيْرِنَا وَكَبِيْرِنَا وَذَكَرِنَا
وَأُنْثَانَا، اَللّٰهُمَّ مَنْ اَحْيَيْتَهُ مِنَّا فَاَحْيِهِ عَلَى الْاِسْلَامِ وَمَنْ تَوَفَّيْتَهُ مِنَّا فَتَوَفَّهُ
عَلَى الْاِيْمَانِ ،

"O Allah, pardon our living and our dead and our present and our absent and our young and our old and our men and our women. O Allah, whoever from among us lives, make him live adhering to Islam and whoever from among us dies, let him die adhering to the Faith."

In some *ahadith*, the following prayer has also been mentioned:

اَللّٰهُمَّ اغْفِرْلَهُ وَارْحَمْهُ وَعَافِهِ وَاعْفُ عَنْهُ وَاَكْرِمْ نُزُلَهُ وَ وَسِّعْ مَدْ خَلَهُ
وَاغْسِلْهُ بِالْمَاءِ وَالثَّلْجِ وَالْبَرَدِ وَنَقِّهِ مِنَ الْخَطَايَا كَمَا يُنَقَّى الثَّوْبُ الْاَبْيَضُ
مِنَ الدَّنَسِ وَاَبْدِلْهُ دَارًا خَيْرًا مِّنْ دَارِهِ وَاَهْلًا خَيْرًا مِّنْ اَهْلِهِ وَزَوْجًا خَيْرًا
مِّنْ زَوْجِهِ وَاَدْخِلْهُ الْجَنَّةَ وَاَعِذْهُ مِنْ عَذَابِ الْقَبْرِ وَعَذَابِ النَّارِ ،

"O Allah, pardon him and have mercy on him and give him security and forgive him and ennoble his descent and widen his place of entry and bathe him in water cooled and cleanse him from sins as clothes are cleansed white from filth and give him an abode better than his home (in the mortal world) and a family better than his family and a wife better than his wives and admit him to paradise and be his refuge from the punishment of the grave and the punishment of the Fire."

If both these prayers are recited, that too is good. The fact is that Allamah Shami, in his Radd al-Mukhtar, has written these two prayers as one. Apart from these two, there are other prayers cited in *Hadith*. Muslim jurists have reported these as well. One can go by any of these at his discretion.

If the deceased is a minor boy, recite the following prayer:

اَللّٰهُمَّ اجْعَلْهُ لَنَا فَرَطًا وَّاجْعَلْهُ لَنَا اَجْرًا وَّذُخْرًا وَّاجْعَلْهُ لَنَا شَافِعًا وَّمُشَفَّعًا ٠

And if the deceased is a minor girl, the prayer stays the same with the difference that you say *ij'alha* in place of *ij'alhu* which appears at three places and *shaf'atan wa mushaffa'atan* in place of *shaf'an wa mushaffa'an.*

When you have recited this prayer, say *Allahu-Akbar* once and do not raise hands this time as well. When you have said the *takbir,* release your hands and turn for *salam* exactly as you do your *salam* in usual *salats.* In this particular prayer, you do not recite *At-Tahiyyat* or portions of the Holy Qur'an.

(Bahishti Gauhar)

Rulings:

1. If a person has not committed the prayer recited in *salatul-janazah* to memory, he can simply recite:

اَللّٰهُمَّ اغْفِرْ لِلْمُؤْمِنِيْنَ وَالْمُؤْمِنَاتِ

"O Allah, forgive Muslim men and Muslim women."

If even this much is not possible, the saying of four *takbirs* only will make the *salah* valid, for the *du'a* and *darud* are not obligatory; they are *Sunnah*.

(Bahishti Gauhar)

2. Making a prayer by raising hands on the spot immediately after the *janazah salah* is *makrooh* (reprehensible). This has no proof in the *Sunnah* because *salatul-janazah* is in itself a prayer for the deceased.

3. The *salatul-janazah* is the same for the Imam and for those who follow him in the congregation (*muqtadi*) with the only difference that the Imam will call the *takbirs* and *salam* in a raised voice while the *muqtadis* say it in a lowered voice. Everything else, such as, the *Thana'*, the *Du'a* and the Darud, will be recited in a lowered voice both by the *muqtadis* and the Imam.

(Bahishti Gauhar)

4. It is desirable *(mustahabb)* that those present in the *janazah* prayer be made to stand in three rows, so much so that one man, out of a total of seven men present, should be made the Imam with three men standing in the first row, two in the second and one in the third.

(Bahishti Gauhar)

Things which make *'Salatul-Janazah' fasid*

Ruling:

Things which make usual *salats* incorrect are things which make *salatul-janazah* incorrect. The only difference is that, in the *salah* of *janazah*, a loud laugh does not make the *wudu* invalid nor does the proximity of women, opposite or parallel.

(Bahishti Gauhar)

The Masjid and places where *salatul-janazah* is reprehensible:

Offering the *salah* of *janazah* in a *masjid* (mosque) - which has been constructed for the five daily prayers, or the special prayers of Friday or the two 'Ids *('Idul-Fitr* and *'Idul-Adha')* irrespective of whether the *janazah* is inside the *masjid* or out of it with the congregation being inside[1] - is *makrooh al-tahrimi*, that is, reprehensible in the degree of prohibition. But, it is not so in a *masjid* which has been built specially for the *salah* of *janazah*.

(Bahishti Gauhar)

If there is no place outside the *masjid* and there be a situation of compulsion, offering the *salah* of *janazah* in the *masjid* is not *makrooh* (reprehensible).

(Imdadul-Fatawa, p. 543, v.1)

This is why *salatul-janazah* is offered inside the *masjid* at the two Sacred Mosques of Makkah and Madinah.

---

1. The situation where the *janazah*, the Imam and some *muqtadis* are outside the *masjid* while rest of the *muqtadis* (those who follow the Imam in congregation) are inside the *masjid* has been ruled as *makrooh* (reprehensible) by 'Allamah Shami and the author of al-Durr al-Mukhtar, but this has been recorded as permissible in Imdadul-Muftiyin on the authority of Fatawa *Bazaziyah*. Therefore, the cautions course is to avoid such a situation without a valid excuse. (Rafi Usmani)

Rulings:

1. Performing the *janazah salah* on a thoroughfare which may cause inconvenience to passers-by is *makrooh* (reprehensible).

(Imdadul-Fatawa, p. 533, v.1)

2. Performing the *janazah salah* on a private property without due authorization from the owner is *makrooh* (reprehensible).

(Shami, p. 827, v. 1)

4. Performing the *salah* of *janazah* while sitting or riding is not permissible, specially so when there is no valid excuse.

(Bahishti Gauhar)

The case of several *janazahs* gathering at one place and time

Rulings:

1. Should there be several *janazahs*, all at one time, it is better to offer *salah* for each *janazah* separately. And should there be one single *salah* for all the *janazahs*, that too, is permissible. In the latter situation, all *janazahs*, should be placed in a row, preferable by placeing one *janazah*, then placing another ahead of it, so that everyone's legs point to the same uniform direction and everyone's head rests in the other. This form is better because by doing so, everyone's chest will become parallel to the Imam which is a *sunnah* of the Holy Prophet صلى الله عليه وسلم.

(Bahishti Gauhar)

2. Should the *janazah* be of different sexes and ages, their rows should be arranged in a way that the male, adult *janazahs* are placed close to the Imam

followed by those of boys, then those of adult women and then, those of minor girls.

(Bahishti Gauhar)

Rules for *Masbuq* and *Lahiq* in *Salatul-Janazah:*

1. A *masbuq* is one who joins in to catch up the prayer after missing one or more *raka'at*. If a person arrives at the *janazah salah* at a time when some *takbirs* have already been called before he arrived, he will be regarded as *masbuq*[1] in terms of whatever number of *takbirs* he has missed. He should not, immediately on arrival, join[2] in the congregation by saying his *takbir al-tahrima (Allahu-Akbar)* as he would normally do in other *salahs,* instead he should wait for the next *takbir* to be called by the Imam. When the Imam calls the *takbir,* he should also say *Allahu-Akbar* with him, whoch will be the initial *takbir al-tahrima* as far as he is concerned. When the *Imam* has turned for *salam,* this person should call[3] his missed *takbirs* and

---

1. As explained earlier, every *takbir* in *salatul-janazah,* including the *takbit al-tahrima,* legally represents one full *raka'ah.* So, the number of *takbirs* missed means the missing of an identical number of *raka'at.*

(Shami, Rafi Usmani).

2. Because this *takbir* is like the missed *raka'ah* and a *masbuq* does not offer any *raka'ah* he has missed immediately as he joins in the *Salah* instead, he completes those after the Imam has turned for *salam* in the same way, these missed *takbirs* too will be called after the Imam of *Janazah Salah* has turned for *salam.*

(Shami, Rafi Usmani).

3. But, if this person, without waiting for the next *takbir* of the Imam, immediately on arrival says '*Allahu-Akbar*' and joins in the *salah,* even then, his *salah* will come out correct. However, the *takbir* he said while joining in will not be counted among the four *takbirs* which are obligatory in *salatul-janazah.* Therefore, when the Imam turns for *salam,* it is necessary for this person to say *takbirs* he had missed before his joining in the *salah* and then turn for *salam.*

(Shami, Rafi Usmani).

thus complete the *salah*, wherein no recitation is needed.[1]

2. If a person arrives at a time when the Imam has called even the fourth *takbir*, he will not be considered a *masbuq* as far as the fourth *takbir* is concerned, he should immediately join in by saying *Allahu-Akbar* before the Imam turns for *salam* and once the *salah* is over, he should call his three missed *takbirs*.

(Bahishti Gauhar)

3. If a person was not present at the time of *takbir al-tahrima*, the first call of *'Allahu-Akbar'*, or any other *takbir*, but was ready to participate in the *Salah* but could not join in[2] because of lethargy or some other reason, he should not, then, wait for the next *takbir* of the Imam, instead, he should say his *takbir* and join in the *salah*. He will not have to say that *takbir* later[3], if he says that *takbir* before the Imam calls the next one, even though it may not be with the Imam. However, this person shall be a *masbuq* as far as the saying of *takbirs* he missed earlier than this one is concerned. Those *takbirs* he should say after the Imam has turned for *salam*.

(Shami, Bahishti Gauhar)

4. As indicated earlier, when the *masbuq* in a *janazah salah* says his missed takbirs and fears that by the time he recites the supplication *(du'a)* it will be too late and the *janazah* will be moved away from his

1. When a *masbuq* in *Janazah* says his missed *takbirs* (after the Imam turns for *salam*), and he fears that by reciting the supplication (*du'a*) he will be left behind, that is, the *janazah* will be removed away from his front, then, let him not recite it. Instead, he should simply say his *takbirs*, one after the other, and turn for *salam*.
2. That is, he did not say his *takbir*. (As in Shami - Rafi Usmani)
3. That is, after the Imam has turned for *salam*. (Shami, Rafi Usmani).

front, he should not recite the *du'a*.

(Bahishti Gauhar, Shami)

5. If a person becomes a *lahiq* in the *salah* of *janazah*, he is governed by the same rule which governs the *lahiq*[1] in usual *salats*.

(Bahishti Gauhar)

---

1. Details are given below:

There are two kinds of a *muqtadi* (those who follow behind the Imam): (1) *masbuq*. (2) *Lahiq*. A *Masbuq* is a *muqtadi* who has missed one or more *raka'at* before: joining in the congregation. A *Lahiq* is a *muqtadi* who has missed one or more or all *raka'at* after joining in the congregation. This could be under any excuse such as sleeping off during the *salah* or becoming unmindful. Or it could be plain lethargy which is no excuse.

Since *takbirs* in *salatul-janazah* are governed by the same rule which applies to other usual *salats*, therefore, anyone who has missed some *takbirs* before joining in the *salah* will be a "*Masbuq*"; and the one who misses his *takbirs* after having joined in the *salah* will be a "*Lahiq*".

There is a difference between the rule governing the *Masbuq* and the *Lahiq*. The *Masbuq* says his missed *takbirs* after the Imam has turned for *salam*. The *Lahiq* performs his missed *raka'at* first, then, subject to the congregational prayer still in progress, he follows the Imam onwards. Otherwise, he completes the rest of the *salah* as well, individually, and turns for *salam*.

In *satatul-janazah*, the rule governing a *Masbuq* is somewhat different from other *salats*, details of which have appeared earlier, but the rule governing a *Lahiq* is the same in *salatul-janazah* and other usual *salats*. So, a person who becomes a *Lahiq* in *salat ul-janazah*, that is, should he, after having said '*Allahu-Akbar*' and having joined in the *salah*, misses one or more *takbirs*, he should first say his missed *takbirs* and then follow the Imam. But, should it be that the Imam says the next *takbir* before he was able to say his missed *takbirs*, he should not, then, follow the Imam in saying this particular *takbir* with him. Instead of that, he should complele his missed *takbirs* and say this *takbir* too all by himself. Following that, if there remains a *takbir* still due to be called by the Imam, he should follow the Imam and say that *takbir* with him and turn for *salam* when the Imam turns for *salam*. If this person finished saying his missed *takbirs* at a time when the Imam had already turned for *salam* as well, he could turn for *salam* doing it alone.

These details are from al-Bahr al-Ra'iq and Bahishti Gauhar

(Rafi Usmani).

Who deserves to lead the *salatul janazah* ?

Ruling 1:

The Muslim ruler of a given time is the most deserving of leading the *salah* of *janazah*, even though there be people better than him in fear of Allah and piety. If the ruler (king/head of the state) is not there, the next person deserving is his deputy in the area, even though there be people better than him in fear of Allah and piety. In case, he too is not there, the judge of the area and if he too is not there, his deputy. With these people around, making anyone else lead the prayer as Imam is not permissible without their permission. They are the ones who should necessarily be made the Imam. If they are not present, the Imam of the locality deserves to lead the *salah* subject to the condition that there be no one more merit-worthy than him from among the relatives of the deceased. Otherwise, relatives who have the right of guardianship over the deceased are deserving of leading the *salah* of *janazah* - or anyone they permit. If anyone who does not have the deserved right to be the Imam had led the *salah* of *janazah* without the permission of the guardian of the deceased who did not participate in the *salah*, the said guardian has the right to perform his *salah* over the deceased later. He can do so even at the grave, if the deceased has been buried, of course, unless there be no apprehension about the corpse having been disintegrated.

(Bahishti Gauhar, Al-Bahr Al-Raiq)

Ruling 2:

If, in the absence of a permission from the guardian of the deceased, the *salah* of *janazah* was led by a person who has a deserved right to be the Imam, the guardian of the deceased cannot repeat it on his own.

Similarly, if the guardian of the deceased has, in absence of the ruler of the time or his appointees, led the prayers, then the ruler of the time or his appointees have no right to repeat it. In fact, the correct position is: If the guardian of the deceased has already led the *janazah salah* despite the presence of the ruler of the time who would, then, not have the right to repeat it, although under such a situation, by not having the ruler of the time as Imam, the guardians of the deceased will incur the sin of abandoning an obligation.

(Bahishti Gauhar)

Salatul-Janazah in absentia

The Holy Prophet صلی اللہ علیہ وسلم did not perform *salatul-janazah* in absentia. But, it is also true that he did it for *Nagus (Najashi),* the King of Ethiopia; also for Sayyidna Mu'awiyah Laithi رضی اللہ عنہ But, it is possible that (the body of the deceased was imaged before him, or) this was something special[1] to the Holy Prophet صلی اللہ علیہ وسلم.

(Shami)

---

1. The proof of which is that several noble Companions, other than the two persons named above, died during the very life-time of the Holy Prophet صلی اللہ علیہ وسلم. The group of Companions known for their recitations of the Holy Qur'an who were most dear to him became martyrs while travelling. Sayyidna Ja'far al-Taiyyar رضی اللہ عنہ his cousin and Sayyidna Zaid ibn Haritha رضی اللہ عنہ, his adopted son met their death while on journey and in *jihad*. When he received the news in Madinah al-Taiyyibah he did not offer *Salatul-Janazah* in absentia for them, although he was very particular about offering the *salah* of *janazah* for those who died in Madinah al-Taiyyibah. There was an standing instruction to everyone: "Whenever anyone from among you dies, do inform me because my offering the *salah* for the deceased is a source of mercy for him."

From here we know that the *salatul-janazah* in absentia he offered for the two persons named above was either peculiar to those two, or

Salatul-Janazah in absentia is absolutely prohibited with Imam Abu Hanifah and Imam Malik, رحمة الله عليهم اجمعين (Madarijun-Nubuwwah), and leading Hanafi jurists concur on its inadmissibility.

Being present before[1] the *janazah* is a condition that makes the *salah* of *janazah* correct.

(Shami, al-Bahr, Bahishti Gauhar and Madarijun-Nubuwwah)

The Blessing of a large attendance in *janazah*

In a narration from Sayyidah 'Aishah رضی الله عنها the Holy Prophet صلی الله علیه وسلم has been reported to have said:

> 'The deceased for whom a large number of Muslims perform *salah*, even as many as one hundred, and all of them plead for the deceased before Allah, then their plea and prayer will certainly be accepted.'

(Sahih Muslim)

Sayyidna Malik ibn Hubairah رضی الله عنه narrates that he heard the Holy Prophet صلی الله علیه وسلم saying:

> 'The Muslim servant of Allah who dies and three rows of fellow Muslims who offer the *salah* of *janazah* for him (praying that he be forgiven and blessed with Paradise), surely then, Allah Almighty grants it (forgiveness and Paradise) for him.'

---

special to the Holy Prophet صلی الله علیه وسلم himself as Allah Almighty had imaged the deceased before him during the performance of the *salah* of *janazah*. Allamah ibn al-Hummam has discussed this subject in great detail in his Fath al-Qadir. (Rafi Usmani)

1. The presence of *janazah*, before the Imam only will suffice to fulfil this requirement. (Shami, p 813, v.1)

Because of this *hadith*, it was the practice of Sayyidna Malik ibn Hubairah رضی اللہ عنہ that he would, whenever he felt the attendance was on the lower side, divide people over three rows.

(Sunan Abi Dawood)

1. Once the *salah* for the deceased is over, the *janazah* should be immediately taken to the grave site for a quick burial. The method of raising and carrying the *janazah* has been explained earlier.

(Bahishti Gauhar)

2. One should not return before burial without seeking permission from the family of the deceased, but no permission is needed once the burial is over.

('Alamgiri, p. 165, v.1)

The Obligation of Burial

The burial of a deceased person is *Fard 'alal-Kifayah* (an obligation which, if discharged by some, will absolve others) just like the bathing, the shrouding and the *janazah* prayer for the deceased. If this obligation is not discharged by anyone at all, everyone will incur the sin of abandoning an obligation.

(Bahishti Gauhar, 'Alamgiri)

The Type of Grave

In its depth, the grave should be dug measuring at least half the height of the deceased. If it is dug deeper, as deep as the full height of the deceased, it is much better, however, it should not go any deeper than that height. Then, length-wise, the grave should match the measurement of this height. The width of the grave will be equal to half this height. The lateral[1] grave is better than the medial[2] one, the former being the niche type and the later being the box type. But, should the earth crust be very soft and there be the danger that digging into the side-wall for a niche to hold the body will cause the grave to cave in, then, the niche type grave should not be dug.

(Shami, Madarijun-Nubuwwah)

In the event that it is not possible to dig out a niche type grave because of the earth being soft or flood-ridden, it is also permissible to place the deceased in some box or chest and bury the body in that manner. The box or chest *(tabut* or coffin - the later without the ever-ascending price tags placed by commercial funeral homes in the West for 'state-of-the-art' caskets) could be from wood, rock or metal, but simple. It is better if earth is spread on the floor of the box.

(Shami, Baḥr and Bahishti Gauhar)

The niche' type grave should be sealed up using mud bricks or reeds or something similar. It is reprehensible *(makrooh)* to close it with baked bricks or wood planks. But, where the earth is soft or flood-ridden and which could cause the grave to cave in,

---

1. This type of grave is known as *lahd* (in which the grave is dug up all the way down to the desired surface). Then, it is in the wall on the side of the Qiblah that a niche' is made (which is a recess or hollow space to place the body of the deceased). This is something like a stark miniature roomette in the earth, and of the earth. (Calling it a burial chamber or charnel vault or sepulchre would be an overstatement, even affectation.) (Shami, Rafi Usmani)
2. This type of grave is called '*Shaqq*' in Arabic. The method is to first dig the grave upto the depth of about one foot. then going deeper from the center, a hole is dug out the length of which is equal to the height of the deceased and its depth is equal to half his or her height, or full height, which is better. The width of this box-like hollow should be equal to half the height of the deceased, at the most.

(Shami, bidiadatil-'ldah, Rafi Usmani)

using baked bricks or wood planks to close the niche is all right-under such conditions; it is also permissible to bury the deceased in a box *(tabut* or coffin). As far as the medial grave is concerned *(Shaqq* or box type grave), it is correct to place wood planks or cement slabs (or rock splinters) with the body of the deceased resting underneath. There is no element of reprehensibility *(karahat)* in doing so.

(al-Durr al-Mukhtar)

The noble Prophet صلی اللہ علیہ وسلم never raised a grave high; he would not 'build' it firmly with baked bricks or stones or similar materials, nor would he coat it or plaster it with mud-putty or mortar that would later harden, nor would he mount any structure, dome or cupola over the grave. All this is *bid'ah,* later-day innovation in religious matters, and is *makrooh* (reprehensible).

The fact is that the blessed grave of the noble Prophet صلی اللہ علیہ وسلم and the graves of his two very dear Companions are almost close to being at the ground level. Only some red pebbles are placed on the raised top.

(Madarijun-Nubuwwah, Safarus-Sa'adah)

The blessed grave of the Holy Prophet ﷺ resembles the hump of a camel in its shape.

(Shami with reference to al-Bukhari)

Sayyidna 'Amir, the son of Sayyidna Sa'd ibn Abi Waqqas رضی اللہ عنہ says that his father (Sayyidna Sa'd رضی اللہ عنہ had made a will on his death-bed saying: For me make a grave with a niche' and close it by placing mud bricks one on top of the other just like it was done for the Holy Prophet صلی اللہ علیہ وسلم .

(Muslim)

It was the good practice of the Holy Prophet صلى الله عليه وسلم that he would order *lahd*[1] (niche' type grave), have it dug deep and would see that enough room[2] was provided near the place where the head and the feet of the deccased were to rest.

(Zad al-Ma'ad)

Rulings:

1. No deceased person, big or small, should be buried in the house, for this is something special to the noble prophets, may peace be upon them.

(Bahishti Gauhar, al-Durr al-Mukhtar, Bahr)

2. If a grave-site for burial is not available in the public graveyard of the Muslims, or entry therein is not permitted for some particular reason, a plot of land for the grave should be purchased. The cost of this land will also be paid from the inheritance of the deceased just like the payment of other funeral arrangements from it.

(Mufidul-Waritheen p.32)

Inter-City Transfer of Body

Ruling:

Taking thd body for burial from one city to the

1. The Blessed grave prepared for the Holy Prophet صلى الله عليه وسلم was of the type known as *lahd*, a grave the side of which is dug hollow. According to some narrations, there are indications that the box type grave known as 'Shaqq' in Arabic has been made as and when needed even during the blessed times of the Holy Prophet صلى الله عليه وسلم But, the preferred method of preparing a grave is still that of *lahd*, that is, a grave with a hollow side, the niche' or baghli type. (Ma'ariful-Hadith, Rafi Usmani)

2. It means that the length of the grave was given more room, a litile more than the height of the deceased, so that there remains good enough space by the side of the head and the feet. (Rafi Usmani)

other is against the preferred choice *(khilaf aula)*, specially so when the other place is not more than one or two miles away. If it beyond that distance, it is not permissible. And taking the dead body after digging, it out from the grave where it was buried is certainly impermissible under all conditions.

(Bahishti Gauhar)

Lowering the body into the Grave

First place the *janazah* by the side of the grave in the direction of the Qiblah in a way that Qiblah should be on the right of the deceased. Then, those responsible for lowering the body of the deceased should stand facing the Qiblah, lift the deceased off carefully and put the body in the grave.

(Bahishti Gauhar)

Rulings:

1. While putting the body in the grave, it is desirable *(mustahabb)* to say:

بِسْمِ اللهِ وَعَلٰى مِلَّةِ رَسُوْلِ اللهِ

With the name of Allah and according to the practice of the community of the Messenger of Allah.

(Bahishti Gauhar, Zad al-Ma'ad)

2. That those who lower the deceased into the grave should be in a certain odd or even number is not proved from the practice of the Holy Prophet صلى الله عليه وسلم. He himself was lowered in his sacred grave by four persons.

(Bahishti Gauhar)

3. Saying *Adhan* (the call for prayer) while lowering the deceased in the grave, or after the burial, is *bid'ah* (innovation in established religious practice).

(Bahishti Gauhar)

4. According to the *Sunnah* of the Holy Prophet صلى الله عليه وسلم once the deceased has been put inside the grave, the body should be turned on its right side in order to face the Qiblah. Turning only the face towards the Qiblah is not enough, rather the whole body should be neatly turned.

(Bahishti Gauhar, Islahi-Inqilab-i-Ummat)

5. After the deceased has been put in the grave, the knot tied in the *kafn* (shroud) to keep it in place against any likelihood of its opening up should be untied.

(Bahishti Gauhar)

6. While placing a deceased woman in the grave, it is desirable *(mustahabb)* to have the body shielded from public view (purdah), and if, there be the apprehension that the body of the deceased may show up in the process, then, making arrangements for purdah becomes obligatory.

(Bahishti Gauhar)

7. The grave need not be shielded from public view while burying men. However, if there be an excuse, such as, the rain or snowfall or scorching sun, then it is permissible.

(Bahishti Gauhar)

8. Once the deceased has been placed in the grave, the niche' type grave *(lahd)*, if that is the case,

should be closed up with mud bricks and reeds or something similar. If the grave is box type *(Shaqq)*, it should be closed from the top by placing wood planks or cement slabs or rock splinters over the shoulders of the side walls. Any holes or crevices left in-between should be sealed with clods of earth, pieces of rock or kneaded clay. After that, start tossing the earth into the grave.

(Bahishti Gauhar)

9. While tossing the earth into the grave, it is desirable *(mustahabb)* to begin from the side of the head. Everyone should scoop out earth in both hands and throw it into the grave doing it three times. While throwing earth the first time, one should say: مِنْهَا خَلَقْنَاكُمْ "From this We created you..." And the second time, say: وَفِيهَا نُعِيدُكُمْ "And in it We shall return you..." And the third time, say: وَمِنْهَا نُخْرِجُكُمْ تَارَةً أُخْرَى "And from it We shall take you out once again".

(Bahishti Gauhar)

10. The amount of earth excavated from the grave dug for the deceased should be put back in there, all of it. Amassing earth on the grave, more than this, is *makrooh* (reprehensible), specially so when it is too much, so much so that it ends up raising the height of the grave way beyond a span which can be readily measured by extending the thumb and the little finger horizontally, tip to tip. The addition of a small amount of earth from around the grave which actually did not come out from it makes no difference and it is not *makrooh* (reprehensible).

(Bahishti Gauhar)

11. Making the grave square-shaped is *makrooh*. The desirable *(mustahabb)* way is to make it a little

raised like the hump of a camel. Its height should be as much as a finger-span explained under ruling 10 above, or somewhat higher than this.

(Bahishti Gauhar)

12. After the throwing of earth into the grave is over, it is desirable *(mustahabb)* to sprinkle water on the grave.

(Bahishti Gauhar)

THE BURIAL: Miscellaneous Rulings

1. In case the deceased has not been turned towards the Qiblah inadvertently during the process of burial in the grave and this is realized only after burial and earth-filling, in which case, it is not permissible to open the grave just to turn the deceased towards the Qiblah. However, should it be that burial has reached a stage when wood planks or slabs have been placed on the grave opening but earth has not been filled yet, then, the planks or slabs should be removed and the deceased should be turned towards the Qiblah.

(Bahishti Gauhar)

2. If a person dies on a ship or boat at sea and land be far enough to cause the dead body being spoiled, then it is necessary that washing of the body, shrouding and the *salah* of *janazah* (prayer for the deceased) be carried out immediately, following which the body should be wrapped and tied nicely in the shroud and lowered into the waters with added weight, stone or iron, so that it sinks down. But, if the land is not that far, keep the body and bury it on the land when you reach there.

(Bahishti Gauhar and 'Alamgiri)

3. Taking the deceased out of the grave after earth has been filled is not permissible. However, if it comes to depriving someone of his rights, it will be permissible to take out that body. For example: 1) The land in which the deceased has been buried belongs to someone else and he is not willing to have the deceased buried there. 2) Anything valuable belonging to someone has been left behind in the grave.

(Bahishti Gauhar)

4. If a woman dies and she be carrying alive child in her womb, the child should be taken out through operation. Similarly, if someone swallows up something valuable belonging to someone else and dies, then, if the owner wants to have what belonged to him back, that item of value should be recovered through operation. However, should it be that the deceased has left assets behind, payment for the lost belonging should be made from his inheritance and the deceased be spared the opening of his abdomen.

(Bahishti Gauhar)

5. Burying more than one dead body in a single grave should be avoided. However, given some compulsive need, this would be permissible, in which case, should all those dead be males, the most pious among them should be placed ahead (towards the Qiblah), with all others placed behind him in a receding order of preference. If there be some men and some women and children, then, men should be placed ahead followed by children and then women. Make a modest buffer of earth between each two deceased persons.

(Bahishti Gauhar, 'Alamgiri)

After The Burial

After the burial was over the Holy Prophet

صلى الله عليه وسلم and his Companions would stand near the grave of the deceased and pray for the deceased that he remains steadfast while answering to the angels *Munkar* and *Nakir* in the grave. While making this prayer himself, he would advise others to do the same and pray that their brother-in-faith remains steadfast.

(Zad al-Ma'ad)

Rulings:

1. After the burial, it is desirable *(mustahabb)* to stay by the grave for a little while[1], pray for the forgiveness of the deceased,or to recite from the Holy Qur'an for the good of the deceased *(thawab)*.

(Shami, Bahishti Gauhar)

2. It is also desirable *(mustahabb)* to recite, after the burial, the first verses of Surah al-Baqarah upto *'muflihun'* from the head-side of the grave and the last verses of Surah al-Baqarah from *'amanar-rasul'* to the end of the Surah from the leg-side of the grave.

(Baihaqi - Shu'b al-'Iman)

A Post-Burial Prayer

If the deceased is male, reciting the following prayer *(du'a:* supplication) after the burial is also advisable:

---

1. How long is a 'little while'? It appears in Fatawa 'Alamgiri that it is desirable (*mustahabb*) to stay there for a time during which a camel could be slaughtered, and its meat distributed (p. 166, v.I). It does not mean that a camel be slaughtered and its meat distributed for this purpose. The purpose here is to point out an approximate time-frame, that is, one may stay there as long as it takes to finish of these two things. The Arabs were used to doing it without much loss of time. For instance, if they would start after '*asr* prayers, they had it all finished much earlier than *maghrib*, as mentioned in *Hadith* narrations.

(Rafi Usmani)

اَللّٰهُمَّ اغْفِرْلَه وَارْحَمْهُ وَعَافِه وَاعْفُ عَنْهُ وَاَكْرِمْ نُزُلَه وَوَسِّعْ مَدْخَلَه وَاغْسِلْهُ
بِالْمَاءِ وَالثَّلْجِ وَالْبَرْدِ وَنَقِّه مِنَ الْخَطَايَا كَمَا نَقَّيْتَ الثَّوْبَ الْاَبْيَضَ مِنَ
الدَّنَسِ وَاَبْدِلْهُ دَاراً خَيْراً مِّنْ دَارِه وَاَهْلاً خَيْراً مِّنْ اَهْلِه وَزَوْجًا خَيْراً مِّنْ
زَوْجِه وَاَدْخِلْهُ الْجَنَّةَ وَاَعِذْهُ مِنْ عَذَابِ الْقَبْرِ وَ عَذَابِ النَّارِ ،

"O Allah, pardon him and have mercy on him and give him security and forgive him and ennoble his descent and widen his place of entry and bathe him in water cooled and cleanse him from sins as clothes are cleansed white from filth and give him an abode better than his home (in the mortal world) and a family better than his family and a wife better than his wives and admit him to paradise and be his refuge from the punishment of the grave and the punishment of the Fire."

If the deceased be a woman, reciting the following prayer is better:

اَللّٰهُمَّ أَنْتَ رَبُّهَا وَأَنْتَ خَلَقْتَهَا وَ أَنْتَ هَدَيْتَهَا لِلإِسْلَامِ وَأَنْتَ قَبَضْتَ رُوْحَهَا
وَأَنْتَ أَعْلَمُ بِسِرِّهَا وَعَلَانِيَتِهَا، جِئْنَا شُفَعَاءَ فَاغْفِرْلَهَا.

'O Allah, you are her Lord and You created her and You guided her to Islam and You took her spirit away and You know best the open and the secret of her deeds. We have come pleading and praying, so, forgive her.'

(Ma'ariful-Hadith)

Ruling:

After the *salah* of *Janazah* has been offered, one should not leave the burial-site before burial without seeking the permission of the family of the deceased.

But, once the burial is over, one can leave without having to seek such permission.

('Alamgiri p. 165, v.1)

Placing a Grave-Stone

According to an authentic *hadith*, the Holy Prophet صلى الله عليه وسلم when he buried Sayyidna Uthman ibn Maz'un[1] رضى الله عنه he picked up a heavy stone and put it at the head of his grave (as a sign) and said: 'Through it, I shall be able to identify the grave of my brother.'

(Madarijun-Nubuwwah, Shami)

Ruling:

Writing or inscribing anything (names etc.) on the grave as mementos serving to preserve the remembrance of the dead is no permissible according to some scholars. Some others permit it if needed. But, writing or inscribing on the grave or on its headstone the verses of the Holy Qur'an or poetic compositions or exaggerated eulogies is *makrooh* (reprehensible).

(Shami)

The Making of Structures on the Grave is Prohibited

Making any structural edifice on the grave, such as, a dome or cupola or arch is *haram* (forbidden), if made to serve as ornamentation; and is *makrooh* (reprehensible), if the intention is to fortify the grave.

(Bahishti Gauhar)

---

1. He was a foster-brother of the Holy Prophet صلى الله عليه وسلم (Tirmidhi).

Walking and Sitting on Graves is also Prohibited

Not walking and sitting on graves and not reclining against them is included in the many blessed practices of the Holy Prophet صلى الله عليه وسلم Therefore, avoid.

Practices against Sunnah

Raising the graves (too) high is not a *Sunnah* of our noble Prophet صلى الله عليه وسلم ; neither is the making of the graves firm with solid masonry, nor with baked bricks and stones, nor with mud bricks. Also against *Sunnah* is the making of domes over graves.

(Zad al-Ma'ad)

The Holy Prophet صلى الله عليه وسلم has prohibited the lighting of lamps over the graves and the making of graves the places of *Sajdah* (prostration in prayer).

(Zad al-Ma'ad)

Refilling of Earth in a Collapsed Grave

Ruling:

If a grave caves in, it is permissible to refill it with earth.

(Imadadul-Fatawa, p. 525)

Patience in Death: Its Reward

As narrated by Sayyidna Abu Hurairah رضى الله عنه the Holy Prophet صلى الله عليه وسلم said: 'Allah Almighty says when I made a believing servant of mine part with someone dear to him, and he then shows patience and fortitude hoping for a better return from Allah, for him I have no less a return than the Paradise.'

(Sahih al-Bukhari)

Mourning in Death

The Holy Prophet صلى الله عليه وسلم has said: 'It is not permissible for a true Muslim that he mourns for somebody for anymore than three days, except a widow in whose case the period of her mourning,[1] following the death of her husband, is four months and ten days.'

(Tirmidhi, Abwabut-Talaq and al-Bukhari)

The Sunnah is that one should be content with what has been decided by Allah and keep praising and glorifying Him, and (when sorrow hurts) keep reciting إِنَّا لِلّٰهِ وَإِنَّا إِلَيْهِ رَاجِعُوْنَ (To Allah we belong and to Him we are to return). One should show his distaste for those who rend clothes because of what has befallen them, and for those who break into loud lamentations and wailing and mournings, and those who shave off their hands as a mark of greif.

(Bahishti Gauhar)

Treating the Deceased and his Survivors gracefully

The Holy Prophet صلى الله عليه وسلم treated the deceased with ultimate grace and favour, something that would serve the departed soul well in the grave and in the Hereafter. He would also conduct himself most generously before his family and relatives - he would pray for the forgiveness of the deceased, take part in his *janazah* prayers and accompany it all the way to the burial-site, stand by the head of the grave and pray

---

1. Here 'mourning' means leaving off personal adornments, that is, a widow must observe a period of mourning following the death of her husband for four months and ten days which is known as *'idda* or waiting period wherein she ababdons personal adornments. Other than a widow, nobody is permitted to mourn for more than three days on any occasion whatsoever.
Detailed rules governing the *'Idda* will appear later.

(Rafi Usmani).

with his Companions that the deceased remains steadfast in his adherence to the Faith, then, he would also go back to visit his grave, greet the occupant of the grave and pray for him.

(Madarijun-Nubuwwah)

Offering Condolence to Survivors (*Ta'ziyat*)

The Holy Prophet صلى الله عليه وسلم has said that anyone who comforts a person in suffering receives a reward similar to the one reserved for the sufferer.

(Jami' Tirmidhi, ibn Majah)

It was the blessed practice of the Holy Prophet ﷺ that he himself went out to offer condolences.

Ruling:

It is desirable *(mustahabb:* recommended) to visit a house afflicted by death in the family to offer condolences once within the first three days. As for a visit where the persons related to the deceased are given solace and comfort in their hour of suffering and are told about the great merits of patience *(sabr)* and its supreme returns and rewards from Allah and are persuaded to stick to the ideal course of forbearance through *sabr*, it is the proper thing to do. Doing all this and praying for the forgiveness of the deceased is not only that it is permissible, instead, it is an act of sheer goodness. This is what *'Ta'ziyat* is (and which has been referred to as 'condolence' of English, a somewhat formal social grace in the West bereft of the spiritual).

It may be noted that offering condolences after three days is termed as *Makrooh Tanzihi* (reprehensible in the degree of taste and propriety). But, should it be that the person offering condolences is in travel, or the family and relatives of the deceased (to whom one has to go to offer condolences) be on the same status of travel and return after three days, in which case, going to offer condolences to them even after the three days mentioned earlier will not be reprehensible *(makrooh)*.

(Bahishti Gauhar)

A LETTER OF CONDOLENCE

From the Holy Prophet صلى الله عليه وسلم to his Companion, Mu'adh ibn Jabal رضى الله عنه on the demise of his son

Sayyidna Mu'adh ibn Jabal رضى الله عنه narrates that the Holy Prophet صلى الله عليه وسلم after he heard about the death of his son, had a letter of condolence written to him, a translation of which is being given below:

With the name of Allah, the All-Merciful, the Very-Merciful. From the Messenger of Allah, Muhammad to Mu'adh ibn Jabal. Peace be on you. I begin with the glorification of Allah Almighty except whom there is no god. After praising Him, I pray that Allah bestows upon you the greatest of returns and gives you the ability to bear by your loss patiently and make you and us fortunate enough to be grateful, for there is no doubt about it that our lives, our belongings and properties and our children and families are all a pleasant gift, in fact, trusts placed in our care for a certain period of time (meaning that your son too was given in your care as a trust of Allah under this rule). Allah Almighty allowed you the time to enjoy and be benefitted by his company so freely and happily. Now that He has taken him back in lieu of that supreme return of His, I give you the significant tidings of His very special favour to you, and His mercy and guidance - if you stay patient hoping for the best of returns from Allah. So, be patient and stay patient (and grateful too). See that your lamentation does not go on to destroy your returns for which you may feel sorry later. Remember, weeping and crying can never bring the deceased back, nor does this lighten the burden of sorrow. And what has to be, must be; and what was to be, has already come to be. *Wassalam.* Peace on you.

(Tirmidhi, Hisn Hisin)

Sending Meals for Family of the Deceased it Desirable *(Mustahabb)*

As stated by Sayyidna 'Abdullah ibn Ja'far رضی اللہ عنہ when the news came that his father (Sayyidna Ja'far ibn Abi Talib رضی اللہ عنہ) was martyred, the Holy Prophet صلی اللہ علیہ وسلم said that food should be prepared for the family of Ja'far as they are in a state in which they would be unable to attend to the cooking of their own meals.

(Jami' Tirmidhi, ibn Majah)

It was also blessed practice of the Holy Prophet صلی اللہ علیہ وسلم that he did not favour the idea that the family of the deceased suffer from the added burden of preparing food for those who came to offer their condolences to them. Instead of that, he instructed that others (relatives and friends) should prepare the food and send it to them. This is a sample of good morals and an act of grace which relieves survivors of the deceased from a burden not in line with the sad occasion.

(Zad al-Ma'ad)

Ruling:

1. It is desirable *(mustahabb)* for neighbours and distant relatives of the family of the deceased that they prepare food for one day and one night and send it to the family of the deceased. In case, they avoid eating because of their sorrow, one should gently plead and induce them to eat.

(al-Durr al-Mukhtar, Shami, p. 84)

A feast thrown by the family of the deceased is *bid'ah*

There is a custom among ignorant people these days that they would, as the family of the deceased, prepare special food and invite those who come to offer condolences to partake of it. Because this is against the practice of the Holy Prophet صلى الله عليه وسلم so, this is not permissible. It is a *bid'ah*, a laterday innovation in the true and correct practice of religion, for a feast suits a happy occasion, but certainly not a sad death. It is reasonable enough that those who come to offer their condolences to the family of the deceased - and do not send food for the bereaved family - should at least have the courtesy of not inflicting themselves on the hospitality of the already aggrieved family.

(Shami, p. 841-842, v. 1)

On visiting the Graves: Hadith

Sayyidna 'Abdullah ibn Mas'ud رضى الله عنه narrates that the Holy Prophet صلى الله عليه وسلم said: (the meaning of which is:) 'I had prohibited you from visiting the graves; (now, I permit you to) visit the graves because it builds an attitude of disinterestedness towards the blind pursuit of material gains in the present life, and helps create an awareness of the life-to-come and the readiness to act in that direction.'

(Sunnan Abi Majah)

Rulings:

1. To make *ziarah* of graves, that is, to go and see them, is desirable (*mustahabb*) for men. It is better if done at least once a week, and it is still better if that day is a Friday.

(Bahishti Gauhar)

2. Travelling to see the graves of pious elders is permissible on condition that there is nothing against the Shari'ah of Islam in matters of doctrine or deeds while doing so. An example of this can be seen these days in what is known as '*urs*[1] in some Muslim countries, a custom full of harmful practices.

(Bahishti Gauhar)

3. An occasional visit to the graves in the Night of *Bara'a* (freedom from Fire) falling in the middle of Sha'ban and praying there for the forgiveness of the inmates of the graves has its proof in *Sunnah* (see treatise on the Night of *Bara'a*). When one enters the graveyard, he should make an intention that he is addressing all inmates of the graves there, and thus offer his greeting to them once. It appears in *Hadith* that anyone who passes by the grave of someone (a Muslim) he knew and offers his greeting, the deceased recognizes him and returns his greeting (although this response is not heard by the person who first greeted him).

(Bahishti Jauhar with reference to Kanz al-A'mal)

1. ***'Urs***: a custom-oriented annual gathering of those claiming devotion to a pious elder credited with spiritual excellences or some chief of a mystic order, from history or folklore, on fixed days of the year, at the burial site, featuring activities and practices for which there is no sanction in the Shari'ah of Islam based on the Qur'an and Sunnah.

4. The inmates of the graves should be greeted in the following words:

اَلسَّلَامُ عَلَيْكُمْ يَا اَهْلَ الْقُبُوْرِ يَغْفِرُ اللّٰهُ لَنَا وَلَكُمْ اَنْتُمْ سَلَفُنَا وَنَحْنُ بِالْاَثَرِ

'Peace be on you, O inmates of (these) graves. May Allah forgive us and (forgive) you. You went before us and we are to follow.'

When the Holy Prophet صلی اللہ علیہ وسلم passed by some graves of Madinah al-Tayyibah, these were the words he used to greet them.

(Jami' Tirmidhi)

5. After having offered the greetings *(salam)*, one should stand, back towards the Qiblah and face towards the deceased in the grave, recite as much as convenient from the noble Qur'an and pray that its reward reaches the deceased. For example, one may recite *Surah al-Fatihah, Surah Yasin, Surah Tabarakal-Ladhi, Surah Alhakumut-takathur, Surah Qul huwal-lahu Ahad,* eleven or seven times, or less, whichever could be done conveniently. After this recitation, one should pray to Allah that He, in His infinite mercy, makes the reward for this recitation reach the person in the grave.

6. One should also pray for the forgiveness of the deceased. It was the blessed practice of the Holy Prophet صلی اللہ علیہ وسلم that he would, at times, visit graves for the particular reason of praying for their forgiveness.

(Madarijun-Nubuwwah)

On the Visit of Women to the Graveyard

That women go to the graveyard is totally

impermissible in the view of some Muslim jurists. The *fatwa* (religious decision in a given situation) is on the ruling that it is just not permissible for a young woman to go there, while it is permissible for an aged woman on condition that she goes there observing the required *hijab* or purdah without wearing any make-up or perfume, and that she better be sure that she is not going to do anything against the rules laid out by the Shari'ah of Islam, for example, weeping and crying loudly, asking people in their graves to grant favours and wishes and countless other deviationary activities which are innovations *(bid'ah)* associated with graves and are, as such, patently impermissible. All these should be avoided.

The mention of the curse of Allah on women who go to the graveyard appears in a *hadith*. Muslim jurists say that women who go to the graveyard without observing the conditions set for them come within the range of this curse.

(Shami, p. 843, v. 1. Imdadul-Fatawa, p. 520, v. 1, Imdadul-Ahkam, p. 720. v. 1)

The *Sunnah* method of *'Isal ath-Thawab'*

The term means that the reward of a merit-worthy act be given to one or more than one person. Its reality in the Shari'ah of Islam can be explained simply by saying that someone does something good and merit-worthy and the reward that he gets for it is given by him to someone else (be he dead or alive). This is done by saying: 'O Allah, the reward that You have given me for what I have done, may be given to such and such person, in other words, make it reach him.' For example, someone spends something in the way of Allah - food, cash, clothing, or offers voluntary prayers or fasts, or performs voluntary Hajj or 'Umrah, or recites the Holy Qur'an, makes *Dhikr*, or establishes ongoing acts of charity, such as, the making of mosques, religious schools, the publication of religious readings in the way of Allah, and then makes the prayer before Allah pleading that the reward so earned by him may reach such and such person through the grace of Allah Almighty - the result is that the reward for such good deeds, done that day or on any other day prior to this during one's entire life-time, does reach the designated person. This much is all that is proved under the Shari'ah of Islam.

(Bashishti Zewar, Shami)

All other different kinds of customs and forms of the *'Isal* of *Thawab'* invented by people are all baseless. As a matter of fact, being a party to any of these is a sin. Some of these reach the limits of *shirk* (ascribing of partners to Allah) and are straight *bid'ah* (later-day innovations in religion). Therefore, staying away from these is essential because one hardly gets any reward for what is not reward-worthy to begin with, instead, one gets involved with major sins.

For this *'Isal* of *Thawab'*, the Shari'ah has not fixed a particular day or time which would have made it impossible to participate in this act of good grace outside such days and timings. Then, there is no fixed place, nor any prescribed act of worship for this purpose. It is also unnecessary that people 'get together' to perform this act, or that food or other eatables be placed in front and be formally blessed, or that some religious scholar or a *Hafiz* or *Qari* be necessarily invited to conduct such ceremony. It is also not necessary that the whole of Qur'an be finished in one sitting, or that a specified Surah of the Qur'an, or a prayer, be recited in a specified number. People have invented these on their own and have added up all these restrictions, otherwise, the Shari'ah has made the graces of the *isal* of *thawab* so simple and easy that anyone who wishes to do it can do so any time, any day, just by offering some voluntary act of worship and can thereby hope that the reward of his deed will reach the deceased.

Can the reward of obligatory acts of worship be given to someone

Among Hanafi jurists, there is a consensus on the validity of bequeathing the reward of voluntary acts of worship *(nafl 'Ibadat)* to another person. This can be done in favour of the alive and the dead both. But the question - whether or not the reward of obligatory acts of worship *(fard 'Ibadat)* can be bequeathed to another person - has been answered variously. Some jurists have ruled this too as Permissible, while there are others who prohibit it.

On bequeathing the reward of some act of worship to several persons

It is possible to bequeath the reward of some act of worship in favour of several persons combined together. For example, someone gives a dollar in charity and asks Allah to let the reward for spending in charity reach ten persons. Now the question is: Will each deceased person get the reward equal to one dollar each? Or, the reward of spending one dollar will be distributed over all deceased persons proportionately? This has no clarification in the Holy Qur'an and Sunnah. Both are likely, but a group of jurists prefers the first likelihood which is more befitting of the all extensive mercy of Allah Almighty.

(Shami, p. 845, v.1)

'Isal' of *'Thawab'* as in *Hadith*

Praying for Allah's mercy after a person's death and performing the *Salah* of *janazah* for him are acts which issue forth from the Holy Prophet صلى الله عليه وسلم himself. Along with these, there is yet another method of serving the dead to their advantage. One may spend in charity on behalf of the deceased, or may engage in an act considered good by the Shari'ah and let the consequent reward coming to him be given to the deceased. This is *'Isal'* of *'Thawab'*. Quoted below is a *hadith* in this connection:

Sayyidna ibn 'Abbas رضى الله عنه narrates that the mother of Sayyidna Sa'd ibn 'Ubadah died at a time when he was not there in town (being with the Holy Prophet صلى الله عليه وسلم in a battle). When he returned, he went to the Holy Prophet صلى الله عليه وسلم and said to him, *'Ya Rasul Allah,* my mother died during my absence. If I spend in charity on her behalf, would that be good for her? (meaning: Would its reward reach her?)'

He said, 'Yes, it will.'

Thereupon, Sayyidna Sa'd رضى الله عنه said: "Then, I make you my witness that I give my fruit farm in charity for my mother (so that the reward for this act of charity reaches her).'

(Sahih al Bukhari, Ma'ariful-Hadith)

CHAPTER V

Rules of Burial For a *Shaheed*

A Muslim who is blessed with death by *Shahadah*[1] (شهادة) is called a *shaheed*[1] (شهيد). The Qur'an and Sunnah give a great rank to *shahadah* and speak highly about its many enviable virtues. But, we should understand that there are two kinds of *shaheed* in terms of bathing and shrouding (غسل و كفن):

The Two Kinds of *Shaheed*:

1. The first kind of *shaheed* is not bathed or shrouded and is, rather, buried after offering *Salatul-Janazah* in the clothes he is wearing, without bathing, details of which follow.

2. The second kind of *shaheed* is one who shall certainly have the rank of *shaheed* in the Hereafter *(Akhirah)* as the glad tidings of the Holy Prophet صلى الله عليه وسلم have predicted, but the rules governing a *shaheed* do not apply to him during the life of this world, that is, he too is given the bath and the shroud like the Muslims in general. There are many forms of this kind of *shahadah*, a list of which will appear later. Let us first understand the first kind and its rules.

The First Kind of *Shaheed*:

The first kind of *Shaheed* (who is neither bathed nor shrouded) is one who is killed while the following seven conditions are found:

---

1. Usually, *Shaheed is* translated as **'martyr'** and *Shahadah* as **'martyrdom'**. But, in view of the special nature of this subject, we have elected to retain the original Islamic terminology, hoping to let our readers have a synchronized perspective on the application of these two terms which have become victims of context-less usage in our time.

Condition 1

Being a Muslim. Therefore, no kind of *shahadah* can be established for a non-Muslim *(kafir:* disbeliever).

Condition 2

Being *Mukallaf,* that is, sane and adult. Therefore, for anyone killed in a state of insanity or non-adulthood, the rules of *shahadah* appearing later will not apply.

Condition 3

Being free from *al-Hadth al-Akbar,* that is, major impurity (which makes taking a bath obligatory). If a man dies in a state of *janabah* (major impurity) or a woman in a state of menstruation or childbed, the rules of *shahadah* would not apply to them either.

Condition 4

Being killed unjustly *(zulman).* Therefore, for a man who was not killed while innocent but was killed in retaliation against a crime recognized by Islamic Law, or was just not killed but died due to some other reason, for him too the injunctions governing a *shaheed* will not apply.

Condition 5

If a person was killed by a Muslim or *Dhimmi* (a non-Muslim citizen of *Dar al-Islam,* country ruled by the Muslims), the additional condition is that the act of killing was done with some sharp-edged instrument. If a person was killed by a Muslim or *Dhimmi* with an instrument not sharp-edged, for example with something like a stone having no sharp edge, the rules of *Shahadah* will not apply to him.

However, iron (inclusive of a bullet-Shami, v. 5) is ruled as a sharp-edged instrument in the absolute sense, even if it has no edge; and if a person is killed by belligerent disbelievers *(harbi kafir:* one who is a resident of a country ruled by disbelievers) or by rebels or bandits, or is found killed in their battle zone, the condition that the killing instrument be sharp-edged will not apply even if he is hit by stones and its likes and which causes his death - the rules of *shahadah* will immediately apply to him. In fact, it is not binding either that these people be directly involved in the act of killing, rather their very being instrumental in the killing, that is, they cause a chain of events that lead to such killing, even then, the rules of *shahadah* will become immediately operative.

Example A

A belligerent disbeliever, while riding an animal or vehicle, crushed a Muslim down.

Example B

A Muslim was riding an animal. Some belligerent disbeliever scared the animal and put it to flight. This caused the Muslim to fall off his mount and die.

Example C

Some belligerent disbeliever put the house of a Muslim, or a shop, on fire which caused someone to die.

In all three situations given above, the rules of *Shahadah* will become operative, that is, *ghusl* (bath) and *kafn* (shroud) will not be given to him.

(Shami, Maraqi al-Falah & Bahishti Gauhar)

Condition 6

In punishment of this killing, there be no financial compensation fixed initially by the Islamic law, instead of that, *qisas* (even retaliation) be ruled as *wajib*[1] *(necessary* or obligatory). Therefore, even if financial compensation be fixed, the rules of *shahadah* will not apply to the killed, even if killed unjustly.

Example A

A Muslim kills another Muslim with an edge-less instrument.

Example B

A Muslim kills another Muslim with a sharp-edged instrument - but, by mistake - for example, he was aiming to hit some animal or target while he ended up hitting a man.

Example C

In a situation where a person is found killed in an inhabited locality or somewhere close to it[2], other than a battle-field, and the killer be unknown[3], then, the rules of *shahadah* will not become operative here because it is blood-money which becomes necessary as compensation against such killing and not *Qisas* (even retaliation).

The restriction of 'initially' (in Condition 6) regarding the fixation of financial compensation has

1. If the nature of killing is such that there is nothing to punish through 'retaliation' or 'blood-money', the rules of *Shnhadah* will come into force. For instance, a person was found killed in a forest or desert far away from inhabited areas and the killer cannot be identified, then, he will not be given bath and shroud *(ghusl* and *kafn)* (Shami, Rafi Usmani)
2. In this situation, blood-money is paid from the Bait al-Mal (public exchequer) (al-Durr al-Mukhtar, Shami v 1, p 851)
3. Shami, ibid.

been placed there to cover the eventuality - if retaliation was fixed initially, but was waived due to some prohibitive factor and blood-money became necessary in lieu of it - in which case, the rules of *shahadah* will come into force.

Example A

Someone was killed with a sharp-edged instrument, intentionally and unjustly, but conciliation was arrived at on payment of blood-money between the killer and the inheritors of the killed person, then, in this situation, since retaliation was the only option deemed necessary and blood-money was not initially declared necessary but did so become because of the conciliation, therefore, the rules of *shahadah* will become operative here.

Example B

If a father kills his son with a sharp-edged instrument, it is a situation in which *Qisas* (even retaliation), and not blood-money, was initially ruled as necessary, but it was because of the respectable position of the father that caused *Qisas* to be waived and replaced by blood-money in lieu of it, which has now become necessary. Therefore, here too, the rules of *Shahadah* will apply.

(Shami, Maraqi al-Falah & Bahishti Gauhar)

Condition 7

Once wounded, no enjoyment of the routines of life, such as, eating, drinking, sleeping, undergoing medical treatment, buying and selling etc. should issue forth from him, nor should he be found in his normal senses for a period which does not exceed the time for one *salah*, nor is he to be carried away from the battlefield while still in his state of consciousness.

However, should he be carried away from the battlefield lest he gets trampled by animals or vehicles, then, it does not matter. Therefore, should a person talk too much after having been wounded fatally, he too would not be included under rules that govern a *shaheed*, for to keep talking is a mark of the living. Similarly, if he makes a will after having been wounded and the will be related to something worldly and mundane, he will stand excluded from being classified as a *shaheed*. But, should the will be about a religious matter, he will not be so excluded.

If a person met his death as a *shaheed* on the battlefield and such things did issue forth from him, he shall be excluded from the rules govering a *shaheed*. If otherwise, he will not be so excluded. But, if this person was killed in combat and the battle was still on, he would be a *shaheed* despite having had all these enjoyments.

(Bahishti Gauhar)

Rules for this kind of a *Shaheed*

1. The first rule for a *shaheed* in whom all these conditions are found is that he should not be given *ghusl* (bath) and his blood should not be cleaned away from his body. However, if some other impurity, except the blood, appears to linger on his body or dress, that should be washed off.

(Shami)

2. The second rule is that the clothes a *Shaheed* is wearing should not be removed from his body. But,

should the clothes he is wearing be less than the number identified by the Holy Prophet صلى الله عليه وسلم the missing number of clothes should be supplemented in order to match the *masnun* number. Similarly, if his clothes turn out to be more than the *masnun* number, the extra clothes should be removed. And if there are clothes on his body which are not shroud-worthy like a garment of leather or fur or their likes, these too should be removed from his body. But, should it be that he has no clothes on his body except such clothes, then these should not be removed.

(Shami & Maraqi al-Falah)

3. The cap, shoes, weapons and armour etc. shall be removed under all conditions. Rest of the rules that apply to all other Muslims, for instance, the *salah* of *janazah* and the burial, shall remain operative for him as well.

If any of the conditions mentioned above is found missing in respect of a *shaheed*, he shall be given *ghusl* (bath) as well as a new *kafn* (shroud) like any other dead person.

(Bahishti Gauhar & Shami)

The Second Kind of *Shaheed*

As already defined in the beginning of this chapter, *shaheeds* of this kind will have the rank of *shahadah* in the Hereafter with all attending rewards and honours, but the rules of *shahadah* do not apply to them in this world, that is, they are given the required bath and shroud like Muslims at large which is not done in the case of *shaheeds*.

The kinds of Muslims who are included under this

category reach upto more than forty, but all these are not mentioned in one single *Hadith* report. They have been identified from many different narrations. So, scholars have compiled regular works collecting and commenting upon such *ahadith.* Allama Ibn 'Abidin Shami has given a summary of these researches in his famous book, Radd al-Mukhtar. This we reproduce here as a concise list.

Muslims included in this category are:

1. A person killed unjustly but not included as *shaheed* of the first kind because some qualifying condition mentioned therein was found missing in his case.

2. One who mounts an attack on a *kafir*, rebel or bandit but the weapon of his charge inadvertently hits him which causes his death.

   (al-Durr al-Mukhtar)

3. A border guard of Muslim countries who dies a natural death on duty there.

4. One who has honestly and sincerely prayed to lay down his life in the way of Allah and then died a natural death.

5. One who is killed fighting aggressors in order to save his life and that of his family members.

6. One who is killed fighting aggressors to protect or retrieve his belongings.

7. The oppressed prisoner of a government who dies because of the rigours of detention.

8. One who hides away (seeking sanctuary against tyranny) and dies in that state.

9. One who dies in plague. It includes one who dies during the epidemic without having been affected by it, subject to the condition that he continues to stay in the affected area he is already in, with patience and fortitude, in the hope of Allah's ultimate reward, without having made efforts to run away.

10. One who dies in abdominal disorders (dropsy or diarrhoea).

11. A pneumonia patient.

12. A tuberculosis patient.

13. One who dies of epilepsy, or one who dies by having been thrown off from one's mount.

(See Shami, v.1, p. 533)

14. One who dies in fever.

15. One who dies because of vomiting at sea.

16. One who recites: لا إلٰهَ إلا أنت سبْحانك إنّي كُنْتُ مِنَ الظَّالِمِيْنَ

(There is no god but you. Pure are you. I, surely, I am but one of the unjust) forty times during his sickness, and then dies.

17. One who dies by choking.

(*'Bish-Sharaq'*, Shami, v.1, p. 533)

18. One whose death is caused by a bite from some poisonous creature.

19. One who has been torn by a beast.

20. One who dies by burning in fire.

21. One who dies by drowning in water.

22. One who dies under a wall or structure which collapses on him.

23. A woman who dies in pregnancy.

24. A woman in *nifas* (childbed) who dies at the time of childbirth or after it, before the expiry of the period of *nifas*.

25. A woman who dies a virgin.

26. A woman who remains patient in her sorrow over her husband's (marital) relationship with some other woman, and dies in that state.

27. A pious lover who conceals his love and dies lovesick.

28. One who dies away from his homeland.

29. A student of religion.[1]

30. A muezzin who gives *adhan* (call for prayers) exclusively for the pleasure of Allah (without salary or wages).

31. One who takes care of his wife and children and obeys the commands of Allah in their matters and provides *halal* (lawfully earned) livelihood for them.

32. A truthful and honest businessman.

33. A businessman who carries eatables to a city of the Muslims.

34. One who has lived his life treating people well (that is, not ill-treating even bad people without having the sanction of a clear Islamic injunction).

1. According to Shami, this includes the religious scholar who teaches, even if it be only one class a day, or that he writes. Being engaged in religious study throughout the day is not a binding condition. (Rafi Usmani)

35. One who adheres to the *Sunnah* (the teachings and the practice of the Holy Prophet صلى الله عليه وسلم while the Muslim community is in a state of decay.

36. One who goes to sleep in the night with *wudu* (ablution) and dies in that very state.

37. One who dies on a Friday.

38. One who makes the following prayer twenty five times every day:

اَللّٰهُمَّ بَارِكْ لِيْ فِي الْمَوْتِ وَ فِيْمَا بَعْدَ الْمَوْتِ

O Allah, bless me in death and in what there is after death.

39. One who makes the *salah* of *Duha (assalatud-Duha:* voluntary forenoon prayer) and keeps three fasts every month and does not leave out *witr*, neither while in town nor while travelling.

40. One who recites the noble *darud* (prayer for peace and blessings) upon the Holy Prophet ﷺ one hundred times (apparently 'daily', and Allah knows best - Rafi Usmani).

41. According to a narration from Sayyidna Ma'qil ibn Yasar رضى الله عنه reported by Imam Tirmidhi, the Holy Prophet said: Anyone who recites:

اَعُوْذُ بِاللّٰهِ السَّمِيْعِ الْعَلِيْمِ مِنَ الشَّيْطَانِ الرَّجِيْمِ

(I seek refuge with Allah the All-Hearing, the All-Knowing, from *shaitan*, the accursed) three times in the morning and supplements it with the last three verses of Suratul-Hashr (59:22-24), for him Allah Almighty appoints seventy thousand angels who keep seeking forgiveness for him right through the evening; and anyone who recites these words and verses in the evening, then the same honour holds good for him right through the morning.

In short, the first kind is classed as *shaheed* both in this world (in terms of the rules of bathing and shrouding) and in terms of the merits deserved in the life-to-come (the *Akhirah*. The second kind is *shaheed* only in terms of the rewards of the *Akhirah* and not in terms of the rules of burial for him in this world. Therefore, the first one is a *shaheed* of *dunya* and *Akhirah* both, while the second one is known as a *shaheed* of *Akhirah*.

A note of warning

A person killed while fighting disbelievers for no other purpose but material gains, with no motive to serve the cause of Faith, shall simply be a *shaheed* of this material world, even if he fulfils all seven conditions listed earlier under the first kind. He will certainly not be classed as a *shaheed* of the *Akhirah*, that is, he will be buried as a *shaheed*, without being bathed and shrouded, but he will remain deprived of the rank and reward of *shahadah* in the *Akhirah* (Hereafter). Refuge with Allah from such a fate!

DEATHS IN ACCIDENTS

Rules of Burial for Dead Bodies and Body Parts

The Tragedy of Contemporary Life

It is the nemesis of our deeds that life in our so called civilized societies of the modern world has become some sort of shooting range where disorders breed and accidents happen in breathless frequency.

The media is loaded with tales of terror and hundred die unnaturally as a matter of routine which, of course, includes a large number of Muslims as well.

There are occasions when the death of Muslims presents very complex and involved situations, so much so that arranging for timely bathing, shrouding and *salatul-janazah* (prayer for the deceased) becomes an embarrassing problem. In the event that there is no knowledgeable person around to guide into the correct Islamic method of burial in a given situation, the confusion is worse confounded. So, it is for the sake of convenience that rules for such special conditions are being given here in order that they could be used when needed. The rules relating to miscarriage appear first because that too is an accident. Other rules governing other conditions will follow. Allah willing.

1. Miscarriage resulting in expulsion of embryo only:

If abortion takes place in that stage, that is, body parts have yet to be formed, the embryo is neither bathed, nor shrouded, neither is *salatul-janazah* offered, nor a regular burial given. Instead, it should be wrapped in some cloth and buried in a ditch dug for that purpose. Also, it should not be given a name.

(Shami, v.1 p. 809)

2. About fetus with partly formed body parts:

If abortion takes place at a stage when the fetus has developed some but not all body parts, it should be given a name, and bathed without given it a regular shroud. Instead, it should be wrapped up in some cloth. No *salah* of *janazah* should be offered and it should be buried as is without that *salah*.

(Shami, v. 1, pp. 830 831 & Bahishti Zewar)

3. The rule in still-birth:

If a child is born still, either through miscarriage or regular pains, and there be no sign of life in it at the time of birth, even though all body parts are there fully formed, then, this child will be governed by the same rule as given in No 2 above, that is, the child will be bathed and named, but regular shroud will not be given and the *salah* of *janazah* will not be offered. Instead, it would be wrapped in some cloth and buried.

(Shami. v.1, p. 830)

4. For a child born alive but dead later in the process of delivery:

The case of a child, who was alive when the head came out at the time of birth but died later, will be handled under the rule given in No. 3 for a still-born child. That is, the child will be given a bath and a name, but not a regular shroud. Instead, the body will be wrapped in a single cloth piece and buried without offering *salatul-janazah.*

(Shami. v. 1, pp 829-830)

5. For a child still alive when a major portion of the body had come out:

If the child dies after having been born in that mode of birth, it will be covered by the rule that governs the birth of an alive child. The child will be given the regular bath and shroud. In case the child is a boy, it is better to give him a shroud like men; and if a girl, a shroud like women. However, if the body is shrouded in only one piece of cloth, and the girl in two, that would also be correct.

Give a name, offer *salah* of *janazah* and bury in the regular way.

(Shami)

(a) If the child dies before the major portion of its body comes out, the rule governing the child born still (No. 3) will apply.

(b) 'If the child's major portion of the body comes out alive' means that the child was born head first, then, its coming out upto the chest will be taken as the coming out of the major portion of the body. If the child is born legs first, then, its coming out alive upto the navel will be taken as the coming out of the major portion of the body.

(Shami, v.1, pp. 829-830)

6. The rule when a child is alive in the womb of the dead mother:

If a woman dies in a state of pregnancy and the child be alive in her womb, the child should be taken out surgerically.

(al-Durr al-Mukhtar, v. 1, p. 840)

If the child dies after having been removed alive, it should be given a name like all other children, bathed, shrouded and buried after offering *salatul-janazah.* If the case be that the child, irrespective of whether the fetus is inert or alive, dies before it could be taken out of the womb, then, the child should not now be removed out through a surgerical operation on the woman. But in case the child is taken out in that condition, it will be governed by the rule which applies to the birth of a still-born child.

(No.3)

7. For one who dies by drowning in water:

If a person dies by drowning in water, it is obligatory to give the dead body a regular bath after it has been taken out from there. Drowning in water is no exemption from *ghusl* (bathing) because giving a bath to the deceased is an obligation imposed on the living. Here, the living have done nothing to absolve them of their obligation - the incidence of drowning does not affect their position. However, if the deceased is moved in the water with the intention of giving it a *ghusl* (bath), before taking the body out of there, the prescribed *ghusl* would be deemed as performed.

(al-Bahr al-Ra'iq)

After this has been done, give the deceased the regular shroud, offer the *salah* of *janazah* and bury the body in accordance with the *sunnah*. But, should it be that he has been drowned in cold blood by rebels, highway robbers or disbelievers of a non-Muslim country and he fulfils all conditions required in the first kind of *shaheed*, rules of burial for a *shaheed* will apply to him.

8. For an inflated corpse:

If a corpse inflates, because of drowning in water, delay in cremation, or for some other reason, to the extent that it cannot be even touched, that is, there be the danger that any touch of hands while bathing it may cause it to burst open, in which case, it is sufficient to pour water all over it since rubbing is not necessary in bathing the dead body. Then, the body should be shrouded, and buried after offering *salatul-janazah*. But, in case the corpse is ruptured before the *salah*, it should be buried without performing it.

('Alamgiri, al-Bahr & Imdadul-Ahkam)

9. A corpse which starts releasing stench:

Salatul-janazah will be offered for a dead body which gives stench but has not yet ruptured.

(Fatawa Darul-Uloom, Deoband, v. 5, p. 335)

10. A corpse which has ruptured:

For a corpse which has ruptured, *Salatul-Janazah* is dropped. It should not be performed in this case.

(al-Bahr & Imdadul-Ahkam)

11. If only a skeleton of bones is found:

In the case of a corpse where everything like flesh and ligaments have disintegrated leaving the bare structure of bones, it is not necessary to bathe the skeleton. Even *salatul-janazah* need not be offered over it. Instead, it should be wrapped in some clean cloth and buried.

(Imdadul-Ahkam, v. 1, p. 738)

12. One who dies by burning:

A person who dies in a fire or is electrocuted should be given the regular bathing and shrouding, *salatul-janazah* should be offered and he should be buried in accordance with *sunnah*. However, if the corpse is swollen or ruptured, the rule to be followed has appeared in No. 8 and No. 10 above.

(al-Durr al-Mukhtar, al-Bahr & Imdadul-Ahkam)

But, should it be that a person has been burnt to death by rebels, highway robbers or disbelievers of a non-Muslim country, or he is found dead on a battlefield and he fulfils all conditions required in the first kind of *shaheed*, the rules of burial for a *shaheed* will apply to him. Details can be seen in "Rules of Burial for a *Shaheed*".

13. The case of a charred body:

For a person who was burnt and totally charred, or the major portion of his body was charred, it is not necessary *(wajib)* to bathe or shroud the body or offer *salatul-janazah* for it. The remains should be wrapped in some cloth and buried as is.

('Alamgiri & Fatawa Darul-Uloom, v.1, p. 345)

If the major portion of the body has remained unburnt, even if it be minus the head, or half of the body including the head has remained unburnt, or the whole body has been affected by burning, though in a minor way, leaving the skin, the flesh and the bones intact, then, it should be buried after the regular bathing, shrouding and *salatul-janazah*.

(Shami, v. 1, p. 809 & Alamgiri)

14. One who is crushed under, is buried down or falls off:

One who dies buried under a collapsed wall or structure, or falls down from some height or is killed as a victim of some airline accident and the major portion of his body remains intact, then, his remains should be buried after the regular bathing, shrouding and *salatul-janazah*. But, should it be that this accident was plotted and executed by hostile disbelievers or rebels or highway robbers, then, the rules governing the burial of a *shaheed* will apply on those killed in this manner. For reference, please see No. 12 above.

15. Rules for victims of common accidents:

For those who die in accidents caused by cars,

motor-cycles, trains, buses and other modes of transport, the same rule as in No. 14 above shall apply.

(al-Durr al-Mukhtar)

16. The corpse which cannot be salvaged from under debris or from out of a well:

If a person dies by falling into a well or some other depth or gets buried under the debris of a fallen building and it is not possible to salvage the corpse from there, then, this is a case of compulsion and the requirement of bathing and shrouding the deceased stands excused. The spot where the corpse was drowned in or buried under will be taken as his grave and it will be in this very state that the *salah* of *janazah* will be offered for him.

(Shami, v. 1, p. 827)

17. For a corpse lost at sea:

In situations when a person dies by drowning into the sea and the dead body cannot be traced, or the death may have occured under some other circumstances and the dead body is either lost or remains untraceable, then, the regular bathing, shrouding, *salah* of *janazah* and burial all stand excused. In addition to that even a *salatul-janazah* in absentia (prayer for the deceased in absence of the dead body) is not to be offered because one of the conditions that makes the *salatul-janazah* correct is that the dead body for which it is being offered should be present in the front.

(Shami, v. 1, p. 827)

18. When dead bodies of Muslims and non-Muslims get mixed up and are unrecognizable:

If an accident causes the dead bodies of Muslims and non-Muslims to be all mixed up, Muslims should be somehow removed out from there by making an effort to identify them by some distinguishing features including circumcision. All last rites for them, such as the bathing, the shrouding, the *salatul-janazah* and the burial, should be performed as done with Muslims. The dead bodies of non-Muslims should be handled in accordance with rules set for them. For details please see chapter II.

(Bahishti Gauhar & v.1, p. 805 & 'Alamgiri v.1, p. 159)

Should it be that the Muslims cannot be identified as distinct from non-Muslims by any means and there be no cue visible enough to tell which dead body is that of a Muslim and which that of a non-Muslim, then, the situation has three solutions:

(i) If the number of Muslims is larger among the dead, all dead bodies should be handled the Muslim way, that is all of them should be given the regular bathing, shrouding and *salatul-janazah* and buried in the graveyard of the Muslims. But, the intention *(niyyah)* made in the *salatul-janazah* should be for the Muslims only. An intention *(niyyah)* of making *salatul-janazah* over dis-believers is not permissible.

(Shami. v. 1, p. 805 & 'Alamgiri, v.1, p. 159)

(ii) If the dead bodies of non-Muslims are larger in number than those of Muslims, all dead bodies should be bathed and shrouded.[1] *Salatul-Janazah* should be offered for them but with the intention

1. According to Fatawa 'Alamgiri, this bathing and shrouding will not be done in the regular way as done for Muslims (instead, the dead bodies will be summarily washed with water and wrapped in a single piece of cloth each). (v. 1 . p. 159).

(niyyah) that it is being offered for Muslims only. After that, all of them should be buried in the graveyard of disbelievers.

(Shami, al-Durr al-Mukhtar, v. 1, p. 805)

(iii) If the dead bodies of Muslims and non-Muslims be equal in number, all of them should be bathed and shrouded, however *salatul-janazah* shall be offered for all of them but with the intention *(niyyah)* that it is being offered for the Muslims only. As far as the site of burial is concerned, Muslim jurists have taken three positions:

(A) All of them should be buried in the graveyard of Muslims.

(B) All of them should be buried in the graveyard of disbelievers.[1]

(C) A separate graveyard should be used to bury them.

Though the third position (C) offers a little more precaution, but it is quite correct to act in accordance with any of the above modalities.

(Shami, v. 1. pp. 805-806, al-Durr al -Mukhtar)

19. When the *Kafir* wife of a Muslim dies while pregnant:

If a Jewish or Christian wife of a Muslim dies during her pregnancy and if the embryo in her womb was still inert, she will be invariably buried in the

1. If all of them are buried in a separate place, that is, neither in the graveyard of disbelievers nor in that of Muslims, then, this approach would appear to be more precaution-prone. Under the next ruling (No. 19) the author of al-Durr al-Mukhtar has himself pointed this out explicitly. (Rafi Usmani)

graveyard of non-Muslims. And if the fetus was alive, then the child died in the womb along with the dead mother, then, this child, being the offspring of a Muslim, should be classified as a Muslim, but because the child is in the womb of its non-Muslim mother and the question of the burial site destined for the mother hinges on the three positions taken by Muslim jurists stated earlier in Rule 18 They are:

(I) In difference to the status of the child, the woman be buried in the graveyard of Muslims.

(II) She be buried in the graveyard of non-Muslims.

(III) The woman should neither be buried in the graveyard of the Muslims nor in that of non-Muslims, but should be buried on some other separate site. This Position takes additional precaution.

Now, whatever course is adopted in the burial, the back of the deceased woman must be turned towards the *Qiblah* after the body has been lowered into the grave, because the child, while in the womb of the mother, faces her back. Thus, the face of the child will become oriented towards the Qiblah.

(Shami, al-Durr al-Mukhtar v. 1, pp. 805-806)

20. When the identity of the deceased is unknown:

In a situation where the dead body of a man or woman is found and it cannot be determined by any marks or signs whether the deccased is a Muslim or a non-Muslim, one should look at the area where the body was found; if it is a Muslim majority area, the deceased will be deemed to be a Muslim and treated as such, that is, bathed, shrouded and buried after offering *salatul-janazah.* In case, the area where the body was found is a non-Muslim majority area, the deceased will be handled under the rules governing non-Muslims.

(al-Durr al-Mukhtar, 'Alamgiri & Bahishti Gauhar including marginal notes)

21. About the deceased buried without *ghusl* or *salatul-janazah*:

If a Muslim deceased was inadvertently lowered into the grave without offering *salatul-janazah*, and if the mistake is realized before earth has been filled in the grave, the body should be taken out of it. After that, if the body was not bathed, it should now be given a bath and buried after offering the *salatul-janazah.* In case, the deceased was already given a bath, then, just offer the *salatul-janazah* and bury.

And should it so happen that earth has been thrown back into the grave and the mistake is realized after that, then it is no more permissible to dig the grave all over again. Now the rule is: Until such time the likelihood exists that the corpse would have not ruptured, the *salatul-janazah* will be offered on the grave site itself. But, in accordance with the weightier opinion, there is no specific time frame for the actual rupturing or bursting of the corpse. This time differs in terms of weather, location and heaviness or slimness of the deceased. Therefore, until such time that there be the major likelihood that the corpse would have not ruptured yet, offering the *salatul-janazah* is obligatory; and when the major likelihood is that the corpse would have ruptured, the *salatul-janazah*, then, should not be offered. Given this situation those who had the capability of offering this *salah* yet did not do so will be incurring a sin. It is incumbent on them that they should repent and seek forgiveness from Allah and make sure that they would not be so heedless in the future.

(al-Durr al-Mukhtar)

Should the doubt - has the corpse ruptured, or has it not? still persist, that will be a condition under which as well, the *salah* of *janazah* will not be offered on the grave site.

(Shami v.1, p. 827)

22. The rule for one who commits suicide:

Anyone who kills himself deliberately or by mistake should be given the regular bath and shroud and buried after offering *salatul-janazah.*

(Shami, v. 1, p. 815 & al-Durr al-Mukhtar)

23. When only parts of a corpse are found:

If the full body of a deceased person is not found, instead only some parts of the body are found, the case rulings given below may be applied:

(a) In case only hand or leg or head or waist or some other part is found, it needs no bathing, shrouding and *salah,* nothing. Instead, wrap in a piece of cloth and bury as it is.

(Shami, Bahishti Gauhar, p. 90)

(b) In case different parts of the body, for example, only two legs or only two hands or only one hand and leg or, similarly, a few other parts are found, and these different parts combined together turn out to be somewhat less than half of the full body of the deceased, that is, the major portion of the body of the deceased is not available, then, there is no bathing, shrouding and *salatul-janazah* for these parts. Wrap in a piece of cloth and bury as they are.

(Shami, Bahishti Gauhar)

(c) In case one half portion of the body of the deceased is found without the head, that too does not require any bathing, shrouding and *salatul-janazah.* Just wrap in a piece of cloth and bury.

(Shami, Bahishti Gauhar)

(d) In case one half portion of the body of the deceased is found with the head, that should be given regular bathing and shrouding and buried after offering *salatuljanazah.*

(Shami, Bahishti Gauhar)

(e) In case the major portion of the body of the deceased is found, even though it be without the head, the rule is thal it will be given the regular bathing and shronding and buried after offering *salatul-janazah.*

(Shami, Bahishti Gauhar)

24. On remaining parts found after the burial:

In case the major portion of the body of the deceased was found but the remaining portion was not found and *salatul-janazah* was offered for the available major portion of the body and the body was buried, however, the remaining portion of the body was found after that, the rule is that *salatul-janazah* will not be offered for this remaining portion at that stage and it would simply be wrapped in some cloth and buried.

(Shami, 'Alamgiri)

25. The rule for parts separated from the living body:

If some part of the body of a living person is cut off from it or removed by operation, it does not require any bathing, shrouding and *salah* of *janazah*. It should be simply wrapped in a piece of cloth and buried.

(al-Durr al-Mukhtar & Fatawa Darul-'Ulum)

26. A corpse, all in one piece, shows up from the grave:

If a grave opens up and the corpse comes out for some reason such as an earthquake or flood or the plundering of a shroudlifter and it be bereft of its shroud, then, if the corpse has been found ruptured, it need not be given a regular shroud under that condition. It should be just wrapped in some cloth and buried.

And if the corpse has not been ruptured, it should be given the regular full shroud according to the *Sunnah*. And should this happen repeatedly with one particular corpse, then, it should be given the full *masnun kafan* every time this happens.

All expenses incurred on this shrouding will be taken from the basic inheritance of that particular deceased, even if the deceased be in debt. However, if the entire inheritance has been distributed over the debtors, or it has been distributed under some other head according to the will of the deceased, in which case the debtors or the receivers of cash or property under the will cannot be asked to pay for the expenses on this shrouding of the deceased.

And if the inheritance of the deceased has already been distributed to the inheritors, each such inheritor will be required to pay for the expenses incurred on the shrouding of the deceased in proportion to the percentage of their shares in the inheritance.

(al-Durr al-Mukhtar & Shami, v.1, p. 809)

27. When robbers or rebels kill or get killed:

If robbers or rebels get killed during a fight, the rule is - to disgrace them and teach others - that they should not be given *ghusl*[1] (bath), nor *salatul-janazah* be offered for them, rather they should be buried casually. But, if they were killed after the fight or if they died their own death after the fight, then, they will be given the regular bath and *salah* for their *janazah* will be offered. This very rule covers those who are killed fighting for tribal national or linguistic prejudice.

If the robbers or the rebels kill someone during the process of robbery or fighting, that person will be a *shaheed*. He will not be bathed and shrouded. Only *salatul-janazah* will be offered for him before he is buried. Please see details in Rules of Burial for a *Shaheed'*.

(Shami. v.1, p. 814, al-Durr al-Mukhtar)

---

1. Shami has approved another Hanafi ruling which says that they should be given *ghusl* but *salatul-janazah* should not be offered for them. (Shami. v. 1. p. 814)

CHAPTER VI

The 'Idda of Death

In the event the husband of a woman dies, or there is divorce by the husband, or the woman seeks to terminate the marriage contract through *khul'*, or the marriage is annulled in some other manner, then, under all such conditions, the woman has to remain staying in one house upto a specified period of time. Until this period expires, it is not permissible for her to go elsewhere. The act of passing this period of time is called *'Idda* (عدة *'Iddat; pausal* form: *'Iddah*: translitrated as *'Idda*). Also, she cannot marry another man during this period. If it is done, the marriage will be void, not having been 'concluded' legally.

(Bahishti Zewar & Islahi-i-Inqilab-i-Ummat)

Special Note

If the *'Idda* or Waiting Period is observed following the death of the husband, it is called, 'The 'Idda of Death'. If observed following *Talaq* (divorce). *Khul'* (divorce at the instance of the wife) or for some other reason, it is called, 'The *'Idda* of Divorce'. There is some difference in the rules and periods of the two types of 'Idda. Given here are rules which relate to the *'Idda* of Death. For rules governing the *'Idda* of *Talaq*, please see 'Bahishti Zewar' by Maulana Ashraf Ali Thanavi or consult religious scholars you trust.

Rules:

1. A woman whose husband dies should remain in *'Idda* for four months and ten days. She should live in the house she used to live in at the time of her

husband's death. Going out of there is not correct.

(Bahishti Zewar)

2. Whether or not a woman has had intimacy with her husband during his life-time, whether or not she had any kind of privacy with him, whether or not she had come to live with him, whether or not she menstruates, whether old or young, pubert or non-pubert - there is one rule for all: Be in '*Idda* for four months and ten days.

However, if the woman was pregnant and the husband died while she was in that state, she would remain in '*Idda* until the child is born. Now the count of months is not taken into consideration. In fact, if the child is born a little after the death of her husband the '*Idda* will be all over.

(Bahishti Zewar, 'Alamgiri, Imdadul-Fatwa)

3. She lives in the house and moves freely where she wants. There is a custom in some families where a woman whose husband has died would confine herself to one fixed place. If she moves from there, it is taken to be something bad. This is meaningless, absurd. The custom must be abandoned.

(Bahishti Zewar)

4. For a woman who had gone out of the house to take care of some family chore, or was away visiting neighbours, or her own parents or relatives for a few days (with or without the husband), it is necessary that she, immediately as she finds out that her husband has died, should return from wherever she may be to stay in the house in which she was living, irrespective of the consideration that her husband had died elsewhere.

(Bahishti Zewar, Imdadul-Fatawa, v.2, p. 442 & 427)

5. A woman whose displeased husband had sent her to her parental home should, in case her husband dies, return to the home of her husband and complete her *'Idda* there because *'Idda* is completed in the house which was the permanent residence of the woman at the time of her husband's death. He temporary residence is not taken into consideration. As obvious, her visit to the parental home was temporary.

(Imdadul-Fatawa, v. 2, p. 427)

6. If the husband died on the first of the lunar month and the woman is not pregnant, she will have to complete the period of four months and ten days in accordance with the lunar calendar. And if the husband died on a date other than the first, she would have to complete the period of four months and ten days by counting each month as of thirty days (that is, 'full one hundred and thirty days' - Ma'ariful-Qur'an). Consequently, when the time at which death had occurred returns after the passage of this waiting period, the *'Idda* will be over.

(Bahishti Zewar & Ma'ariful-Qur'an)

7. *'Idda* begins from the time of the husband's death even if the woman is not aware of this and she has made no intention to observe *'Idda.*

(al-Durr al-Mukhtar)

8. In case the husband of a woman dies and she remained uninformed, so much so that she found it out after the passage of four months and ten days, then, her *'Idda* stands completed, that is, she will not have to observe *'Idda* all over again onwards from the time she was informed of the death of her husband.

(Bahishti Zewar)

9. A woman hears about the death of her husband several days later, but there is a doubt about the exact date of his death, in which case. 'Idda will be counted[1] onwards from a date about which there is a reasonable element of certainty.

(Shami, v.2, p. 838)

10. The custom, wherever it may exist, that a woman keeps sitting in observance of *'Idda* for a whole year, is absolutely *haram* (forbidden).

(Bahishti Zewar)

Maintenance during the period of *'Idda:*

Rule:

The maintenance and the residential quarters[2] for a woman observing the *'Idda* of Death are not the responsibility of her in in-laws. She also does not have the right to take her maintenance out of the inheritance of her deceased husband. She will, nevertheless, positively get her share in the inheritance as fixed by the Shari'ah.

(Bahishti Zewar)

***'Idda* in Pregnancy and Abortion:**

As stated earlier, the *'Idda* of a pregnant woman ends with the birth of the child, but the ruling differs in the case of an abortion, the details of which follow. If the fetus shows the formation of any body part, such as the mouth, the nose or finger, the *'Idda* will end. If

1. For instance, there are two probabilities here: The death occurred on Rajab 4 or Sha'ban 4. Therefore, the period of *'Idda* will be counted from Sha'ban 4 as a matter of precaution. (Rafi Usmani)
2. Details about the house may be seen later on under "Shifting Residence...!" No. 1-5 pages 129-131.

there was no formation of any body part on the fetus and it was still in the stage of an embryo, then, *'Idda* will not end on that basis. Rather, the woman would be deemed to be non-pregnant, and as a result, her *'Idda* will be nothing less than four months and ten days.

(Shami v.2, p, 831)

Rules:

1. The Shari'ah does not recognize pregnancy beyond the maximum of two years. So, a woman who was obviously pregnant at the time of her husband's death but did not deliver the child for two years, she will not be considered pregnant Shari'ah-wise. Her *'Idda* ended after four months and ten days from the death of her husband.

(Azizul-Fatawa. p. 542)

2. If a pregnant woman carrying twins gives birth to one, but not to the other, then, her *'Idda* will not end until she has delivered the other baby too.

(Shami. v.2, p. 831)

The death of Husband during the *'Idda* of *Talaq*

For a woman who was divorced by her husband in any manner whatsoever, or she had herself sought a release through *Khul'*, or her marriage was annulled for some other reason and who had completed the *'Idda* of *Talaq* following which her ex-husband dies, then, for this woman there is no *'Idda* because of this death of her husband, and she will not be one of his inheritors either.

(Shami, v.2, p. 833)

The case of a woman whose husband dies before the *'Idda* of *Talaq* ends has some details which follow:

(1) If the husband had given a revocable divorce, in sickness or in health, the woman would set aside the *'Idda* of Death afresh from the time of her husband's death. She will also be entitled to inherit from the deceased husband.

(Shami, v.2, p. 833)

(2) If the husband had given an irrevocable divorce while being in good health, irrespective of whether the divorce was given with or without her consent, then, the husband dies before the *'Idda* of Divorce could end - now, in this situation, the woman would complete only whatever period remains of the *'Idda* of Divorce. She will not go through the *'Idda* of Death and she will not inherit from the husband either.

(Shami. v.2, p. 833)

(3) If the husband was sick while giving the irrevocable[1] divorce and the divorce was given with the consent of the woman, the situation will be governed by the same rule as stated above in No. 2, that is, the woman would complete only the remaining period of the *'Idda* of Divorce, whatever the period may be. She will not observe the *'Idda* of Death and she will not inherit from the husband either.

(Shami, & Hidayah)

(4) If the husband had given an irrevocable divorce during his sickness without the consent of the

1. The rule relating to the irrevocable divorce *(al-Talaq al-Ba'in)* given here applies identically to the triply pronounced divorce (*al-talaq al-mughallazah* : the declaration of divorce pronounced three times which makes it binding). As in Hidayah under the Chapter on *al-'Idda*. (Rafi Usmani).

woman, this will be a situation in which it will have to be determined as to which of the two waiting periods takes more days to complete. Does the *'Idda* of Divorce take more days? Or, does the *'Idda* of Death take more days? Whichever of the two periods takes more days to complete, that will be the period of *'Idda* the woman will complete and she will inherit from the husband.

(Shami, v. 2, p. 832, & Bahishti Zewar)

Things not permissible during *'Idda*:

For a woman whose husband had died, the rule is that she should neither go out of the house during the period of *'Idda*, nor remarry, nor indulge in make-up. During *'Idda*, all these things are *haram* (forbidden) for her. This absence of make-up and lack of concern for being well-dressed signify 'mourning' on her part.

(Bahishti Zewar, part 4)

Mourning in *'Idda* is *Wajib*:

Rules:

1. Mourning on the death of her husband is necessary *(wajib)* for a woman who is a Muslim, sane and adult. It is not obligatory on a woman who is a disbeliever or is insane or is a non-pubert girl. For them, wearing make-up is permissible. But, going out of the house and remarrying is not correct even for them.

(Bahishti Zewar, part 4)

2. For a woman whose marriage was not correct or was irregular, then her husband died, this is a situation in which it is not necessary[1] for her to observe

---

1. But, the observance of *'Idda is* obligatory on her as well, that is, it is not permissible for her to remarry during the period of *'Idda* (al-Durr al-Mukhtar, v. 2. p. 825). Such a woman should, after her husband

mourning.

(Bahishti Zewar, part 4)

3. Proposing to a woman observing the *'Idda* of Death in clear words or making her a party in betrothal is *haram* (forbidden). However, short of making a direct proposal, saying something in the manner of a veiled hint is permissible. To a woman who is observing her *'Idda* of Divorce, even saying this much, no matter how veiled the hint, is not permissible.

(al-Durr al-Mukhtar, v. 2, p. 852 & Ma'ariful-Qur'an, Suratul-Baqarah)

4. Until such time that the *'Idda* expires, wearing perfume, anointing body or dress, donning ornaments, jewellery or decorations of any sort, sporting bangles (even if made of glass), wearing eye make-up, such as *kohl* or galena, chewing or applying something to show colour on lips, teeth or gums, applying oil on the head, combing hair, using henna, wearing silken or other gaudy dresses (specially new) are acts patently *haram* (forbidden). However, wearing clothes which are coloured but not new and showy is correct, the purpose being to avoid adornment, decoration or distinction in dressing up.

5. Washing of the head and bathing is permissible during *'Idda.* Combing hair when needed is also correct, but combing hair in a manner which gives sheen or style should be avoided. It is better to use a thick-edged comb which leaves the hair dull but functionally in place.

(Bahishti Zewar & Shami - abridged)

---

dies, not sit in *'Idda* for four months and ten days but she should sit in *'Idda* until she completes three full menstrual periods. If she does not menstruate, she will be in *'Idda* for three months and if she is pregnant, it will be till delivery.

(Bahishti Zewar & al-Durr al-Mukhar v. 2. p. 850)

6. For a woman who has clothes all of which are elegant and becoming, and none of them are ordinary and simple, then she should get some ordinary clothes from somewhere and wear them, even if she has to sell her good clothes for this purpose. For her the rule will be that she continues wearing the elegant clothes she has (without intending to look elegant) until she gets hold of the simple ones to wear.

(Shami, p. 115)

7. After *'Idda*, all these restrictions are over. She can remarry too.

(Bahishti Zewar)

8. Mourning at anyone's death, except that of the husband, is not permissible. However, unless the husband prohibits her, it will be correct if a woman was to forsake her usual make-up for three days while mourning the death of one of her relatives. Doing anymore than this is totally *haram* (forbidden). If the husband does prohibit her, she should not forsake her make-up even for three days.

(Bahishti Zewar, Part 4)

Hadith

The Holy Prophet صلى الله عليه وسلم has said that it is not permissible for a believer to mourn for anyone for more than three days except the widow whose period of mourning (when not pregnant) on the death of her husband is four months and ten days.

(Tirmidhi - Abwabut-Talaq, al-Bukhari)

Using beauty aids as medicine

Rules:

1. If there be need to put oil on the scalp because of headache or lice, it is correct to use an oil without scent.

(Bahishti Zewar& Imdadul-Fatawa, v.2. p. 450)

2. For a woman who strongly apprehends that she will get a headache if she does not rub oil on her scalp, a practice she is used to, then she can use an oil without scent to offset the likelihood of a headache, even if the headache has not started yet.

(Hidayah. v.2,. 'Alamgiri)

3. Using *surma (kohl*, powdered galena, NOT antimony which is an erroneous rendering, and quite dangerous too, as antimony is an ingredient of explosives and no liner of eyestr.) to heal eyes is correct when needed. But, apply at night and clean off during the day.

(Bahishti Zewar)

4. If there be need to wear silken clothes as medical measure against itching skin, there is leeway for that too. Still, it is better not to wear these with an intention to look good.

(Hidaya v.2)

Going out of the house because of need

Completing *'Idda* in the same house in which the womenn lived permanently at the time of her husband's death is obligatory. Going out is not permissible. However, if she is so poor that she does not have enough to pay for her living expenses, it is permissible for her to go out properly covered *(purdah, hijab)* to work on salary or wages during the daytime. But, she should make it a point to stay at her house during nights and also to return home during days as soon as she is free from her work. Spending anymore time outside the house is not permissible.

(Bahishti Zewar, Imdadul-Fatawa, Shami)

Rules:

1. Travelling is also not permissible during *'Idda*. It includes any travel, even that of Hajj.

(Imdadul-Fatawa, v.2, p. 428)

2. If the job done by a widow in *'Idda* takes up some part of the night as well, this too is permissible, but she should spend the major part of the night at her own home.

(al-Durr al-Mukhtar. v.2, p. 854)

Travelling under a situation of compulsion during *'Idda*

Rules:

1. A woman who owns some cultivated land, farm, property or business which requires that she personally go there to control, execute or manage affairs and that there be no one else around her family who could be asked to do this job on her behalf while she is in *'Idda*, then, this would be a situation of compulsion in which it will be permissible for her to go out of the house properly covered. But, she should spend the night at her own house and make an effort that she returns home as soon as her job is over.

(al-Durr al-Mukhtar & Shami)

If the land farm is far from where she lives and one has to 'travel' in order to get there, then she can go there as well with a *Mahram* (person with whom marriage is unlawful for ever) for as many days as necessary.

(Imdadul-Fatawa, v.2, p. 429)

2. If a woman observing the *'Idda* of Death is sick and it is not possible to arrange for a house-call by a physician or give her any alternate treatment, then, it is also permissible to take her to the physician or, if there be a situation of urgency, getting her admitted into a hospital is also permissible. If treatment or diagnosis is not available around her residential area, then, it is permissible to take her to another city for this purpose for whatever number of days necessary. But, should this other city be at a distance the covering of which is termed as 'travel', then, she has to have a *Mahram* (person with whom marriage is unlawful forever) accompanying her.

(Imdadul-Fatawa. v.2, p. 428)

Shifting residence during *'Idda* under circumstantial compulsion

Rules:

1. If the house in which a woman lived at the time of her husband's death was a rented house and she has the ability to pay rent, then, she should pay rent and live there until the period of her *'Idda* expires. If she does not have the ability to pay rent, then she should move to the nearest possible place where she could live with all possible security of life, property and honour and with full regard for her modesty *(purdah)*. She should not shift to a house far out unless

necessary. Once she does shift this residence of hers, she should spend the rest of her waiting period (*'Idda)* in there.

(al-Durr al-Mukhtar & Shami. v.2, p. 854)

2. If the house in which a woman lived at the time of her husband's death belonged to her husband and was now distributed among inheritors and the part of the house which came into her possession as her share in the inheritance is not sufficient to live in and the rest of the inheritors do not let her live in their portions, or it may be that it is sufficient all right but there are people, from whom she should observe *purdah* in obedience to the Shari'ah, who also live there and do no respect her concern of observing purdah as a religious duty - this, then, will be a situation in which she could move to the nearest available house where she could live with all possible security of life, property and honour and with full protection of *purdah.* She should spend the remaining period of her *'Idda* there.

(al-Durr al-Mukhtar, Shami & Hidayah)

3. If the house in which she is observing *'Idda* collapses, or there be the danger that it will, or there is a strong apprehension that she is likely to lose her honour, life, property or health if she stays there, or it may not be possible for her to observe *purdah* from those the Shari'ah has identified as those from whom *purdah* be observed, then, under all these situations as well, she can move from that house.

(Imdadul-Fatawa, Shami, al-Durr al-Mukhtar)

4 If a woman is scared of living alone in the house where she is observing her *'Idda* and she does not have a trustworthy person to live with her, then,

she has two choices. If the fear is so severe that she cannot bear it, this will also be a situation in which she could shift her residence from this house. But, if the fear is not that severe, shifting from the house is not permissible.

Similarly, if the house in which she is passing her *'Idda* be haunted and she is so scared of demons that she cannot bear the very thought of living in a haunted house or there is some open evidence of hurt caused by such evil presences, then, this is also a situation in which it is permissible to shift her residence to another house. If the above conditions do not exist, it is not permissible.

(Imdadul-Fatawa v.2, p. 433)

5. In situation rulings given above where shifting from the house of *'Idda* has been declared permissible, it is necessary in all of them that the woman should shift from there to such nearest possible house where she could live with security of life, property and honour along with the freedom to seek protection through *purdah*. Unless necessary, she should not move to the house farther away and she should pass the remaining days of her *'Idda* in the house she shifts to. Now this house will be governed by the same rule as was applied to the original one, that is, from here she cannot go out without any compulsion to move.

(al-Durr al-Mukhtar & Shami. v.2, p. 854)

Family feuds are no excuse

If the woman in *'Idda* and her mother-in-law are at odds with each other, so much so that they find it terribly difficult to live under one roof, then, shifting to another house on the basis of this sole reason is not permissible. This mutual bickering would certainly be painful but not so painful that it cannot be patiently cushioned out during the period of *'Idda*.

(Imdadul-Fatawa. v.2, p. 448)

Where does a woman who is in travel at the time of her husband's death pass the period of *'Idda?*

This question involves separate rulings in different[1] situations details of which are given below:

(1) If she was still somewhere enroute at the time of her husband's death (or at the time of receiving the news of his death), in some town or in an unpopulated place, it should then be determined at to how far in distance is her own town from that spot. If this distance is less than the "travel distance"[2], she should immediately return to her town of residence, whether or not she has a *Mahram* with her, and whether the town she was travelling[3] to is on "travel distance" or is at a lesser distance.[4]

(Hidayah, Inayah, Fath al-Qadir, v.2, p. 299)

---

1. Whether or not the husband is with her, details under both situations remain the same as stated later.
(al-Durr al-Mukhtar, Shami, Hidayah, Fath al-Qadir)

2. "Travel Distance" denotes a standard distance because of which a person is considered to be "a traveller" in the terminology of the Shari'ah and because of which the prescribed *salah* is shortened (*Qasr*). On plains, this distance is the equivalent of 48 miles.
(Awzan ash-Shara'iyyah by Mufti Muhammad Shafi).

3. From here onwards we shall be using the word, "destination" for this town. (Rafi Usmani)

4. However, some Hanafi jurists have said that in the event the "destination" too is at a distance less than the standard "travel distance", then the woman has the option of either going there and completing her *'Idda* or doing it in her own town by returning there. But, even they think that it is much better if she returns to her town of usual residence.
(Shami, v.2. p. 856)

(2) And should it be that her own town is at the "travel distance" from there and the destination is at a distance less than that, then she should continue travelling onwards, reach the destination and complete the *'Idda* there, whether or not she has a *Mahram* with her.

(al-Durr al-Mukhtar, Shami, Hidayah)

(3) If both towns are at "travel distance" from there and if the place is unpopulated and uninhabitable, she has the choice of either returning to her home town or reach the destination and complete her *'Idda* there. But, returning to her home town is better, whether or not she has a *Mahram* with her.

However, if there is an inhabited town enroute her own home town, or the destination, where she could stay with assured protection of life, property and honour, or if she already was in such a town at the time of her husband's death, then she should stay there and complete her *'Idda,* whether or not she has a *Mahram* with her[1].

(al-Durr al-Mukhtar, Shami, Hidayah, Fath al-Qadir)

Shortcomings and Misdealing customs in *'Idda*

As a result of the modern curse of following the West, widows and divorced women do not sit at home

1. This is an accordance with the juristic position taken by Imam Abu Hanifah. According to Imam Abu Yusuf and Imam Muhammad, if a *Mahram* is with her, the rule shall remain as it is, that is, she should complete her *'Idda* in that town. If the woman has no *Mahram* with her, she has the choice to either complete the *'Idda* in that town or return to her home town and complete it there. This difference between these respected jurists is restricted just to this last situation here. Under all previous situations where the appendage - 'whether or not she has a *Mahram* with her' - appears, the unanimous ruling is the same as stated there. (Shami, al-Durr al-Mukhtar, Fath al-Qadir)

to complete *'Idda* as obligated on them. Going out openly, visiting bazaars and attending social functions are activities undertaken in absolute disregard to this injunction of the Shari'ah. This is a serious failing and certainly a major sin. Those concerned must repent and stay home during *'Idda* as prescribed by the Shari'ah.

Unfortunately, similar other shortcomings and false customs have crept in and around *'Idda* these days. Staying clear from them is necessary. Some of these are mentioned here:

Breaking the bangles worn by a widow on the death of her husband

We already know from rule 4 under 'Mourning' (p.140) that wearing bangles (even glass bangles) is not permissible during *'Idda*. But the custom in some parts of the Muslim world that women would break off bangles worn by the widow instead of taking them off, or at times the widow would herself break them off, is a Hindu custom. Apart from being a waste of good money, this is clear extravagance as well. So, do not break, take them off so that they remain available for use after *'Idda*. Incidentally, if there is some pain or difficulty in taking them off, break them off, of necessity.

(Imdadul-Fatawa v.2, p. 451)

Going out of the house during *'Idda* without an excuse admitted by the Shari'ah

Some women do sit in observing *'Idda* but they would go out of the house prompted by flimsy excuses, such as, to show up at a meeting, a ceremony or function, or to take care of some family chores, such as, shopping for groceries, medicines and things like that which could be easily handled by men in the family. This is done inspite of the fact that it is not permissible to ignore the restriction of *'Idda* and come out of the house on the basis of such excuses. The excuses under which going out of the house during *'Idda* is permissible have been listed earlier with appropriate details. If there comes a situation of a different nature under which going out of the house is supposed to be inevitably necessary, the problem may be discussed with trustworthy religious scholars in order to arrive at an admissible solution. To go out or not to go out in *'Idda* is a question the answer to which must be based on the dictates of the Shari'ah and not on personal choice. So, the wiser course is to follow the Shari'ah-based advice of the *'alim:* Go out if he permits, otherwise do not.

Going out in *'Idda* without valid excuse does not annul it

There are uninformed people who assume that the *'Idda* of a widow who comes out of the house without a valid excuse breaks thereby and that it would be necessary for her to observe *'Idda* all afresh. This is totally incorrect. *'Idda* does not break in that manner. But, going out of the house without a valid excuse admitted by the Shari'ah is certainly impermissible and a grave sin.

(Islah-i-Inqilab-i-Ummat)

Using things of personal adornment during *'Idda*

Some women indulge in personal adornment without bothering to think whether what they are doing is permissible or not, although wearing make-up, using oil or perfume or cosmetics, combing for hair styling, application of *surma/kohl*/eye-liner, lipstick, henna, putting on gaudy dresses and using everything that serves as aid to beauty and looks is *haram* (forbidden) which has been already discussed in detail under No. 4, 'Mourning' (pp. 139-141).

Marriage or betrothal during *'Idda*

Some people act imprudently when they marry a widow still in *'Idda.* They do not even wait for her *'Idda* to be completed. Then there are others who, in their own estimation, take 'precaution' when they marry a widow during her *'Idda* but avoid entering into any kind of marital relation with her. Let us remember that *nikah* (marriage) during the period of *'Idda* is not permissible. If done, it will not be deemed as duly concluded. In fact, even the making of initial betrothal or the giving of explicit proposal during the period of *'Idda* is not permissible. The Holy Qur'an forbids it.

(Islah-i-Inqlab-i-Ummat, v.2, p. 62)

Adding some days to the prescribed period of *'Idda* as a matter of precaution

If the *'Idda* of the widow is four months and ten days, some people make the mistake of adding ten more days to the period to make up for one or two missing days in case the lunar months remain of twenty nine days. This is wrong. The calculation of the days of *'Idda* should be precise and well-remembered.

(Islah-i-Inqilab-i-Ummat)

The gathering of women to 'release' a widow from *'Idda*

There are places where many women would assemble in the house of the widow on the occasion of the completion of her *'Idda* and claim that they have come to help the widow to get out of *'Idda.* Some women consider it necessary that the widow must go out of her house and enter some other house in order to be 'released' from *'Idda*, and they make a ceremony out of it. Both these practices are wrong. Once the period of four months ten days is over, or the pregnancy is vacated, the widow is automatically released from *'Idda*, whether she continues living in that very house.

(Islah-i-Inqilab-i-Ummat)

Considering the post-*'Idda* marriage of widow disgraceful

Unfortunately, this terrible Hindu custom has seeped into a lot of Muslim families, particularly in South Asia.

Consequently, some women whose husbands have died or who have been divorced consider that second marriage will become a matter of disgrace for them even after they have completed their *'Idda*, although the Holy Qur'an induces widows to remarry after *'Idda* and sternly warns those who stop them from remarrying.

None of the blessed wives of the Holy Prophet صلى الله عليه وسلم except Sayyidah 'A'ishah رضى الله عنها, was a virgin. Instead, most of them were widows or divorced. The noble Companions also followed this practice. Now such a benedictory practice which was supported by the Holy Qur'an and which was consistently adhered to by the Holy Prophet صلى الله عليه وسلم and the noble Companions رضى الله عنهم, can hardly be regrded as a matter of disgrace by any stretch of imagination. This is rank ignorance, and a very dangerous error, for some women say things about this delicate matter which touch the borders of *kufr.*

Some women do not, though, consider remarriage as something disgraceful, yet they believe that staying away from remarriage is more respectable. This is another error, though not being *kufr* as such, but very close to it. Otherwise, why would a believing-practicing Muslim take what is contrary to *Suunah* as something more worthy of respect?

In short, the Muslims must shun this absurd custom. As far as possible, widows should be married soon after the completion of *'Idda*. Not only that it is appropriate, it is, in a way, much more important than the marriage of a virgin. Unlike her, the widow has seen married life and neglecting her marriage may cause emotional mal-adjustment in her which could result in loss of health, or honour, or faith or everything in one drift.

(Islah-i-Inqilab-i-Ummat)

Some widows do wish to remarry but members in their family circle stop or reproach them for thinking on those lines. It should be borne in mind that preventing widows from remarrying, or telling them to be ashamed of the thought, is a sin and is rated as *haram* (forbidden).

Some people take the plea that the widow would not listen to them. But, the truth of the matter is that the widow initially demurs knowing that a prompt yes from her would give her family an excuse to chide her for being all too ready to get a husband. It is this fear of being disgraced which forces the poor woman to say 'no' or 'not yet'. It is the duty of her family members that they should talk to her in good faith, explain the advisability of marriage, remove her misgivings showing all possible concern and wisdom. If she is still unwilling, these people stand excused from any blames of not having made the effort.

(Islah-i-Inqilab-i-Ummat, v.2, p. 32)

In the case of a woman with children who is in her declining age and financially well-covered, if she refuses to remarry, which in turn is proved by her overall indifference to the need of a husband, then it is not necessary to go about making efforts to get such a woman married.

Rules:

1. A widow who does not remarry because she fears her children will be ruined or because nobody accepts her stands excused. In fact, not marrying lest children are ruined is an act deserving of reward and blessing from Allah.

(Islah-i-Inqilab-i-Ummat, v.2, p. 42)

2. If one has the urge to marry and the capability and the will to fulfil the rights of the husband, marrying is *wajib* (necessary). Not doing it will be a sin. And if the urge is strong, so much so that not marrying might land her into what is unlawful, then, marrying becomes *fard* (obligatory).

(supra, pp. 39-40)

3. If one does not have the urge to marry but does have the capability to fulfil the rights of the husband, then, marrying is an act of *sunnah*. In absence of such capability, it is forbidden.

(supra)

4. If a sane and adult woman were to arrange for the preliminary negotiation of her marriage contract on her own with someone equal to and at par *(kaf'u)* with her and supported by a dower matching with her family status *(mahrul-Mithl)* and goes through the process of offer *('Ijab)* and acceptance *(Qabul)* in the presence of witnesses, the marriage will stand solemnized. But, acting in this manner is derogatory. The marriage should be solemnized through the mediation of her guardians. But, should it be that the guardians are heedless and insensitive or refuse to let her marry at her choice, then, there is nothing derogatory about it if the woman elects to get married on her own. However, the condition is that she marries a man who is equal to and at par with her *(kaf'u)*. If she marries outside her *kaf'u* (the *fatwa* is that) the marriage contract will remain unconcluded. And if she marries with a lower dower not matching with her family status *(mahrul-mithl)* without the permission of her guardians, they can file a suit for the dissolution of such marriage.

(Imdadul-Fatawa v.2. p. 189, with marginal notes)

CHAPTER VII

Inheritance and its Distribution

Whatever is owned by a person at the time of his or her death - wealth or property, movable and immovable, cash, jewellery, clothes, virtually everything big or small, even an ordinary needle and thread - comes under his or inheritance (ترکہ) according to the Shari'ah. This also includes clothes the deceased was wearing at the time of death. In addition to that, any loans given by the deceased to someone which remain unrealized but are received after the death of the deceased shall also be counted as part of the total inheritance.

There are four claims (rights) on the total inheritance of the deceased in the order given below. Their disbursement, in accordance with the rules laid out in the Shari'ah, is *wajib* (obligatory). That this is done faithfully and precisely is the crucial responsibility of the inheritors, so much so that nobody is permitted to take out even a cardamom[1] lying inside some pocket of the deceased and put it in one's mouth without the express permission of the sharers of the inheritance, for that cardamom is not the share of one person alone.

These four claims or rights are:

1. The preparation of the deceased by bathing and shrouding.
2. The financial claim or debt owed by the deceased to someone.

---

1. Cardomom: *Ila'ichi, qaqula, Alpinia Cardamoms:* common eastern mouth-freshener, also additive in desserts, and in hot drinks like the Arab Cahva with green mint leaves.

3. The valid will or testament made by the deceased.
4. The distribution of the inheritance among inheritors.

It means that expenses on the bathing, shrouding and burial should be paid from the inheritance as a matter of first priority. What remains should be used to pay off all debts owed by the deceased. Then, what remains should be applied against any valid will made by the deceased which should not exceed the limit of one-third. After that, the remaining two-third of the inheritance should be distributed among all inheritors in accordance with shares fixed by the Shari'ah. If the deceased had no debt to pay back, nor had he made a will about the inheritance, then, what ever of inheritance remains after paying for the bathing, shrouding and burial, will all belong to the inheritors who will inherit it in accordance with the shares fixed by the Shari'ah. Details about these four claims shall appear later under relevant subject headings.

Things not included under inheritance

Before we take up the details of these four claims, it is necessary to understand that things in the possession of the deceased, things of which he was not the owner, even though he had been using them freely like an owner, will not be included in his inheritance. All such things should be returned to their real owners. Spending or using them in the bathing, shrouding and burial of the deceased is not permissible. Examples:

(1) Things which the deceased had borrowed from someone for temporary use (*'ariyah)* or things which someone had placed with him in trust *(amanah)* will not be included in the inheritance. All such things

should be returned to their owners.

(Mufidul-Warithin, p. 27)

(2) If the deceased had kept something by extortion, theft or breach of trust *(khiyanah)*, that too is not included in the inheritance and should be returned to its owner.

(Mufidul-Warithin, p. 28)

(3) If the deceased had gifted *(hibah)* something which belonged to him before *maradul-maut* (literally, 'the disease of death', meaning 'a disease during which the deceased died') and had seen that it goes in the actual possession of the receiver of the gift, then, this thing has gone out of the possession of the deceased and the one who has received it becomes its owner. So, this will not be included in the inheritance of the deceased after his death. But, should it be that he had simply said this verbally or in writing, to the effect - 'I give this to you' or 'I have gifted this to you' - and had not made him take the actual possession, then, this act of saying or writing will not be taken into consideration. This is neither a gift *(hibah)* nor a will *(wasiyyah)*, therefore, this thing will remain within the ownership of the deceased and will be included in his inheritance after his death.

(Bahishti Zewar, v.5, p. 60)

And if this thing was given during *maradul-maut* and the deceased had also made him take it in his possession, then, this act of giving will fall under the rule governing a will. Therefore, this thing will be counted as part of the inheritance and, after the total cost of the funeral and the debts have been paid off, this too will be handled like other wills are handled subject to their governing conditions. Details of this question will appear later under a separate heading concerning wills.

(Mufidul-Warithin, Shami, Bahishti Zewar)

The pension received after death is not included in inheritance

Pension until received does not form part of ownership. Therefore, whatever amount of pension is received after the death of the deceased will not be counted in the inheritance because inheritance is what the deceased owns at the time of his death and this amount had not yet passed into his ownership until his death. Therefore, the four financial claims which it is obligatory to disburse from the inheritance shall not be so applied on this amount. Also, the rule of inheritance will not become operative here. However, to whomsoever the government (or the company) decides to give this amount will become its owner because this is a sort of award, not salary or wages. So, should the government or company award this pension to one of the relatives of the deceased, he will become its sole owner. And if this is given for all inheritors, all inheritors will distribute[1] it among themselves. But, this distribution will not be because of the factor of inheritance, rather, it would be deemed as an award given to them by the government or company.

---

1. في الدرالمختار ان اوصى لورثة فلان فهو للزكر مثل حظ الانثيين لانه اى الموصى اعتبر الوراثة وقال الشامى تحتة لان التنصيص على الاسم المشتق يدل على ان الحكم يترتب على ماخذ الاشتقاق فكانت الوراثة هى العلة، زيلعى، ثم قال الشامى وظاهره ان قوله للزكر مثل حظ الانثيين ليس عامًا فى جميع الورثة، بل خاص بالا ولاد والاخوة والا خوات وفى غيرهم يقسم على قدر فروضهم وهوالمركور فى الاسعاف والخصاف فى مسائل الاوقاف، والوصية اخت الوقف انظر ردالمحتار، ص ٦،٢ ج ٥، (رفيع العثمانى) قول الظاهرانه يقسم على قدرسها مهم فى الارث وان لم يكن المال موروثا من الميت لما

Some possessions of the deceased are also not included in his inheritance

The gist of what has been said upto this point is that everything owned by the deceased at the time of his death is his inheritance and things which he did not own at that time are not included in his inheritance. But, this rule has some particular exceptions, that is, some things which by right belong to someone else, will not become part of the inheritance inspite of being in the possession of the deceased. Two examples are given below:

(1) There may be something the deceased had purchased but had neither paid for nor taken possession, of it, rather, it was still present[1] in the hands of the seller, and the deceased left nothing behind other than this (which could be used to first pay for the funeral expenses and then pay for the cost of the thing hc had purchased) in which situation this thing, though it had become the property of the deceased, will not be included in his inheritance.

(2) Similarly, something the deceased had mortgaged against a loan and had left behind no cash or property to help pay back the debt, then, this thing, irrespective of naving been in the possession of the deceased, will not be included in his inheritance. It means that in a situation where the deceased has left no cash or property, the seller who has not received payment for what he sold and the mortgagee who has not yet received what he loaned can arrange to sell things they hold in their possession and can thus settle

1. In case the deceased had taken possession and had not paid for it, then, the seller cannot take it back. This will be included in the inheritance and it will be used to pay for the expenses incurred on the funeral services following which, the seller will be paid the purchase price observing the rule governing the payment of debts. These rules have been described laler under 'Debts'. (Rafi Usmani)

their claim before anybody else. It is only after their claim has been settled, anything that remains, if it remains, shall be deemed as the inheritance out of which funeral expenses and debts will be paid off, and the will and the legacy will be taken care of according to rules set for each. In case, nothing is left behind, the relatives should themselves bear the funeral costs.

(Mufidul-Warithin, Shami, al-Durr al-Mukhtar)

We have given only two examples here. Should there be some other situation corresponding to these in which somebody else's claim is tied up with something particular and fixed under the possession of the deceased, then, it is advisable to consult a learned and trustworthy religious scholar and to act in accordance with his advice. Please never take action based on your personal opinion or analogous deduction because the slightest of change in the situation (which everyone cannot discern) changes the relevant ruling.

What has been set aside for a particular person during one's life-time is included in the inheritance

If a person had, during his life-time, collected cash, clothes or jewellery for the marriage of his children and hoped to use it when a son or daughter of his gets married or give it as marriage[1] portion (*Jahez*: dowry) of his daughter, but, as fate would have it, this person died without making that particular child the owner-possessor of these things. In this case, all such things shall be included in the inheritance and that particular son or daughter will have no special right on or claim to it. On the contrary, they will get just what comes to them as their share in accordance with the rules of inheritance after the funeral expenses,

1. If this happens in the case of a non-pubert son or daughter, please consult reliable scholars.

payment of debts and the execution of wills have been taken care of.

(Mufidul-Warithin)

Now that we understand the nature and composition of inheritance, let us take up the four claims on inheritance in some details. The disbursement of these claims will be made in accordance with the order given below.

1. Funeral Expenses

First of all the funeral expenses should be taken from the inheritance of the deceased. But, this obligation must be discharged simply and functionally in accordance with *Sunnah* as laid down by the Shari'ah (details of which have appeared earlier). The shroud too should match the general status of the deceased. Select white cloth of a price the deceased used to wear while going out to meet people or to visit the mosque or market. Do not buy too cheap a cloth causing disgrace to the deceased, nor something so expensive which may touch the limits of extravagance and thereby chip off money from the pool of inheritance and cause loss to debtees and inheritors. Make the grave in mortar whether the deceased be rich or poor. If a bather of the body or the grave digger has to be hired, make the cost average within limits of capability. If space in the general graveyard for the Muslims is not available, a plot of land for the grave should be purchased. The cost of the land should be taken from the inheritance like everything[1] else procured for the funeral.

(Mufidul-Warithin, p. 32)

1. A complete list of things needed for the funeral has appeared earlier. Everything, including fragrance, can be taken out of the inheritance. (Shami)

Rulings:

(1) The large sheet used to cover the *janazah* is not included[1] in the prescribed 'shroud'. The prayer-spread saved from the shroud cloth for use by the Imam is extra to the prescribed shroud and simply useless. Therefore, should it be that the inheritance of the deceased have no more than what is enough for liquidation of the debt, or the inheritors are minors, then, making this prayer-spread and covering sheet and thereby causing loss to debtees or orphans is not permissible under any condition, in fact, it is strictly prohibited. Some people who do not know might laugh at this ruling, but they will soon be chastened with surprise when they hear about the limits to which authentic books of Shari'ah go in this matter. They say if the deceased is under a lot of debt, his debtees can force the inheritors to restrict the shroud to only two cloth pieces. It means that they can have one cloth piece (shroud-dress or under-wrap) eliminated even from the standard *sunnah kafan* (the shroud prescribed by the Holy Prophet صلى الله عليه وسلم). So, who can think of pleading for the provision of extra covering sheets and prayer-spreads?

(Mufidul-Warithin, p. 33)

(2) The senseless customs of all sorts, innovations (*bid'at*) and spendings including, for instance, a feast by the family of the deceased, other than the normal funeral process in accordance with the Shari'ah, are things for which it is not permissible to take any money from the inheritance under any condition. Similarly, it is not permissible to spend anything out of the inheritance to entertain those who come to offer their condolences. Anyone who does it, inheritor or non-in-

1. Details of things needed for the funeral have appeared earlier. Please see again. (Rafi Usmani).

heritance will have to compensate for the extra expenditure. Or, in case he is an inheritor, it will be deducted from his share in the inheritance.

(Mufidul-Warithin, p. 33)

(3) Some people who do not know the rules give out things in charity before the distribution of the inheritance, such as grains, money and clothes. These give-outs will never be counted as valid expenses on the funeral, instead, it will be necessary that the giver pays compensation for them. This matter is very delicate. Great restraint and care should be exercised. There are situations when among the inheritors left behind by the deceased, there are young orphaned children who deserve all sympathy, or the deceased is under debt while relatives care more for following customs and go about spending callously what is not theirs on unauthorized activities inviting in this process the punishment of the *Akhirah* on themselves, because this action of theirs violates the rightful claims of the debtees or inheritors. The forms of this injustice are many. It is fairly common that sewn clothes belonging to the deceased are given out in charity on his behalf. When a husband dies leaving behind the widow and minor children, the widow would start giving things from the inheritance in charity not realizing that innocent children have claims on this inheritance. No doubt, she is their mother, but she is not entitled to unnecessarily spend out what belongs to them - even if the children were to allow her to do so for their permission is not valid in the sight of the Shari'ah.

Giving of charity on behalf of the deceased is, without any doubt, very desirable and merit-worthy. The deceased does get its reward *(thawab)*. But, charities *(sadaqat)* can be good and beneficial if they are in line with the dictates of the Shari'ah. The Shari'ah commands: Do not make your hands dirty by illspending what belongs to the claimants and orphans. Instead, whoever has the ability and the desire should come up with charity from his own lawfully earned property. Therefore, it is necessary that the inheritance should first be distributed in accordance with the rules of the Shari'ah. It is only after that, that the adult inheritors can give what they wish out of their share. Never give before the distribution.

(Mufidul-Warithin, p. 34 & Bahishti Zewar)

(4) If the deceased is a woman with her husband alive, the funeral expenses must be paid, as a matter of obligation, by the husband. This should not be taken from the wife's share in the inheritance. However, if she does not have her husband, it should be taken from it as usual.

(Mufidul-Warithin, p. 36 and Shami, v. 1, p. 810)

(5) If a near relative or someone else desires to take care of the cost of the funeral willingly as an act of parting service for the deceased, man or woman, and the inheritors too agree to this, then he can do so subject to the condition that he be sane and adult. Under this situation, the funeral expenses should not be taken from the inheritance.

(Mufidul-Warithin. p. 35)

(6) If, by chance, beasts wreck the grave, destroy the shroud and pull the dead body out, or the shroud-lifters leave the dead body naked, in which case, the cost of the second shroud will also have to be given from the inheritance of the deceased. In this situation, bathing and prayer are not repeated.

(Mufidul-Warithin, p. 35 and Shami)

(7) If the deceased left nothing behind, who will pay for the funeral? Full detail about this question have already appeared and may be seen there.

(8) The funeral is the first of the four *seriatim* claims due against inheritance. If nothing remains after paying for the cost of funeral, the debtees get nothing, there is no disbursement against a will, if made, and the inheritors inherit nothing from the inheritance.

(Mufidul-Warithin. p. 36)

2. The Payment of Debts

After funeral expenses have been taken care of, the most important task is to pay debts owed to others[1] by the deceased. If the dower (*mahr*) of his wife was not paid by the deceased, that too is a debt and its payment is as necessary and binding as is the payment of other debts. So, it is obligatory to first pay off all debts owed by the deceased from his inheritance, from what remains of it, after defraying the cost of the funeral, whether or not a will to this effect was made and regardless of the likelihood that this remaining inheritance, the whole of it, is consumed in the very payment of these debts. If any part of inheritance does remain after the payment of debts, it will be further applied to payments as in the will of the deceased in accordance with rules laid down by the Shari'ah and, in case of further left-overs, the inheritors too will get their shares. If nothing remains, there will be nothing to spend on the fulfilment of the will and the inheritors will have nothing to receive because, in the Shari'ah,

---

1. This concerns debts owed to people created by Allah. Then there are the debts of Allah which may have remained unserviced by the deceased such as the *qada'* of missed prayers, the *fidyah* of missed fasts, *Zakah*, *Hajj*, vows etc. Relevant rules for these will appear later under distinct headings. (Rafi Usmani)

the payment of debts takes precedence over will and inheritance under all conditions.

(Mufidul-Warithin, pp. 36-51)

The Holy Prophet صلى الله عليه وسلم has spoken very strongly about the need to pay debts. He would not lead the *janazah salah* for people who left unpaid debts in their name and, worse still, left nothing in their inheritance to help clear them with. In such cases, he used to ask his Companions to lead the necessary *salah* of *janazah* for the deceased. As obvious, such people remained deprived of his *salah* and his prayers for their forgiveness.

Hadith:

Sayyidna Abu Hurairah رضى الله عنه narrates:

"When the body of a deceased person who was in debt was brought before the Holy Prophet صلى الله عليه وسلم for the *salatul-janazah*, he would ask, 'Has he left enough to pay for his debt?' When he was informed that he has, then, he would lead the *salah* for him. Otherwise, he asked his Companions to do it."

(Sahih Muslim, v.2, p. 35)

Although the debt these people incurred was never beyond normal limits - they borrowed only when in need - yet the Holy Prophet صلى الله عليه وسلم was so strict about it. Here, in our own time, people go about borrowing huge sums of money to engage in all sorts of wasteful activities and then die and their inheritors find them no good to think about.

Hadith:

It has been reported in an authentic *hadith* that

the spirit of a Muslim is stopped (from entering Paradise or from being rewarded) until his or her debt is cleared. Someone present said: 'O Messenger of Allah, my brother has died leaving his young children behind. Shall I spend on them (and not pay the debt)?' He said: 'Your brother is under detention because of this debt. Pay the debt'.

(Mufidul-Warithin, p. 40 as in Mishkat)

Rulings:

(1) If, after payment of funeral expenses, the remaining inheritance is good enough to clear all outstanding debts, then all debts should be paid off without any discrimination. In case, it is not enough and the debt has to be paid to one single person, then whatever of inheritance remains, after defraying the cost of the funeral, should be given to him. As for what remains unpaid, it shall be upto him. He may forgo and forgive it if he so chooses, or he may postpone it for settlement in *Akhirah* (the life-to-come).

(Mufidul-Warithin, p. 38)

(2) If the inheritance as after payment of funeral expenses is not enough and there are several debtees to take care of, then we have to go in great details to determine who among them would receive what, and in which proportion, and what sort of debts would be given priority over others. The best time to find these details out is when you need to know and the wisest course is to consult an authentic religious scholar entitled to give rulings. Tell him everything about the situation you are in and he will certainly resolve the question within the parametres of prescribed religious practice. If, for some reason, this is not possible, a careful study of 'Mufidul-Warithin' by Maulana Sayyid

Mian Asghar Husain Muhaddith of Deoband will be useful since it has full details.[1]

(3) If, after the funeral, nothing remains of the inheritance, or whatever is left is not sufficient to clear all debts, the payment of remaining debts is not more obligatory on the inheritors.

However, not simply that love so demands, but it is better and desirable too that, as far as possible, debts owed by the deceased should be paid off to give his soul relief on that account. If nobody comes forward to pay such debts, the debtees should patiently wait for the justice of their Lord in the world-to-come where every person shall have his lost right returned to him and whoever has held back a right which was the due of other shall see that his good deeds are taken away from him and given to those whose rights he failed to fulfill. But, it is much better that claimants too forgo and forgive their claim. This act of grace alone will bring them a reward of such magnitude that all possible good deeds of the debtor combined when given on the Day of Judgement will be unable to match the Divine reward for this act of forgiveness. The act of remitting a debt and the grace of giving more time to a penniless debtor have been highly praised in the Qur'an and *Hadith*, so forgiveness is the best.

(Mufidul-Warithin, p. 41)

Hadith:

As narrated by Sayyidna Abu Hurairah رضی اللہ عنہ

---

1 There is a lot of difference in rules governing a debt against the deceased which was established during his *maradul-maut* and that which was already established before that time. When you approach a religious scholar for a solution of this problem, do tell him as to which of the debts was established during *maradul-maut* and which was already established as such before that time and was it established through a confession of the deceased or through the testimony of witnesses.

(Rafi Usmani)

the Holy Prophet صلى الله عليه وسلم said that a certain person used to give loans to people. His instruction to his assistant for recoveries was: When you go to someone poor, be lenient and forgiving (accept what is given, give respite or forgive), may be Allah Almighty treats us with the same leniency and forgiveness (in *Akhirah*). So, when he appeared betore his Lord (after death), He forgave him.

(Sahih Muslim. v.2, p. 18)

In yet another narration, it is reported that this person had no other good deed in his account except this one, yet all his sins were forgiven.

(Ibid)

Sayyidna Abu Qatadah رضى الله عنه narrates that he heard the Holy Prophet صلى الله عليه وسلم say: Anyone who likes that Allah Almighty delivers him from the distress of the Day of Doom, he should deliver the poor from distress, or forgive them (their debt).

(Ibid)

Paying Debts owed to Allah Almighty

Upto this point, we have talked about debts of living human beings that remain uncleared by the deceased. Then, there are the debts of Allah, that is, His rights which must be fulfilled. These are the *Fara'id* and the *Wajibat* or obligatory acts. For example, there may have remained some such acts - *Salah*, the *Fidyah* of fasts, *Zakah*, *Hajj*, *Sadaqatul-Firt*, *Nadhr* (vows), *Kaffarah* (expiation) etc. - which the deceased had not accomplished. For these, the rule is: If, after paying off all debts owed to human beings, some funds still remain and the deceased had made a will too that these rights of Allah due on him be cleared, then, these should be cleared off from one-third of the remaining funds. If this one-third turns out to be insufficient for full payment, then, pay whatever can be paid. It is not binding on the inheritors to spend anymore than one-third to liquidate the total due because the remaining two-third of the property belongs to the inheritors. Once the distribution is over, all sane and adult inheritors may elect, at their discretion, to spend from their respective shares and redeem the deceased from the burden of undischarged obligations and thus save the deceased from the accountability of the *Akhirah* and, in the process, become personally deserving of Divine reward. Please note that it is strictly impermissible to spend the share of insane or minor inheritors for this purpose, even if they permit it gladly. It is also possible that all inheritors, if they so elect, disiribute the remaining two-third of inheritance among themselves in accordance with the shares fixed by the Shari'ah and do no more. In this situation, the responsibility of the rights of Allah Almighty which remain unredeemed shall rest with the deceased. The inheritors will not be held accountable.

(Mufidul-Warithin, p. 39, and Islahi-Inqilabi-Ummat, v.1, p. 185)

Similarly, if that one-third of the property be just about enough to redeem all those unfulfilled rights of Allah Almighty, but the deceased has, in his will, asked for the redemption of some rights and not for others remaining, or allocated a lower amount of money in his will which was insufficient for the redemption of all rights; for instance, the one-third of the property was valued at $ 2000 which could redeem all such rights, but the deceased allocated only $ 1500 for this purpose in his will, in which case, the inheritors will be obligated to pay within the limit set by the will. It will not be necessary for them to spend the total of

$ 2000 to redeem these rights. However, the deceased will incur the sin of not having made provision in his will for the redemption of all unfulfilled rights.

(Dalailul-Khairat, p. 28)

Summary:

In short, there are three differences between debts of human beings (servants of Allah) and the debts of Allah Almighty (His rights over human beings):

1. The liquidation of human debts does not depend on the will of the deceased. On the contrary, even if the deceased has made no will, it is obligatory to pay these debts after paying for the funeral expenses. As for the fulfilment of the rights of Allah Almighty, it depends on the will made by the deceased. If he does not make a will to this effect, the inheritors do not necessarily have to clear such debts.

2. The second difference is that there was no limit imposed on the payment of human debts. Once the funeral expenses have been paid, spending off the entire inheritance, if it comes to that, to clear the debts is obligatory. As compared to that, when it comes to redeeming the rights of Allah Almighty, all debts owed to human beings have to be paid first, following which, the rights of Allah Almighty have to be redeemed from only one-third of whatever remains of the inheritance. Apart from this obligation of one-third, the inheritors do not necessarily have to spend anymore

3. The third difference is, as obvious, that the redeeming of the rights of Allah Almighty is obligatory only when all debts owed to Allah's servants have been cleared.

(Mufidul-Warithin, p. 40)

Special Note:

Since this second kind of debt, that is, the redemption of the financial rights or claims of Allah Almighty, depends on will which, if not made by the deceased, requires no compliance. Therefore, we shall take it up again under "WILLS" immediately after, where the readers will find what has to be done to compensate for missed prayers, fasts and also a full listing of other rights of Allah in terms of quantities and measures.

The Execution of Valid Wills

Two of the four *seriatim* claims which it is obligatory to apply against the inheritance of a deceased person have appeared previously. These are:

1. The Funeral Expenses
2. The Payment of Debts

The necessary details of the third claim, that is, the will, are being presented here.

Saying that, "I make a will for so much cash or property," or, "Give so much cash or property to such and such person after my death." or, "Put it to such and such use," is the making of a will, whether said in sickness, or health and whether the maker of the statement died of the disease which took away his life, or died later.

(Bahishti Zewar)

If death was not mentioned at all, nor the word, "will" was uttered, instead, what was said was no more than - "Give such and such thing from me to such and such person," or, "Put it to such and such use" - then, this is no will and the rules relating to a will are not going to apply here, because the Shari'ah of Islam recognizes only that will as valid in which the deceased has left some instructions to be carried out after his death.

(Al-Durr al-Mukhtar, p. 568. v.5)

Similarly, if somebody had saved money to build a mosque, or to have a well made for public use, or to give it out in the way of Allah or to present it as a gift to someone; or, had collected things or had money saved up for performing Hajj pilgrimage; then, as God would have it, he left this mortal world, a happening which would cause everything mentioned above to be included in his total inheritance and which, in turn, will be distributed among heirs. These will not be counted as the subject of some will since he did not give any such instructions to survivors which could be termed as 'the will'.

(Mufidul-Warithin, p. 29)

Valid and Invalid Wills

Rulings:

1. Everyone, sane and adult, has the right to make a will against his property in a way that the inheritance which remains, after the payment of the funeral expenses and the debts, should be good enough to help execute that will within the mandatory limit of one-third. If the will was made for more than that, the heirs do not, of necessity, have to fulfil it beyond the one-third, for the remaining two-third belongs only to the heirs as a matter of right. However, sane and adult heirs who wish to fulfil the additional portion of the will out of their respective shares in the inheritance may do so. (al-Durr al-Mukhtar, Shami)

2. If somebody has no heir at all, he has the right to leave a will for everything that remains after the payment of the funeral expenses and the debts. If he has his wife as the only heir, a will upto three-fourth is correct. Similarly, if there is no heir of a woman, except her husband, a will upto half of the property is correct - because these are situations in which the rights of any heirs are not compromised.

(Bahishti Zewar al-Durr al-Mukhtar p. 572, v.5)

3. If the amount of debt owed by the deceased is so high that its payment leaves nothing of the inheritance, then, every will, whatever the nature, is redundant and invalid. May be, if the debtees forgo some of the debt the deceased owed to them and this leaves some property open for distribution, then, the will is to be applied to the remainder upto the limit of one-third, the rest will go to the heirs.

(Mufidul-Warithin, p. 63)

4. The will made by the minor or the insane is invalid under the rules of the Shari'ah. It is not obligatory to execute it even within the limit of one-third.

(al-Durr al-Mukhtar Shami. p. 576, v.5)

5. If the deceased makes a will for any of his or her heirs, for example, mother, father, husband, son, or others, then, this will too shall be invalid, because the Shari'ah has itself fixed the share of every heir in the inheritance. This is what the heir will get. No heir can be given anything on the basis of a will so that the rights of other heirs are not compromised. However, if the deceased has no heir other than that particular heir, or, if the rest of the heirs are willing, it can be

given by their permission. But, the permission given by persons, insane or minor, is not valid. Only sane and adult heirs can, if they so wish, give out from their own respective shares.

(Bahishti Zewar, Mufidul-Warithin)

6. A will which excludes one's entitled heir from the inheritance, or which seeks to curtail the heir's share in it, is also invalid. Executing such a will is categorically impermissible. Moreover, making such a will is a sin as well.

(Mufidul-Warithin, p. 57, al-Durr al-Mukhtar)

7. Also invalid is a will which calls for spending on a sinful purpose. Spending from the inheritance to fulfil such a will is not permissible even if it be with the permission of the heirs.

(al-Durr al-Mukhtar Shami p. 605, v. 5, Bahishti Zewar)

8. If the deceased made a will for his killer, before being killed or after being injured, the situation presents two solutions, that is, if the killer was not minor or insane, this will too is invalid in many circumstances, and valid in some others. When confronted with some such problem, it is recommended that necessary action may be taken in consultation with trustworthy scholars of Islamic jurisprudence.

(al-Durl al-Mukhtar, Shami, p. 569 575, v.5)

9. If the maker of the will takes it back within his life-time, for example, he says, "I take this will back", or, "This will may not be executed", or, "I cancel this will", then, that will shall be rendered invalid, like it was never made. Until such time that the maker of the

will is alive, he is fully entitled to invalidate[1] his will. Similarly, if he, during his life-time, acts in a way which indicates that he has gone back on his will, even then, the will shall become invalid. Some down-to-the-earth examples could be like when the maker of the will builds a house for himself on the very plot of land he had earlier bequeathed for someone; or, bequeathed household furniture, then sold it off later; or, bequeathed cloth yardage to someone, then went on to cut the same and had dresses made out of it for himself. All such situations will lead to the conclusion that he has gone back on his bequeathal or will. As a result, the will shall become invalid.

(Mufidul-Warithin, p. 64)

10. If the will was made for a particular plot of land, house, cloth, domestic animal, or something else, and which went out of his ownership somehow, or was wasted, or died, then, the will becomes invalid, because the particular thing for which the will was made does not exhist anymore.

(Mufidul-Warithin, p. 64)

11. If the person for whom the deceased had provided cash or property in his will refuses to accept what was willed by the maker of the will and says, "I am not going to take it," then, the will shall become invalid. Now he cannot claim it later on. But, if this refusal took place during the life-time of the maker of the will, the will shall not become invalid, because the only valid acceptance or rejection of a will is what comes

---

I. But, if he lies and says that he never made that will, although witnesses exhist and people generally know that the will was made, then this false refusal would not render the will invalid and, in addition to that, the liar-denier will be incurring a sin without the fun.

(Mufidul-Warithin)

after the death of the maker. Pre-death acceptance or rejection is not valid.

(al-Durr al-Mukhtar, Shami. p. 577, v.5)

The Method of Executing Wills

After taking care of the funeral expenses (and after the payment of debts owed by the deceased, if that was the case), if there remains something left over, it should be seen whether or not the deceased has made a valid will concerning his inheritance. If he has not done so, the left-over property will all be distributed among the heirs, because they are its rightful recipients in the absence of a will. And if the deceased had made a will, verbally or in writing, expressing his wish to have a mosque built after his death from out of his property, or a public well; or instructed that a certain amount be donated to a religious school or spiritual seminary; or requested that money or thing be given to a specified person; or asked that certain specified things be given in charity to the poor and needy; or, may be, thinking of some of the obligatory prayers and fasts he missed, he gave the instruction that *fidya*[1] (payment in redemption) be given against them after his death; or, conscious of the need to redeem some of the unperformed obligations on him as the due of Allah Almighty, such as the Hajj, the *Sadaqatul-Fitr*, any *Kaffarah* (expiation) or *Nadhr* (vow), he instructed that these should be 'paid' back after his death - then, all this counts as 'will' and the method of executing it is that the inheritance that remains, after paying the

1. If *fidya* was not specifically mentioned, rather, the will simply said, "Offer so many prayers, or fasts on my behalf," then, this will is not valid because acts of worship, such as, the prescribed prayers and the fasts, which are to be performed physically, cannot be performed by anyone on behalf of anybody else. There is no proxy in *'Ibadah*. However, one can hope to redeem what he failed to perform through *fidya*.

(Mufidul-Warithin, Rafi Usmani)

funeral expenses and debts, will be divided in three equal portions. Two portions (2/3) out of these will be given to heirs only, as their due right, and which will be further distributed[1] over them in accordance with the rules set by the Shari'ah. One portion (1/3) goes to take care of the will, whether or not this one-third is good enough to execute the will in full.

Rulings:

1. If something still remains after the execution of all wills from this one-third, that too shall belong to the heirs.

(Mufidul-Warithin)

2. For more than one will, the same rule applies, that is, execute as many of them as it is possible within the limit of one-third. Leave the rest because the fulfilment and execution of remaining wills is not incumbent on the heirs.

(Shami, Bahishti Zewar)

3. The sane and adult heirs present on the spot can fulfil the remaining part of the will made by the deceased, if they wish to do so, but this has to be out of their own accord and from their own respective shares. However, it is not permissible to use the share of a minor, insane or absent heir in what is being spent over and above the limit of one-third. This is because the permission of a minor or insane person is not admissible Shari'ah-wise, and the mind of the one absent is unknown, may be he permits, may be he does not. Therefore, in the event that someone from among the heirs is absent, or is a minor, or is insane, spend one-third to cover the will and, after that,

1. The section on the distribution of inheritance among the heirs will follow immediately after the present discussion on wills.

distribute the remaining two-third among all heirs in accordance with their shares fixed by the Shari'ah. Once this is done, anyone from among the adult and sane heirs is free to fulfil the remaining part of the will made by the deceased, at his discretion and from his share (or even by adding more from his own pocket.)

(Mufidul-Warithin)

The Order in Executing Wills when More than One

Rulings:

If the deceased had made some wills which could not be implemented within one-third of the property and spending more was not authorized by the heirs, then, the wills which are more important in the sight of the Shari'ah should be implemented first. In case something is left over after such implementation, carrying out less necessary wills as well is obligatory. If there still remains something, it is also obligatory to carry out unnecessary wills too, as far as possible. For instance, if the deceased willed the payment of *fidaya* for his missed fasts, and the payment of his unpaid *Sadaqatul-Fitr*, and willed the building of a public well, all at the same time, then, the *fidya* for fasts should be paid first because fasts are obligatory. After that, if something remains of the inheritance, pay from it whatever can be paid against the *Sadaqatul-Fitr*. Leave the rest because this is necessary *(wajib)*, not obligatory *(fard)*. As for the building of a public well, just leave it out totally because this is not even necessary *(waiib)*; it is simply desirable or recommended *(mustahabb)*. Had there been some inheritance left, building this too would have become necessary.

(al-Durr al-Mukhtar, Shami & Mufidul-Warithin)

If all wills carry equal effect, that is, the difference of being more necessary', 'necessary' and 'unecessary' does not exist between them, then, the will which was made first by the maker of the will should be fulfilled first. After that, if inheritance remains, fulfill the other; if nothing remains, just leave. For example, a will was made to pay *fidya* for fasts and prayers both. As both, being obligatory, are equal, therefore, the one willed first should be the one to be paid first. Take the case of a will asking for the performance of obligatory Hajj and the payment of *zakah* which cannot be fulled simultaneously. So, the one willed first shall be the one to be complied with first. (Some authentic scholars say that, in case Hajj and *zakah* cannot be taken care of simultaneously, *Zakah* should be given precedence and paid off). Take yet another example. In a situation when $ 1,000 were bequeathed for a mosque and another $ 1,000 for a religious school but the one-third is no more than $ 1,000, then, the first bequeathal shall be executed first because none of the two is *fard* (obligatory) or *wajib* (necessary). Both are *mustahabb* (recommended).

(Mufidul-Warithin, p. 60, 61; Shami p. 580, 581, v.5)

Special Note:

The rule just cited above, that is, if all wills are of equal effect, the one made first shall be given precedence, operates when wills are not made for specified persons. If wills were made for specified persons - for example, one-third of the property was bequeathed in the name of A, then, one-third of the property was bequeathed in the name of B as well - the first will shall not be given precedence over the second one, instead of that, that one-third of the property will be distributed equally between A and B.

(Shami. p. 580, v. 5)

This question is full of details and subsequent subtleties. When actually confronted with a question of this nature, it is better to act in consultation with expert and trustworthy religious scholars.

How to calculate the *fidya* of prayers and fasts

1. Daily prayers, including *witr*, will be calculated as six a day. The *fidya* for each prayer *(salah)* will be 1.62 kilo of wheat or its price. As a measure of precaution, give full two kilo of wheat or its price. Thus, the *fidya* for prayers missed on one day will be a full 12 kilo of wheat or its price.

2. The *fidya* of one fast is equal to the *fidya* of one *salah* (prescribed prayer), that is, 1.62 kilo - (precaution-wise: 2 kilo - of wheat or its price. In case there was a vow (*nadhr, mannat)*, other than the fasts of Ramadan, *fidya* for it will have to be paid as well.

3. *Zakah* will have to be calculated in terms of the number of years and the amount of holdings in each, according to which payment will have to be made.

4. If the deceased was unable to perform the obligatory Hajj, someone from his neighbourhood will be sent to perform Hajj on his behalf *(Hajj Badal)* and all expenses covering return transportation and boarding and lodging will have to be paid. If the one-third of inheritance is not sufficient to cover that, someone from a place costing less may be sent.

5. For every *Sadaqatul-Fitr* (fixed amount of charity tied with the fortunate completion of the fasts of Ramadan), 1.62 kilo - (precaution-wise: full 2 kilo.) of wheat or its price should be paid.

6. For any sacrifice *(Qurban* or *Qurbani)* missed,

the price of one goat or one cow should be estimated as in that year and the price so arrived at should be given in charity.

7. If the correct number of *qada'* or missed (literally expired, dead, taken away or lost fully) prayers and fasts and other obligations is not known, an estimated calculation should be made.

(Hila-i-Isqat by Mufti Muhammad Shafi)

Impermissible Wills:

Some Examples

The rules described upto this point relate to wills which are, Shari'ah-wise, correct. What is false and invalid about wills was taken up alongside. Also invalid are wills in which the deceased has desired the spending of his wealth in what is impermissible, for example, making a will to celebrate the third, or the tenth, eleventh, twelfth, twentieth or the fortieth day following the death of the deceased; or to hold ceremonial gatherings of *Milad* or *'Urs*; or to have a reinforced grave or have a dome built over it; or to have a *Hafiz*. (reciter from memory) of the Holy Qur'an hired on payment of wages[1] charged with sitting hy the grave and reciting it so that the dead person in the grave could receive the reward out of such recital; or to deprive a legal heir; or to build a cinema house. One who makes such wills is a terrible sinner. Acting to fulfil such wills ic also not permissible.

(Shami, 605. v.5; Bahishti Zewar)

1. Accepting wages for reciting the Holy Qur'an is *haram* (forbidden). The reward of such recitation against wages neither reaches the reciter, nor the deceased. On the contrary, one becomes an unwitting sinner. (Shami - Sharh al-'Uqud Rasm al-Mufti)

The Emphasis on Making Wills and Related Instructions

If someone has the *fidya* of missed prayers or of fasts due against him, or has not performed Hajj, or has not paid *Zakah*, or has failed to fulfil the *Kaffarah* (expiation) for an oath or to pay the unpaid *Sadaqatul-Fitr* or to clear off a vow *(nadhr, mannat)* or, for that matter, any act of worship *fard* (obligatory) or *wajib* (necessary), which required financial coverage and which remained unperformed, then, subject to having enough money, it is necessary for such a person that he makes a will for the payment of what is due on these things well before his death. If one fails to do so, he will be in for sin.

(Bahishti Zewar, al-Durr al-Mukhtar, p. 568, v.5)

Rulings:

1. A person who owes money to people, or who holds cash or things in trust which belong to others and for which there is no receipt or proof which could help the debtees and the trusters to take back what belonged to them, or who may have similar other matters under his supervision in which the absence of a will may cause the rights of people to be compromised, then, it is incumbent on and necessary for that person that he should spell out and place on record, written or verbal, a list of rights these people have, otherwise he will be committing a terrible sin.

(Bahshti Zewar, Mufidul-Warithin, Shami)

There is no assurance of life. Who knows when the angel of death is going to knock at the door? So, be prepared for death all the time - this is the demand of faith; and when in good health, take the first opportunity to make a will about such matters. As in a *hadith* narrated by Sayyidna 'Abdullah ibn 'Umar رضى الله عنه the Holy Prophet صلى الله عليه وسلم said, "A Muslim who has something regarding which he must make a will, then he does not have the right to spend even two nights in a state in which he does not have a written will with him".

(Sahih Muslim, p. 39, v.2)

2. If the legal heirs of a person are already rich, or they are likely to get so much of inheritance through their share in it that they will become very very rich, then it is recommended *(mustahabb)* for such a person that he should make a will regarding part of his property having it donated to mosques, religious schools etc., or leaving it for relatives who will not get a share in the inheritance. In other words, the will, if made, shall bring reward; and not making the will brings no sin. But, making a will for more than one-third of one's property is impermissible under all condilions. As a matter of fact, making a will for even less than one-third is better.

(Bahishti Zewar, Mufidul-Warithin)

And if the legal heirs of a person are neither already rich nor does he have a property so large that the inheritance would make them any richer, then, it is recommended *(mustahhab)* that he should do nothing of the sort, that is, make no will that charities be given out of his property. He should leave all his inheritance for the heirs, because the benefit these people, being in need, will receive from the property of the deceased will be twice as rewarding for the deceased as compared with charity on his behalf. However, if the will is necessary, such as the one for payment of *fidya* concerning missed prayers and fasts, then, making a will for that is *wajib* (necessary) under all conditions, otherwise it will be a sin.

(Mufidul-Warithin, p. 59, Bahishti Zewar, Shami)

3. It is also recommended *(mustahabb)* that a will be made to the effect: 'Please let my funeral be in accordance with the *sunnah* of the Holy Prophet صلى الله عليه وسلم There should be no wailing, mourning or crying on my death. All customs and conventions and innovations contrary to the Shari'ah should be avoided'.

If such impermissible doings are in vogue among the relatives of a person and there be the strong likelihood that what is prohibited will be what is going to be practiced there, then, acting to forbid these things becomes mandatory.

(Mufidul-Warithin, p. 58)

4. As for matters relating to the funeral, making a will for any of them, subject to their not being religiously forbidden or reprehensible, is permissible - for example, the wish to be buried at a certain place or the wish to have a certain person lead the funeral prayer. The heirs are not really bound to follow these instructions, however, if there is nothing repugnant to the Shari'ah, it is better to fulfil such a will.

(Mufidul-Warithin, p. 59)

5. Making a will for a type of people to receive from the inheritance, people who openly disobey Allah and are involved in all sorts of sinful activities, is reprehensible (*makruh*). There is the overwhelming likelihood that these people will spend whatever they receive from the deceased on these very activities. If the deceased has made a will for this type of person,

his share will certainly be given to him in accordance with the rules of a will, but the maker of the will is going to end up being a sinner.

(Shami, al-Durr al-Mukhtar, p. 605, v.5)

The Will: The Making of a Document

Known as *al-Wasiyyah* or *Wasiyyat Namah,* a simple method of getting a will started is to set up a thick enough diary or note-book giving it the title of 'Will' or 'Important Memoranda'. Divide the pages under separate heads given below allotting several pages to each head. (Most of these relate to religious obligations one has failed to perform while some others concern debts, due or owed; and trusts, held for others or kept with others; and the will itself. The present form is an indicator of essentials. The functional format is left to individual discretion.)

Obligations to be fulfilled

1. Number of prayers due
2. Amount of *Zakah* due
3. Number of Ramadan and *Nadhr* fasts due
4. Obligatory Hajj, if due
5. *Sadaqatul-Fitr* due
6. *Sadaqah* of price against sacrifices not offered in specified years (because sacrifices cannot be offered after the passage of the prescribed days of sacrifice - so what is *wajib* (necessary) later is the *Sadaqah* (giving in charity) of its price.
7. *Sadaqatul-Fitr* due on behalf of one's children

8. The *Sajdah* of *Tilawah* due (special) prostration made during the recitation of the Holy Qur'an at places so indicated in the text.)

9. Number of *Kaffarahs* (expiations) of oaths due

Debts

10. Debts to be paid to others

11. Debts to be realized from others

Trusts

12. Trusts held for others

13. Trusts kept with others

The Will

14. *Al-Wasiyyah* or *Wasiyyat Namah*

After having set up appropriate subject headings, keep recording whatever state of affairs you are in. In case you have no obligations to fulfil under one of these headings, just say so. If otherwise, write down the details of the unfulfilled obligation. Then, as you go along keep subtracting what you keep fulfilling during your life-time. If something extra becomes necessary, add it up.

In short, what is important is that a full account in writing under each head should be ready at hand, which should also include a note under the section entitled, 'the Will', with a request to refer back to previous entries in order that payments could be made in accordance with what and how much has been recorded as due. In addition to that, keep making entries in the Will in the light of your circumstances making deletions and additions as and when needed. It is wise to let someone trusted know where to find it, so that, any time the call of death comes, the rights of Allah and the rights of human beings could be fulfilled in peace and the person concerned remains free of any onus from the present life and in the life-to-come.

Giving gift or charity during a disease resulting in death amounts to making a will

It is hoped that the rules of will have made it abundantly clear that a will, made in *maradul-maut,*[1] or in health, is governed by one single rule, that is, it is legally applied to only one-third of the property which remains after the payment of funeral expenses and the debts. Every sane and adult individual has a standing right to bequeath his property upto the limit of one-third to anyone before death. The remaining two-third of the property goes to heirs as their due. So, the Shari'ah has ruled that every will which curtails this due right of the heirs is null and void. It is to safeguard this right of theirs that the Shari'ah has also imposed some restrictions on the giving of gifts and charities during *maradul-maut* by a dying person, a summary of which follows.

Allah Almighty has given to every sane and adult person the right to give to anyone he chooses as much money, material and property as he wishes, but well before *maradul-maut.* He can give more than one-third, even the whole of it, without any restriction. Whether the recipient is a heir, or some other relative, or a perfect stranger, it does not matter. The recipient becomes the owner all right. However, the condition is that he should separate whatever he wishes to give from the rest of

---

1. *Maradul-Maut* : the disease in which the patient dies, details of which appear under the next heading.

(Rafi Usmani)

the property he owns, and then give it to the person he wishes should have it, making sure that it has actually passed into his possession. Otherwise, if he gives what is shared, or fails to bring about effective possession, then, this act of giving will not be valid in the sight of the Shari'ah, that is, the giver shall continue to be its owner and it will become part of the inheritance left by him after his death. The recipient so named will get nothing.

(Mufidul-Warithin, p. 42)

But right from the time *maradul-maut* begins, that is, the disease in which the sick person will pass away from this mortal world, the claim of the inheritors gets somewhat tied up with his property and the sick person does not continue to hold full control over it. Now, if he were to present someone with a gift, or to give in charity, then, this giving will fall under the same rule which governs wills. In other words, the conditions and the limit based on which the will is correct shall be the identical conditions and the limit upto which this giving too will be considered valid; and circumstances under which a will becomes invalid shall be the circumstances under which this giving too shall become null and void.

To sum up, all gifts and charities given during *maradul-maut* shall fall under the rule governing wills. The restrictions imposed on wills shall apply here as well. The *masa'il,* or the problems and their rulings which follow are based on this very principle:

Rulings:

1. Similarly, giving more than one-third of one's property during *maradul-maut* and making it free, for example, gift, *fidya* or charity, is not correct, because this undercuts the rights of heirs. If more than one-

third was given, this act of giving will not be correct until such time, after the death of the testator, when all heirs approve of this. The fact is that the heirs have the right to take back whatever exceeds the one-third. As for the minor and the insane, their permission, even if they give it, is not valid. And to give to any heir, even within the one-third and without the permission of all heirs, is not correct. All aspects of this rule stand operative only when what was to be given was given within the life-time of the giver who had made sure that it has passed on into the recipient's possession. In case one just gives as far as 'giving' goes, that is, simply says verbally or in writing, "I have given this much of my property to such and such person" - but, the actual possession has not been taken - then, after death, that act of giving will be absolutely null and void. That person will get nothing. The entire property rightfully belongs to the heirs.

The same rule holds good when things are given in the way of Allah and invested in righteous deeds like setting up a *waqf* (endowment) and its likes, during *maradul-maut*. So, giving out any more than one-third of the property without getting anything in return is just not correct; and giving it to an heir, even from within the one-third, is not correct either.

(Bahishti Zewar, al-Durr al-Mukhtar)

2. Here is a case study. Some people come to visit the sick person during his *maradul-maut*. They stay overnight, then prolong it for several days and keep being entertained out of what belongs to the person they came to visit. Now, there is no problem if their stay is necessary to take care of the sick person. But, in case there is no need for them to stay, then, spending any more than one-third to cover the expenses

on their feeding and entertainment is not permissible. And if there be neither the need nor those people be other than the heirs, then, spending even less than one-third of the property is totally impermissible. In other words, it is not permissible for those people to eat of the property of the sick person in his *maradul-maut.* Nevertheless, it is permissible if all heirs agree and approve of it.

(Bahishti Zewar)

3. When in *maradul-maut,* one does not have even the right to forgive the debt someone owes to him. If it was an heir who owed to him and he forgave it, then, it was not forgiven; and if he forgave some non-heir, then, whatever part of the property is in excess of the one-third will not stand forgiven without the permission of the heirs.

(Bahishti Zewar)

4. It is generally noticed that a dying wife would forgive her dower *(mahr).* This act of forgiveness is also not correct without the permission of all heirs because this forgiving is during *maradul-maut* and for an heir (the husband), which would amount to compromising the rights of other heirs.

(Bahishti Zewar, Islah-i-Inqilab-i-Ummat, p. 238, v.1)

5. If the person in *maradul-maut* confessed that he owed a certain amount to a certain person, or confessed that he has received the amount a certain person owed to him, then, this confession is valid in some situations and invalid in some others, because such confession curtails the share of the heirs. Therefore, when a situation like this actually comes up, it is advisable to consult an expert and reliable

religious scholar and get a solution of the problem from him. Please refrain from acting in accordance with your own inference. (Details on this subject appear in Mufidul-Warithin by Maulana Saiyyid Mian Asghar Husain Muhaddith of Deoband and may be seen there.)

Special Note:

Diseases through which one comes out cured shall be flatly counted as one's state of health and all spending made during the period one was afflicted with those diseases shall be in force and operative. It means that any commitment made with somebody or any gift or charity given to someone or any debt forgiven and several other things of this nature shall be correct and valid, whether those diseases were major or minor.

(Mufidul-Warithin)

How to tell when *maradul-maut* begins?

Maradul-Maut (literally, 'the disease of death' or 'death-disease') is a juristic term of Islamic law and signifies the disease suffering from which one leaves the mortal world. While living, it cannot be said with absolute certainty as to which disease it is that will take a sick person away from this mortal world.

(Mufidul-Warithin)

Rulings:

1. If a person suffers from a disease and dies in it, the state of *maradul-maut* will be counted as to have begun from the time one started suffering from that disease. But, a disease which continues for a whole year, or more, will not be counted as *maradul-maut* from its start. Instead, *maradul-maut* will be counted from the day when the disease became acute, leading

to the possibility of death. And it will be from this day that the rules of *maradul-maut* stated above shall become operative. So, if a person suffered from chronic diseases such as tuberculosis, or paralysis, or hemorrhoids, then, for a week, the disease became so acute that he died of it, in which case, the duration of *maradul-maut* will be counted as one week. All dealings made before that, such as gift and charity, will be taken as perfectly permissible and very much like what is done in one's state of health.

(Shami, al-Durr al-Mukhtar, p. 579, v.5, Mufidul-Warithin)

2. A disease in which the patient went out normally to offer his prayers in the mosque, or went out to the market shopping for groceries, or kept doing one or the other chore within the house, that is, he was not technically confined to bed, then, that disease too will not be counted as *maradul-maut* right from its start.

Similarly, the disease of a woman who kept doing her home chores will not be counted as *maradul-maut*. For example, during the course of many days, she used to run a temperature every third or fourth day. The disease was not that acute. Then, after a month, she was hit by high fever which did not recede for eight days and she died of it. Thus, the eight days will be taken as the duration of *maradul-maut*. The days of the month during which she ran temperature, will be counted like days of health and all dealings made during those days, such as gift and charity, will be permissible and correct.

(Mufidul-Warithin)

In short, a disease in which the patient dies, and

the duration of that disease be less than a year, and in which one cannot take care of himself, is what is known as *maradul-maut.*

(Mufidul-Warithin)

Ruling:

If a woman dies during delivery, *maradul-maut* will be counted from the time the pains started.

(Mufidul-Warithin, Bahishti Zewar)

Disaster, Despair and Imminent Death: Rulings:

1. If on board a ship or boat, there comes a storm leaving no hope of survival and making death imminent; then, the ship or boat drowns and people die - this will be a situation in which the time taken by the prevailing state of despair or the loss of hope in life will be considered as *maradul-maut* in the case of such people. Here too the rules of *maradul-maut* will remain the same as stated earlier. But, in the event that the ship or boat survives the storm, all dealings conducted during the state of despair will be correct and fully enforceable.

(Mufidul-Warithin)

2. The condition of a person who has been condemned to die and is marking his time in jail will not be taken as similar to *maradul-maut.* But, from the time he is taken out of the jail on his way to the death-cell where he is put to death, then, the time-span between his exit from the jail and his death shall be covered by the rule of *maradul-maut.* And if, for any reason, his date with death was postponed on that day, or the very sentence of death was cancelled, then, the state of his exit from the jail and reaching the death-cell shall not be covered by the rule of *maradul-maut*

and the dealings carried out during this state will turn out to be correct and operative.

(Mufidul-Warithin)

The *Wasiy*: the Executor of Will

The person who is appointed by the maker of the will to take charge after his death to pay debts from the inheritance, distribute the legacy and take care of matters relating to his children as his deputy and guardian is called the '*Wasiy*' (trustee). If the person made a *Wasiy* accepts the charge even verbally, it becomes incumbent on him; or, if he does something which indicates his willingness to become a *Wasiy*, even then he becomes the *Wasiy*.

The *Wasiy*, however, does have the right to refuse to become a *Wasiy*, but this has to be within the lifetime of the maker of the will. However, he will not have this right after the death of the maker of the will.

(Mufidul-Warithin, p. 65)

If a person was made a *Wasiy* for some matters while other matters were neither mentioned, nor someone else was made a *Wasiy* for them, in which case, the person named as the *Wasiy* for some matters shall be taken as the *Wasiy* for all matters. If two persons have been made the *Wasiy* in all matters, both of them should work together. If only one person disposes matters unilaterally, that will be impermissible. However, if just one person acting alone goes ahead and takes care of funeral arrangements and fulfils the immediate needs of the family of the deceased, that will be permissible and valid.

(al-Durr al-Mukhtar. p.616, v.5 & Mufidul-Warithin)

To be a *Wasiy* and to be honest at the same time is really something very hard to do. So, one should avoid the charge as far as possible. If one has to do it, one should never say yes unless the circumstance are extremely compelling. In case, he does finally agree to take the responsibility because of some dire need or wise consideration, he should constantly fear being accountable before Allah and apprehend being punished in the Hereafter for any breach of trust, and then do his duty with full honesty having the highest concern for the welfare of the legatees. Spending trust funds needlessly like free wealth and disposing things like an owner is just not permissible. However, should the job of management be so time-consuming that one cannot get away to make a living for himself, in which case it is permissible to draw money from the property of the testator for personal maintenance within the limit of needs. When a situation like this comes up, please consult reliable religious scholars.

(Mufidul-Warithin, p. 65)

The Distribution of Inheritance Among Heirs

Details about three out of the four *seriatim* claims which are obligatory against the inheritance of the deceased have appeared previously, that is, the coverage of funeral expenses, payment of debts and the execution of valid wills. Taken up now is the fourth claim or right - 'the distribution of inheritance among heirs'.

After valid wills have been executed upto the limit of onethird of the inheritance, whatever property remains falls under the ownership of all heirs of the deceased, and this whole will be distributed among them in accordance with the shares fixed by Shari'ah.

Ruling:

If the deceased had no debts to pay, nor had he made some will, all property that remains after the payment for the funeral will be distributed among heirs. And if the deceased had left some payable debt, but no will to be executed, everything that remains after clearance of the debt will go to the heirs.

(al-Durr al-Mukhtar)

The Shari'ah has itself fixed the share of each heir. Nobody has the right to make changes, modifications, additions or deletions in it. However, the Shari'ah has, in its own way, seen that the share of each heir does not remain the same under all conditions. Instead, it has fixed different shares under different circumstances. In other words, it has altered the ratio of their shares on the basis of any increase or decrease in the number of heirs. Some heirs cause the share of some other heirs to be either totally eliminated, or reduced. Relevant details appear in texts of the Science of Inheritance. These cannot be taken up here because the Science of Inheritance is a regular field of knowledge in its own right with so many refinements that it is difficult for everyone to understand its implications.

So, in the event of some one's death, the safest course is to write down a complete list of his parents, sons and daughters, and the husband or wife, whosoever of them is alive at the time of such death (even if living abroad in more than one country), giving their numbers, and their relationship to the deceased. Then, approach some trustworthy *'Alim* or *Mufti* who has the necessary expertise in questions relating to inheritance and ask him, in writing or in person, about the shares of inheritors. Once this becomes available follow the method suggested there and distribute the inheritance as fixed. If, at the time of the deceased person's death, some of the heirs listed above may be alive, and may be some are not alive, in which case, write down the number and the nature of relationship of other relatives of the deceased. Make clear statements about any real brothers and sisters of the deceased, or of those who are from the same father but different mother, or of those who are from the same mother but different father. This is important and should be clarified, separate and distinct. Step parents and step in-laws and other relatives from the in-laws' side are not heirs under Islamic Shari'ah. They should not be included in the list.

If the heir of a deceased person expires before the distribution of the inheritance, his share will be distributed among his heirs. therefore, it is necessary to include this expired person in the list.

The rule governing the death of several relatives in one accident

If several relatives die in some accident and it is not possible to determine as to who among them died first or last, for example, several relatives were drowned all together while travelling at sea, or died in a car or bus accident, or under the debts of a building which collapsed - and it is not possible to determine as to who among them died first or last - then, under this situation, none of them will inherit from the other. Islamic law will take them as having died all together, therefore, no inheritance will pass from one to the other. The inheritance will be distributed only among the surviving heirs.

(Mufidul-Warithin, p. 70)

If the husband dies while the wife is observing her *'idda* of divorce, does she inherit or does she not?

If the wife of the deceased was observing the *'idda* of divorce while he died, she will inherit in some circumstances, and she will not in some others. Details regarding this have appeared earlier and may be consulted there if needed. In case the course of action in a particular case does not still become clear fully, please consult religious scholars you trust.

A missing heir and his share in the inheritance

The heir reported missing before the expiry of the deceased and who cannot be traced, to determine whether alive or dead, is known as *'mafqud'* or a missing person. The Islamic law governing such a person is that his share in the inheritance should be held in trust so that he can take it when he comes. If he does not return, so much so that the legal time limit for waiting expires and the authorized Muslim ruler declares this person as 'dead' in accordance with rules set by the Shari'ah, then, the share being held in trust will also be distributed among the heirs - not among the heirs of the missing person. However, whatever belongs to the missing person himself will certainly be distributed among his present heirs.

(Islah-i-Inqilab-i-Ummat, v.2, pp. 213-218)

There are a lot of details inherent in this question as well. When one actually faces a situation like this, it is advisable to act in consultation with a trustworthy religious scholar who is entitled to give relevant ruling in such matters.

In the case of an unborn heir, the distribution of inheritance will be held in abeyance

If an heir of the deceased is still in the womb of his or her mother when he dies, the yet-to-be-born child holds a share in the inheritance according to Islamic law. But, in the absence of the certain knowledge about the child being a boy or girl, the inheritance should not be distributed until the child is born because the share of a boy and a girl is not equal. In addition to that, unless it is definitely determined whether the child will be a boy or a girl, the shares coming to other heirs can also not be determined with any degree of certainty in many situations. If the inheritance was distributed on the presumption that the child will be a boy but, later on, when the new-born born is a girl, the whole calculation of shares and their distribution will have to be redone from the very start.

(Islah-i-Inqilab-i-Ummat)

Rulings:

1. The killer does not inherit from the person he has killed. In other words, if the deceased was killed unjustly *('zulman')* by a relative who was his heir Shari'ah-wise, the Shari'ah has excluded him from the inheritance of the person killed by him because of his act of killing. It does not matter how close a relative he may be. For instance, he may be a father or a son-still, he will not remain an heir anymore. However, the condition is that the killer be sane and adult. If the act of killing was carried out by a non-adult or insane person, then, he will not be excluded from the inheritance.

(Sharifiah, Sharh Sirajiyyah, p. 11-12)

2. Inheritance does not beome operative between a Muslim and a *Kafir*, that is, a Muslim cannot inherit from a *Kafir* and a *Kafir* cannot inherit from a Muslim. It does not matter how closely they are related, not even when they happen to be a father and a son.

(Sharifiah, Sharh Sirajiyyah, p. 14)

COMMON FAILINGS IN THE DISTRIBUTION OF INHERITANCE

The Shari'ah of Islam rules that all claims on the inheritance which it is mandatory to liquidate must be paid off as soon as possible and the remaining inheritance should be distributed among the heirs. Delay breeds too many complications and suspicions. There are times when excessive delaying results in almost unsurmountable complexities in the usual equitable distribution of inheritance which could border on the compromising of some heir's just right.

Patently absurd are the sentiments that a quick distribution of the inheritance of the deceased will bring social censure - 'look at these people, they were just waiting for that death in the family so that they could grab his property! - but, given the command of Allah Almighty, all such whims and sentiments are ineffectual. All inheritors should be told that the distribution of inheritance is done to obey the command of Allah Almighty and that it has to be carried out as soon as possible.

Given below are some common failings prevailing all over in our Muslim societies, specially about the prompt distribution of inheritance. Please look at them with concern and seek to correct what must be corrected.

Not paying debts owed by the deceased

It is commonly observed these days that a debt proved to be due against the deceased Shari'ah-wise, other than a debt for which documentary proof exhists, is hardly paid from the inheritance. In fact, people flatly refuse to pay such debts as a convenient measure. This is quite similar to the attitude of people who go back on their word of honour and refuse to pay debts owed by them to the deceased. Both these practices are rank injustice. The case of the deceased is special; if the deceased is under debt, his heirs should realize that the soul of their departed relative shall remain detained in suspension before it could be admitted into the Paradise until such time that the debt has been paid off. Who would like to bring upon one's own dear relative a deprivation so terrible?

(Islah-i-Inqilab-Ummat p. 242)

Not executing valid wills

Another lack of concern becoming common is that people do not care enough to respect the valid wills of the deceased, although the Shari'ah has given the right of making wills upto the one-third of inheritance which is owned by the maker and once a will is made nobody has the right to interfere in its execution. If the valid will is not executed, contrary to the wishes of the deceased, this failing will usurp his rights and thus the right of a servant of Allah shall remain unliquidated. Therefore, great care should be taken to fulfil the will of the deceased. However, if the deceased has made a will towards something impermissible, it will not be permissible to execute such a will.

(Thanvai, Islam Haqiqi, Wa'z)

Giving compensation for missed prayers and fasts from the combined inheritance without a will made for that purpose

There is yet another shortcoming. Some people, in an euphoria of piety, would go ahead and pay off the compensation (*fidya*) of prayers and fasts missed by the deceased from the combined inheritance in absence of the necessary will to that effect, or give *zakah* on his behalf, or arrange to have someone perform the Hajj due on him, despite the fact repeatedly stressed earlier that an heir who, in the absence of a will made by the deceased, would still like to pay for *fidya*, *zakah* or Hajj on behalf of the deceased, should do so from his share in the inheritance or from what he already owns personally, an act which has great merit. But, giving out from the share of other heirs without their permission is not allowed, and giving from the share of the non-adult and the insane is not allowed even with their permission.

(Islah-i-Inqilab-i-Ummat, v.1, p. 239)

Ignoring the need to pay compensation for missed prayers and fasts:

Another failing is that the heirs would, in the event someone dies without making a will, blow up the inheritance left by the deceased on heads of expenditure much less in importance than the compensation of missed prayers and fasts, going to the limits of spending wastefully and purposelessly, even in staging impermissible customary functions and on self-designed acts in the name of religion for which there is no precedent or sanction there. The tragedy is that people hardly care to cut down on other expenses and give out something from their share of inheritance as *fidya* on behalf of the deceased, or arrange to take care of the cost of unpaid *zakah* or unmade Hajj on behalf of the deceased.

Although, as seen by some jurists, the deceased person does not get absolved of his missed religiously obligatory acts through such payment made by others without his will to that effect. But, other jurists say that he is so absolved. As for the jurists who take the first position, they too admit that the merit and reward of this act will anyway reach the deccased. Thus, being certainly beneficial, it is not unlikely that this reward may cancel the punishment for the deceased person's act of abandoning his religious obligations.

(Islah-i-Inqilab-i-Ummat, p. 200, vide Al-Radd al-Mukhtar)

The Device of Waiver against the payment of compensation

In some rural areas of Muslim countries people have a custom called *'daur'* or 'the *hilah* of *isqat*'. *'Hilah'* is a device or stratagem, and *'Isqat'* is waiver. Hence, it is a contrivance to escape compliance while still being within the parameters of religious ramifications. So, the custom is that some people would sit in a circle and the heirs of the deceased deposit some cash inside the circle. The Imam of the mosque who is positioned inside the circle takes the cash, recites some words in Arabic, and then gives the money to a person in the circle who gives it to the second who gives it to the third, and like this the money passes on from the next to the next. Ultimately, the money returns back to the first man. The money is circulated in this manner three times. Then, it is distributed off, half to the Imam and the other half to the poor. At the end of the exercise, the ignorant participants are told that this custom relieves the deceased from all his missed religious obligations, such as, the prescribed prayers and fasts, *Zakah* and Hajj and everything else incumbent on observing practicing Muslims.

There is no doubt about the exhistence of a particular method of such waiver in the writings of Muslim jurists, but people just do not know the conditions attached therein, nor do they at all abide by it. There is a whole corpus of Islamic rules governing the area of missed religious obligations which is simply ignored. What has been done is not more than an easy prescription to get rid of all religious obligations through this convenient custom. What can be achieved by a handful of cash hardly warrants that somebody should go about labouring with a life-time of prayers and fasts!

Please let this be very clear that some Muslim jurists had suggested this device of waiver for someone who had, by chance, missed some prayers and fasts and did not get the opportunity to make up for them during his life-time, and who could only make a will at the time of his death without leaving enough of inheritance from the one-third of which his heirs could pay the *fidya* or compensation of all his missed prayers and fasts. What was not intended is the situation that the deceased has enough assets in his inheritance which the heirs very conveniently devour among themselves and then cheat God and the human beings He created by dishing out a handful of money under the cover of false devices. This has been made very clear in major books of Islamic jurisprudence, such as, al-Durr al-Mukhtar & Shami where this device is hemmed by other conditions as well, which are totally bypassed. This voodoo-like exercise never helps the deceased, nor does he get deobligated of everything he had been obligated with. Being absurd and ineffectual, this act results in nothing but a tasteless sin for the actors.

In short, it is possible that the initial introduction of this device had some correet legal bases, but the way it has been vulgarized into compelling custom is certainly impermissible as it breeds many social ills, details of which can be seen in *'Hila-i-lsqat'* by Maulana Mufti Muhammad Shafi, the late Grand Mufti of Pakistan.

Making a will to have funeral prayers led by a particular person, or to be buried in a particular place

There are people who would make a will that a certain named person should lead his *janazah* prayers, or ask to be buried at a place indicated in the will. What happens is that the heirs take great pains to fulfil such demands in the will which sometimes results in the contravention of obligatory religious rules. Please remember that such wills are not binding in accordance with the Shari'ah of Islam. It is permissible to do what the will calls for only if one does not have to act against the clear rules of the Shari'ah, otherwise, carrying out such provisions in the will is not permissible.

(Islah-i-Inqilab-i-Ummat, v.1, p. 243)

Not distributing the inheritance

A grave shortcoming becoming common these days is that the inheritance of the deceased is not distributed as it should be. Whoever holds whatever assets there are turns into their owner overnight. There are excuses after excuses to render what is unlawful to hold as something lawful for the usurper. It is sad, but there are even educated people who ride into the same boat. They think they are all one, same family, same people, everyone can share and use things around, why distribute? This interpretation can only be advanced by the usurping possessor of assets for this is to his advantage.

Other heirs, being young or dependent, demur and say nothing, but the truth is that nobody allows this to happen with an open heart. This surface permission is no act of will and pleasure. Based on this, the act of one heir, that of taking possession of the entire inheritance, becomes totally *haram* and impermissible, specially so when some heirs are non-adult or insane, or are absent. As for the absent, nobody knows about his permission, and the permission of the non-adult or the insane, even if given clearly and with pleasure, is not legally valid. So, one must fear the punishment of the grave and the punishment of the Hell and abstain from any injustice and usurpation and act straight by seeing that all heirs get their due rights in accordance with the dictates of the Shari'ah.

(Thanavi, Wa'z: Islam Haqiqi)

Running a business on usurped inheritance

Another failing commonly seen is that an heir who runs a business during the life-time of the deceased remains in control of that business even after the death of the owner. He simply takes over, runs it, makes it grow and yield profits, all done without the permission of the other heirs, notwithstanding the non-adult heirs whose permission is not valid. So, when the time comes for the ultimate distribution of inheritance at some fairly later stage, disputes arise about the original capital and the recurring profits. Distributing assets becomes a painful process. The fact is that there are great many complications in determining the prorits Shari'ah-wise. Therefore, the rule is: Distribute first, then go in business. Do it under mutual consent, combined or separate. The guardian of the non-adult can transact on his behalf either way.

The injustice of depriving girls from the inheritance

That some people do not give sisters and daughters their share in the inheritance is certainly an act of rank injustice. Just because they are given gifts and things at the time of their marriage, they presume that such givings were enough to take care of their rights. This is totally incorrect; gifts never cancel the right to receive from the inheritance. It is obligatory to give sisters and daughters their share in the inheritance and any effort to exclude them from it is *haram* (forbidden) and is also an act of tyranny committed against them.

(Islah-i-Inqilab-i-Ummat, p. 241)

Asking sisters to forgo their share in the inheritance

This is an injustice one would witness even in families which are fairly well-informed about the dictates of their Faith. Those who make sisters forgo their share in the inheritance should know that a formal nod of approval, and 'agreement', from sisters to the effect that they forgo their share in the inheritance is not enough and will not absolve those who ask them to do so of their responsibility. Unfortunately, sisters consider demanding their share in the inheritance as something derogatory to their position, which is a legacy of the days of Ignorance. They still fear that their brothers will become sore with them, and that people in the larger family circle will taunt at them. This custom is blandly pagan and quite deplorable that it has survived so long, resulting in silencing the voice of these oppressed women. If a tyrant who does that gets away by not having been punished right here in this mortal world, let him not forget that the final day of reckoning is sure to come, about which Allah Almighty says: ولعذاب الاخرة اكبر that is, the punishment of the Hereafter is greater than the punishment of the mortal world.

To begin with, the Shari'ah does not recognize the simple verbal declaration of sisters as formal valid proof of their intent to forgo their share. Chances are that their heart is not behind it. Secondly, even if there is a rare woman who is all too happy to forgo her share like this, even then, this act of making sisters forgive and forgo is against the Islamic principles of justice as there is no way one could find out that this was done willingly and with a happy heart. Moreover, this also amounts to promoting and approving an oppressive Hindu custom which happens to be very much against the Muslim way. Therefore, it is better to stay away from such conduct.

Some people say that sisters let brothers have their share in the inheritance in consideration of gifts they keep receiving on different ceremonial occasions from them, which is a sort of transaction. But, this is wrong since it does not carry with it the agreement of their sisters. They do so because they are helpless against custom. Then, the quantity and the type and the value of such gifts is not known. So, this transaction, that is, the act of buying and selling, is not correct.

In short, all devices engineered to devour the share of sisters who cannot speak up against this tyranny, and all stratagems to make what is forbidden as lawful, have been flatly rejected by the Shari'ah as null and void. The safest course is: Open up your heart, be honest, give them their full share and see that it passes into their actual possession.

On excluding a widow from inheritance if she remarries

Not uncommon at places is the custom that a widow, who marries again after the death of her first husband, is deprived of his inheritance. Such a widow, just to be sure that she does not miss her share in the inheritance, does not remarry, goes on to live with the tragedy of widowhood for the rest of her years, added thereto being the not-too-sympathetic treatment at the hands of the relatives of the late husband. Let us not forget that this too is open injustice and has been strictly forbidden. The fact is that the widow, even if she remarries, remains the owner of her share in the inheritance.

Depriving a widow from her share because she belongs to another tribe

This custom practiced in a certain part of Pakistan is based on ignorance. This is an injustice as the Holy Qur'an has certainly made the share of a widow obligatory irrespective of whether she comes from the family of her husband for from some other family.

A widow taking possession of the whole inheritance without the right

Another form of injustice shows up when some women who, after the death of their husbands, take possession of all immovable property left by them under the impression that they are the owners of everything. The fact is that anything that their late husbands gifted to them during their life time (before their last sickness) and handed it over to them as being theirs is, no doubt, theirs. But, the rest of it is combined inheritance. According to the rules of Shari'ah, this will be distributed among all heirs as a matter of obligation.

(Islah-i-Inqilab-i-Ummat, p. 241)

Stealing from the inheritance

Also deplorable is the act of an heir who just sits on whatever he can lay his hands on. There is no stealing and no usurping in inheritance. Those who do it should not forget that they will have to throw it back on the Day of Doom.

(Ibid)

In case a bride dies while at the home of her parents, or the home of her in-laws, there is a rule about her personal effects

A terrible injustice is committed in the event of a bride dying at the home of her parents when people from her husband's family take possession of everything, such as effcets belonging to her personally which she brought with her as her marriage portion; and if she dies at the house of the in-laws, the husband or his relatives or guardians take over the whole thing. All this is absolutely and totally impermissible. Everyone involved will have to account for every cent thus appropriated here, in the Hereafter. It should be borne in mind that all heirs of the bride have a share in her marriage portion and in any part of the inheritance which comes to her. This includes her husband also, and the parents of the bride as well - irrespective of the place where the bride died.

(Islah-i-Inqilab-i-Ummat, v.1, p. 242)

When the trustee usurps inheritance

Not too uncommon is the happening when a particular heir would use his seniority or position among the rest of the heirs to take possession of the entire property. Passing as its guardian and trustee, he will go on taking unilateral decisions which affect the property and refuses to distribute the property even if so demanded by other heirs, some of whom may be orphans. The Qur'an says: فَمَا أَصْبَرَهُمْ عَلَى النَّارِ (How enduring they must be on the Fire!) (2:175). Devouring what belongs to orphans should make anyone blush. But, one who is reckless enough to ignore the warning of the fire of Hell will certainly have a great deal to find out on the Day of Doom, standing there to account for everything so usurped and misappropriated.

Asking people to pardon and forgo any of their rights, if they have remained unfulfilled

These are known as *Huquq al-'Ibad*, that is, the rights of the servants of Allah. This is serious matter because these rights cannot be forgiven by anyone other than the person to whom they belong. The Holy Prophet صلى الله عليه وسلم has said: 'Whoever has son right of a brother (a Muslim, or any human being) partaining to his sense of honour, or to something else due against him, should go and have it forgiven by him this very day, before the Day (of Doom), when he would have no *dinar* and *dirham* to use.

(Mishkat, on Injustice)

The rights of the servants of Allah are of two kinds-financial and non-financial. Rules covering financial rights have appeared earlier under Inheritance, Debts, Wills and the Distribution of Legacies. A description of non-financial rights is given below:

Non-financial rights of people

When you live in a complex human relationship with your relatives, friends, acquaintances and many others, something is likely to go wrong in mutual dealings which may affect rights which are obligatory. Naturally, anyone whose right gets compromised feels the pinch of loss. There are cases when misgivings arise and relations get broken. There are other occasions when tempers go out of control and the other party ends up hurting physically or morally, just because of envy or spite. Sometimes the evil habit of back-biting, lying and cheating causes loss of honour or property to someone. There are many things like these which cause situations when someone's rights are compromised, giving him pain, which is a grave sin. The Holy Qur'an and the Sunnah have prohibited such conduct in strong terms giving warnings of severe punishment in the Hereafter. Therefore, it is absolutely necessary that one should do a real survey of one's life, and of things he has been doing all along, and do something to correct or make amends for what has gone wrong, much before death overtakes. Miss no time, go and ask the person who suffered at your hands to forgive you for what happened. Not only that, one should also turn to Allah Almighty and seek His refuge against such sins, moved by genuine remorse of the heart, repenting and praying that Allah forgives you. If, for some reason, it does not remain possible for one to approach people whose rights have been compromised and who cannot be reached for pardon in such cases, may be they have died or have moved away leaving no address, then, one should become very particular about praying for their forgiveness, doing it regularly, always. May be the deeds so offered to seek Allah's mercy for them turn out to be sincere and Allah Almighty, in His infinite grace, may take the responsibility to see that such aggrieved people are satisfied and pleased, and willing to forgive and forget.

(Bahishti Zewar)

The same thing happens to us when others trespass the area of our rights. So, personal nobility and rational need, as well as the Shari'ah of Islam, demand that we too should forgive everyone we are related with in our social circle with an open heart. First of all, this makes you feel good inside, then, this happens to be the sure method of keeping the other person safe against the answerability of the Hereafter. The later is something very dear in the sight of Allah.

The Qur'an and *Hadith* speak of the great merits of accepting the apology of a Muslim brother and forgiving him. In fact the Holy Prophet صلى الله عليه وسلم has said: 'If a person apologizes to his Muslim brother and he does not accept it, then, he will incur a sin similar to what is incurred by an oppressive taxman.'

(Ibn Majah)

It was said in another *hadith:* 'One who does not accept the apology of his Muslim brother made to him, will not be allowed to come to me at the *Hawd al-Kauthar.*'

(Targhib wa Tarhib, from al-'Udhr wa an-Nadhr)

The gist of the submission here is that everyone should, well before his death, clean up his conscience in the light of the dictates of his faith in matters that relate to Allah and those that relate to His created beings.

By the way, it is not necessary that people from whom forgiveness is sought for any omissions and commissions in life should be the people with whom animated relationships through calls, meetings and liason has to be maintained, because doing that is sometimes quite difficult, and not so expedient at others. So, the purpose of forgiving or seeking of forgiveness is not to establish cordial relations based on friendship and informality later on. Instead, the main purpose is to have spiritual relief that comes from having fulfilled the rights of people as envisaged by the Shari'ah.

As for maintaining good relations with one's kinsfolk, the famous dictum of the noble *hadith* is: 'Let them break off relations (if they must), but you (on your part) keep to maintaining relations.' It means that one should be with them when they are hit by sorrows and hardships of life, helping them to the best of one's ability, with money and effort and consolation, and

CHAPTER VIII

Understanding *Bid'ah*

The natural way of handling death, the deceased and the survivors prescribed by Islam has appeared before you as supported by authentic texts of Hadith and *Fiqh*. In its moderation and balance, this is the method *primus* appointed for Muslims in the Qur'an, Sunnah, and *Fiqh*.

So many of those dear to his heart from among his close and distant relatives, and many a devoted Companions, died during the blessed life of the Holy Prophet صلى الله عليه وسلم. Some fell martyrs on the battle field, some breathed their last on the sick bed, some departed leaving no heirs behind and some died leaving mourning children, family and relatives. Some did not leave enough inheritance to cover the minimal cost of a funeral while some others had wealth and property which was distributed among heirs. These were some of the many conditions in which the only guide everyone had was none other than our blessed master, the perennial fountain of mercy, the Holy Prophet Muhammad صلى الله عليه وسلم. It was he who showed the way. Whenever a certain situation came up, it was he, may Allah bless him for ever and ever, who told everyone all about laws and etiquettes relevant to the occasion. What we know as the *Shar'* or the Islamic Law was what he taught, and demonstrated practically, for people to learn. Exactly when he was teaching and grooming his Companions in the discipline of faith, piety and Divine worship along with the rules and regulations that would help them run their lives in the world around them, he was also educating them practically into the many ways of handling happiness and sorrow. The reason was that he was sent to this mortal world for no other purpose but that his teachings and guidance should fill every facet of Muslim community life with light that survives for ever.

So, focusing on the immediate area of our concern, we see that he was with them actively on all occasions of their happiness and grief - he visited them when they were sick, and participated in the preparation of their body for the funeral when they died; he made arrangements for their *janazah* prayer and the ultimate burial; he condoled their death and prayed that the departed soul be rewarded by Allah; he maintained that golden touch of personal concern by visiting even their graves, praying and wishing for their forgiveness in the presence of their Lord; then, he also attended to their post-death obligations, distributing the inheritance they left behind, seeing that debts they owed were paid off, making sure about the execution of wills they had made and also that the remaining inheritance is given to heirs they left behind; he did not forget to console and comfort their survivors; he cared enough to see that widows are taken care of and that orphans are shielded by proper guardians. To put it in a nutshell, the Holy Prophet صلى الله عليه وسلم has bequeathed for his community, through his words and deeds, a complete set of rules to go by in matters relating to death, the handling of the deceased and the amelioration of survivors. It is very unusual that he has left not one aspect of the procedure wanting, or sothething which we have to borrow from some other group of people, or have to invent on our own.

It does not take much to realize that this way of handling death in the family takes into account human needs and natural emotions at every step of its happening. It provides for the consolation of the berieved, institutes a moderate and fairly comprehensive system of equity and justice, ensures the dignity of the deceased throughout the entire process with full consideration of the departed person's well-being in the Hereafter - most importantly, the method prescribed is so easy to carry out, so purificatory, yet so simple and dignified that no civilization of this mortal world has been able to match it even to this day.

The noble Companions of the Holy Prophet صلی اللہ علیہ وسلم learned these set of rules from their master and acted in accordance with them throughout their lives covering each and every aspect of the subject. Not only that, they were also able to transmit their verbal and practical learning to their next generations. The great preservers of the Traditions of the Last Prophet, the *Muhaddithin,* preserved these, as they were, in their books. The Mujtahid Imams explained and explicated them. Later, came the imminent jurists of Islam who handed it over to us through their books, in their very original form, *ipso facto.* It was because of this peerless labour of love from these very people that we have before us right through this day a perfect and authentic guideline in matters relating to death.

But, a look at what we have in the form of these set of rules and then another look at the innovations *(bid'aat)* and customs surrounding death, the deceased and the survivors, which have spread like some epidemic in our society, will certainly leave us stunned with a pinching sense of loss. This is tragedy, so astonishing and so painful. Just imagine the weird line of action taken by a great community which has in its possession such priceless and peerless code of conduct!

It is really unbelievable that they would elect to abandon what was gifted to them, something so efficient and so wise, and stray into devising ways of their own, or stoop to blindly accept and follow the mutilated teachings of other faiths and thus fall into absurd customs, become self-restricted by inventing things not prescribed in their religion, and keep shunting between all sort of wasteful excess and deficiency.

It is, for that matter, a nemesis of our deeds that religious innovations and self-styled customs are finding currency in almost every department of our Faith. But, their proliferation in matters relating to death and the deceased, perhaps, beats its presence in any other department in that proportion. Once death occurs in a family, these wasteful exercises would keep haunting the inmates of the berieved house for months, even years. There are customs and customs - Hindu, Parsi, and the strangest of all: even British! There are occasions when these alien customs are blended with self-introduced additions into the established mores of religion. On top of everything, people tend to do these things with such an air of particularity as if they have been made obligatory or necessary for them. The amount of time, labour and money wasted to go through these pagan customs and innovations beats any sane description. Any effort to collect relevant statistics of this wastage would result in nothing but that the investigator would go crazy. Not unusual are spendings on these needless customs made from the inheritance of the deceased which is a flagrant injustice meted out to orphaned heirs. In short, it is a pity that people would abandon the great life-model of their universally merciful Messenger from Allah, and the set of rules he prescribed for us, and elect to or stray into going along with polytheistic customs of other peoples, or worse still, get lost in the labyrinth of self-designed innovations, although there is with them that loud and clear statement of the Holy Qur'an which says:

لَقَدْ كَانَ لَكُمْ فِىْ رَسُوْلِ اللّٰهِ أُسْوَةٌ حَسَنَةٌ

(There is for you, in the Messenger of Allah, an excellent model.) (33:21)

Though we have been pointing out to such customs and innovations at several places earlier, but it is necessary that this subject should be taken up at this stage with some details and that the more prevalent among these be pinpointed specially, because the Holy Prophet صلى الله عليه وسلم has said:

اذا حدث فِى أُمَّتِىْ الْبِدَعُ وَشُتِمَ اَصْحَابِىْ، فَلْيُظْهِرِ الْعَالِمُ عِلْمَهُ، فَمَنْ لَّمْ يَفْعَلْ فَعَلَيْهِ لَعنةُ اللّٰهِ وَالْمَلٰئِكَةِ وَالنَّاسِ اَجْمَعِيْنَ

(When religious innovations appear in my community, and my Companions are maligned, then, the knowing scholar of the time must make his knowledge manifest before others. Then, whoever fails to do it, on him shall be the curse of Allah and the angels and the human beings, all together).

(Kitabul-I'tisam, Shatibi, v. 1. p. 88, also, Sunnah and *Bid'ah*, p. 26)

Before we proceed to do that, let us first become clear in our minds about the reality of *'Bid'ah'* as a matter of principle, for the simple reason that a lot of people get involved with many of these religious innovations simply because they obviously appear to be something 'good'. People would generally go through these thinking that they were kind of reward-worthy.

This is a misconception based on the ignorance of the true and very clear teaching of the Faith.

What is *'Bid'ah'* ?

Lexically, *'Bid'ah'* (pausal form of *'Bid'at;* referred to here as 'religious innovation' or simply 'innovation') signifies everything new or recent. In the terminology of the Shari'ah, it means some newly-invented method of worship taken to with the intention of receiving a reward (*thawab*), after the Holy Prophet صلى الله عليه وسلم and the most rightly-guided Caliphs, although there existed the motive and reason for it during the blessed times of the Messenger of Allah and his noble Companions, yet there is no proof to support its existence neither in words spoken nor in deeds performed, nor explicitly, nor suggestively.

(Sunnah and *Bid'ah*, p. 11, vide Kitabul-I'tisam)

The definition given above tells us that all new inventions, instruments, gadgets and technologies that keep coming out everyday have nothing to do with what is known as *'Bid'ah'* in the Shari'ah of Islam. The reason is that they are not pursued as an act of religious worship or with the intention of earning *'thawab'* (reward from Allah). All these are permissible and rated as 'allowed', of course, on condition that they do not fall against a religious command. It also tells us that an act of worship which stands proved on the authority of the Holy Prophet صلى الله عليه وسلم or his noble Companions, through their word or deed, explicitly or suggestively, that too cannot be classed as *'Bid 'ah'*.

Further on, it also shows that the need for something which did not exist during the period of prophethood, but did come to exist later on in order to achieve some religious objective, that too is not included under *'Bid'ah'* for example, institutions of Islamic learning, associations devoted to teaching and propagation of the faith, religious publishing houses, sciences required to understand Qur'an and *Hadith* such as, grammar and syntax, Arabic literary forms, aspects of style and eloquence, or books of logic and philosophy to refute anti-Islam forces, or the use of modern arms in *jihad* and the teaching of and the training in modern warfare are all things that enjoy the status of an act of worship in a way and certainly were not present during the blessed times of the Holy Prophet صلى الله عليه وسلم and his noble Companions, yet these cannot be termed as *'Bid'ah'* just because they were not needed in that blessed time. What happened later is that the scholars of the Muslim community saw the need as it manifested during the course of time and they devised appropriate ways and means to meet the challenge, staying within the textual imperatives of the Qur'an and *Hadith*.

It can be further explained by saying that these things are no act of worship as they are, nor anyone pursues them with the intention of receiving a lot more *thawab* or reward from Allah. The fact is that these things are known as acts of worship on the basis of their being the means to that worship. In other words, to go by a new via media as needed in the space-time continuum to achieve a religious objective as determined in the textual authority of Qur'an and *Hadith* is certainly not prohibited.

(Sunnah and *Bid'ah*, p. 13)

These details also point out that inventing some method to do something the need for which is common between the period of prophethood and the periods which followed later, and if the method was not provenly adopted by the Holy Prophet صلى الله عليه وسلم and his noble Companions, then, this will be classed as *'Bid'ah'* and this will be ruled, in accordance with the Qur'an and *Hadith,* as something prohibited and impermissible.

Examples of this abound in our social and religious conduct, for example, imposing the restriction of standing up while reciting *darud* and *salam*, feeding the poor with the intention of bequeathing its *thawab* to the departed soul by placing eatables in front and following a self-imposed restriction of reciting various Surahs of the Qur'an, becoming particular with raising hands of prayer more than once making the entire congregation follow suit, even after the initial *Salah* has been duly offered in congregation, observing the restriction of celebrating the post-death third or the fortieth day to add on to the process of bequeathing *thawab* to the departed soul, offering self-invented prayers during the blessed nights of months like (Rajab) and Sha'ban or setting up illuminations on the locale of such observances and then taking these self-invented, self-promoted practices as if they were religiously obligatory or necessary, and tragically enough, criticising and chiding those who do not take part in such observances.

(Sunnah and *Bid'ah*, p. 14)

It is obvious that *darud* and *salam, sadaqah* and alms, praying that the soul of the deceased may rest in peace, offering voluntary prayers during blessed nights, supplications to Allah following prayers, are included under acts of worship. Their need exhists this day as it certainly did during the period of time graced by the presence of the noble Companions. If a pious servant of Allah living today is fired with the zeal of seeking the pleasure of Allah and the reward of the life-to-come by going through them, it follows that the Holy Prophet صلى الله عليه وسلم in person and his most devoted Companions, may Allah bless them all, were far more zealous about all such acts of worship. Who can, after all these fourteen hundred years, claim that he has a better taste for worship and a greater desire to meet the pleasure of Allah? The noble Companion, Sayyidna Hudhaifah ibn Yaman رضى الله عنه says:

كل عبادة لم يتعبدها اصحاب رسول الله صلى الله عليه وسلم فلا تعبدوها فانَ الاول لم يدع للاخر مقالاً فاتقوا الله يامعشر المسلمين وخذوا بطريق من كان قبلكم ،

> Do not perform an act of worship the Companions did not perform because the former left nothing undone which the later could supplement. O, Muslim people (of the world), fear Allah and take to the way of those who were their earlier than you.

There is another narration on the subject reported from Sayyidna 'Abdullah ibn Mas'ud رضى الله عنه as well.

(Sunnah and Bid'ah, p. 14, vide al-I'tisam)

Why is *'Bid'ah'* prohibited ?

Let us think for a moment. When all these things were being practiced as acts of worship during the very time of the noble Companions, why would someone take to methods which were not put into practice by the Holy Prophet صلى الله عليه وسلم and his Companions? Does it mean that these recently instituted methods of worship were not, God forbid, known to the Holy Prophet صلى الله عليه وسلم and his blessed Companions? Is it that such claimants have come to know of these methods all of a sudden at this late date and that is why they are busy following them?

Introducing any *'Bid'ah'* in the established religion amounts to imputing a breach of trust on the part of the Messenger of Allah.

And if someone was to say that they knew it but he did not communicate this knowledge to his people, would this not be, God forbid, an accusation that he committed a breach of trust in matters of religion and that he failed to fulfil his duties of conveying the prophetic message? Therefore, Imam Malik has said: 'Anyone who originates a *'Bid'ah'* really claims that the noble Messenger of Allah is, God forbid, guilty of a breach of trust in his mission of prophethood by not telling the whole truth.'

(Sunnah and *Bid'ah,* p. 15)

Introducing a *Bid'ah* amounts to claiming that the religion of Islam did not reach its completion within the age of prophethood with the great proclamation of the Holy Qur'an:

اَلْيَوْمَ اَكْمَلْتُ لَكُمْ دِيْنَكُمْ

Today, I have made your religion complete for you.

In short, how can any Muslim accept the introduction of new methods in acts of worship which, for all practical purposes, aim to establish that the Shari'ah of Islam is being completed now? Certainly, not knowingly and consciously.

Therefore, let this be an article of faith with you that any method of acts of worship which was not initiated by the Holy Prophet صلى الله عليه وسلم and his noble Companions, no matter how attractive or preferable it may appear to be, is not good in the sight of Allah Almighty and His noble Messenger. Imam Malik has put this very succinctly in the following words:

> "What was not part of the religion then, cannot be taken as religion now."

So, the fact is that the Holy Prophet and the noble Companions had discarded these methods, God forbid, not because of ignorance, or lethargy, or heedlessness, but because of their being erroneous and harmful as understood by them.

If someone starts offering four *raka'at* in place of the prescribed three *raka'at* of *Maghrib Salah*, or three or four *raka'at* instead of the prescribed two of *Fajr Salah*, or continues on with his fast right upto the time of *'Isha* instead of breaking it at *Maghrib*, the result will be that every sane Muslim of our time will declare this to be bad, false and impermissible, even though this well-meaning simpleton obviously committed no act of sin - what he did was recite a little more of the words of Allah - yet it was unanimously declared as bad and impermissible. Was it not because he acted in excess, adding to and padding on the method of worship given and taught by the Prophet of Islam? Was it not that by doing so he altered the very form of the worship as prescribed, and in a way, claimed that the Holy Prophet صلى الله عليه وسلم had not left the Shari'ah of Islam in its most complete form which, incidentally, he was the one to have completed? Or, is it that the noble Prophet صلى الله عليه وسلم has, God forbid, committed a breach of trust and failed to perform his duly conclusively when he did not pass on these new and useful methods of worship to those he was addressing ?

Now you can see the difference between self-invented offering of four instead of three *raka'at* of *Salah* and the adding of conditions and methods in prayers, supplications, *darud* and *salam,* conditions and methods which have not been reported from the Holy Prophet صلی اللہ علیہ وسلم and the noble Companions. The fact is that adding restrictions and conditions from one's own side amounts to modifying and altering the Shari'ah brought by the Prophet of Islam صلی اللہ علیہ وسلم therefore, it has been strongly checked.

'Bid'ah is a way to alter religion

The worst element of *'Bid'ah'* is that once people are allowed to inject and perpetuate restrictions, conditions and ever-new methods in the area of acts of worship on their own, it would result in altering the originally established religion. Once allowed to take its course, a time will come when it would become impossible to find out the real and original acts of worship taught and practiced by the Holy Prophet صلی اللہ علیہ وسلم in content and manner. Alterations and interpolations in religion professed by earlier Scriptural communities were caused because they invented new methods of their own, superimposing the methods of worship prescribed by their Books and taught by their Prophets. Once these alterations found currency, there came the time when there remained no distinction between the percepts of the original religion and the practice of the newly invented customs.

To sum up, it can be said that anything which constitutes *'Bid'ah'* in the terminology of the Shari'ah is absolutely prohibited and impermissible. However, there are some grades of *'Bid'aat'*. Some are patently *haram* (forbidden) and close to *shirk* which is the ascribing of partners to the divinity of Allah. Some are reprehensible in the degree of unlawfulness (مکروہ تحریمی) while some others are reprehensible in the degree of taste. (مکروہ تنزیہی)

(Sunnah and *Bid'ah*, pp. 14-21)

Great emphasis has been laid on the evils of innovations in established religion, and on the need to abstain from them, in the Holy Qur'an, *Hadith*, reports of the Companions, their Successors and the Imams. Out of the many verses and narrations contained therein, some are being quoted below:

The Refutation of 'Bid'ah' in the Qur'an and Hadith

'Allama Shatibi has cited a fairly large number of Qur'anic verses in Kitabul-I'tisam which deal with this subject. Two of these are being quoted below:

وَلَا تَكُونُوا مِنَ الْمُشْرِكِينَ . مِنَ الَّذِينَ فَرَّقُوا دِينَهُمْ وَكَانُوا شِيَعًا، كُلُّ حِزْبٍ بِمَا لَدَيْهِمْ فَرِحُونَ

Do not be among the *mushrikin*, among those who caused schism in their religion and became sects - every faction pleased with what it has.

(30:31-32)

Sayyidah 'Aishah Siddiqah رضی اللہ عنہا reported an explanation of this verse from the Holy Prophet صلی اللہ علیہ وسلم who said that the reference here is to the factions or parties of the followers of *Bid'ah*.

(al-I'tisam, v. 1, p. 65)

قُلْ هَلْ نُنَبِّئُكُمْ بِالْأَخْسَرِينَ أَعْمَالًا. الَّذِينَ ضَلَّ سَعْيُهُمْ فِي الْحَيَوٰةِ الدُّنْيَا وَهُمْ يَحْسَبُونَ أَنَّهُمْ يُحْسِنُونَ صُنْعًا

> Say: Do you want us to tell you as to the biggest losers deed-wise, those whose efforts in the present life have gone waste, while they are under the impression that they are doing fine.
>
> (18:103-104)

While explaining *"al-akhsarina a'mala"* in the verse quoted above, Sayyidna 'Ali رضى الله عنه and Sufyan al-Thauri have taken it to mean the initiators and followers of *'Bid'ah.* There is no doubt that this verse presents a perfect profile of those who indulge in *'Bid'ah'* in the sense that they are quite pleased with deeds they have themselves invented which they think are the very empitome of good and that by pursuing them, they are investing in what shall serve them well in the life-to-come, although the truth is that such deeds of theirs have no weight or reward in the sight of Allah Almighty and His Messenger صلى الله عليه وسلم, Instead, these are nothing but sin.

(Sunnah and *Bid'ah,* p. 22)

Hadith Narrations about the Evils of 'Bid'ah'

Out of the many *ahadith* on the evils of *'Bid'ah'* and the methods to check them, some are quoted below:

1. Narrated Sayyidah 'A'ishah رضى الله عنها that the Holy Prophet صلى الله عليه وسلم said:

من احدث فى امرنا هذا ما ليس منه فهورد ،

> Whoever introduces something new in our given faith, that does not belong there, stands rejected.

(Mishkat from al-Bukhari)

2. Narrated Sayyidna Jabir ibn 'Abdullah رضى الله عنه that the Holy Prophet صلى الله عليه وسلم used to

say in his sermon:

اما بعد فانّ خيرا لحديث كتاب الله و خيرالهدى هدى محمد صلى الله عليه وسلم ، وشرّ الامور مُحدثاتها وكلُّ بدعةٍ ضلالةٌ

... After that, be sure that the best word is the Word of Allah, and the best Way is the way of Muhammad صلى الله عليه وسلم and the worst of things are innovations therein, and every innovation (in religion) is an error (which leads astray).

This is as it appears in Muslim while a narration from Nasa'i puts it as:

كل محدثة بدعة كُلُّ بدعة فى النّار ،

Every new addition (in worship) is *Bid'ah* (innovation) and every *Bid'ah* leads into the Hell.

(al-I'tisam, v.1, p. 76)

Sayyidna 'Umar رضى الله عنه used to deliver his sermon in the same words and Sayyidna 'Abdullah ibn Mas'ud رضى الله عنه also used the same words in his sermon adding the following words soon after:

انكم ستحدثون ويحدث لكم فكل محدثة ضلالةٌ وكُلُّ ضلالة فى النّار ،

You too will add new things and people will invent new things (in worship) for you. Be warned, every new method (of worship) is error (leading you astray) and every error leads into the Hell.

(al-I'tisam, v.1, p. 76)

3. According to a narration from Sayyidna Abu Hurayrah رضى الله عنه appearing in Sahih Muslim, the Holy Prophet صلى الله عليه وسلم said:

من دعا الى الهدى كان له من الاجر مثل اجور من يتبعه لاينقصُ ذلك
من اجورهم شيئاً ومن دعا الى ضلالة كان عليه من الاثم مثل اثام من
من يتبعه ولاينقصُ ذلك من اثامهم شيئا،

> "Whoever invites people to the right path, for him there is the reward of those who follow him, without the least decrease in their respective rewards. And whoever invites people to error, on him falls the sin of all those who follow him, without the least decrease in their respective sins."

Those who keep inventing ever-new methods in prescribed acts of worship and go about enticing people to follow them should really think about the evil consequences of doing so because they would be suffering not only for what they do in person but the onus of misleading all Muslims who follow them shall fall on them.

(Sunnah and *Bid'ah)*

4. Abu Dawud and Tirmidhi have narrated from Sayyidna 'Irbad ibn Sariyah رضی اللہ عنہ with sound chain of authority: "The Holy Prophet صلی اللہ علیہ وسلم addressed us one of these days. The sermon was very effective and very eloquent. Our eyes shed tears and our hearts trembled with fear. Some of those present there said: 'O Messenger of Allah, your sermon today sounds like some parting testament. If so, tell us how should we lead our lives in the future?'" Thereupon, the Holy Prophet صلی اللہ علیہ وسلم said:

اوصيكم بتقوى اللهِ و السمع والطاعة لولاة الامروان كان عبداًحبشياً
فان من يعش منكم بعدى فسيرىٰ اختلافاً كثيرا فعليكم بسنتى وسنة
الخلفاء الراشدين المهديين تمسكوابها وعضوا عليها بالنواجذ، واياكم
ومحدثات الامور فان كل محدثة بدعة وكل بدعة ضلالة

I advise you to fear Allah, to obey the commandments of Islam - even if you are ruled by an Ethiopian slave - because those of you who live after me will see many differences. So, you must stick to my Way and the Way of the most rightly-guided Successors. Hold it firmly (literally: hold it firmly with your wisdom-teeth) and stay away from newly introduced ways in religion because every new method of worship is *Bid'ah* (innovation in established religion) and every *Bid'ah* is error (which leads into the Hell).

(al-I'tisam)

5. And Sayyidah 'Aishah رضی الله عنها said:

"One who goes to a practitioner of *Bid'ah* (an innovator in religion) and paid his respects to him is as if he helped the person demolish Islam.

(Sunnah and *Bid'ah*, al-I'tisam. v.1, p. 84)

6. And Sayyidna Hasan al-Basri رضی الله عنه reports that the Holy Prophet صلی الله علیه وسلم said:

"If you do not wish to be held up on the Bridge of *Sirat* and that you go straight into the Paradise, then, do not use your personal opinion to carve out a new method in the religion given by Allah."

(al-I'tisam)

7. The noble Companion, Sayyidna Hudhaifah ibn Yaman رضی الله عنه said:

"Out of the many errors which I fear may afflict Muslims, two are most dangerous: One: That they start preferring what they see around them over what they know on the authority of the Sunnah of the Holy Prophet صلى الله عليه وسلم Two: That they go astray unconsciously."

(Sunnah and *Bid'ah*, p. 36)

8. And it was Sayyidna Hudhifah رضى الله عنه who also said:

"By God, time will come when religious innovations (*Bid'aat*) will become so widely spread that a person who dares abandon one of these will be accused by people of having abandoned a Sunnah!"

(al-I'tisam, v.1, p. 90)

9. Sayyidna 'Abdullah ibn Mas'ud رضى الله عنه said:

"O my people, do not take to *Bid'ah* and do not spoil your acts of worship by excess, exaggeration and the search for pseudo-depths. Stay firmly with methods which are original. Go by what you know on the authority of Sunnah, and leave out what you do not know in that manner."

10. Sayyidna Hasan al-Basri رضى الله عنه said:

"The more a practitioner of *Bid'ah* exerts; with his *salah* and *Sawm*, the more estranged he becomes from Allah Almighty."

He also said:

"Do not sit with a man of *Bid'ah*; he will cause sickness in your heart."

(Sunnah and *Bid'ah*, p. 27)

11. Sayyidna Sufyan al-Thauri رضی اللہ عنہ said:

"No word is straight without deed, and no word and deed are straight without the intention, and the combination of the word, the deed and the intention shall not be straight until it corresponds to the Sunnah."

(Sunnah and *Bid'ah*, p. 27)

12. Sayyidna Abu 'Amru ash-Shaibani رضی اللہ عنہ says:

"A man of *Bid'ah* is not blessed with the very motivation to repent (because he lives under the impression that he is really not committing any sin - why then would he repent, and to whom?)"

(Sunnah and *Bid'ah*, p. 27)

This far we have taken up the status of *Bid'ah* as seen through broad principles. Now we point out to specific shortcomings noticed in our contemporary society and to false customs and innovations practiced therein. In view of our subject of discussion, these relate to the incidences of sickness, death, funeral services for the deceased and the care of the survivors. Since a large number of such false practices have seeped into these areas, we have organized our submission under three distinct heads as follows:

1. Customs before death

2. Customs at the time of death

3. Customs after death

We hope our readers would not only keep their distance from them, but would also go a step farther and help others to stay away from them, doing it softly and wisely.

CUSTOMS, FAILING AND DEVIATIONS BEFORE DEATH

During the sickness of a person, the last one in which he is going to die, many shortcomings are witnessed. These issue forth from the person who is going to die on his sick-bed, as well as from those who are related to him. Some of these are as follows:

Not being particular about offering *Salah*

It is really unfortunate that some of those sick do not remain particular about offering their *Salah* when due, although there always exhists the possibility that this sickness of theirs might as well be their last. Let the loud truth that every sickness comes to remind of death be not lost to inertia and negligence. May be one failed to think about it when in good health, but carrying on with the same attitude of heedlessness into one's last sickness and failing to do what must be done with all possible concern, is certainly a matter of great loss loaded with all sorts of dangers.

(Islah-i-Inqilab-i-Ummat, p. 226)

Not uncommon are patients who are very particular about performing their *Salah* when in good health, but once sick, they become thoughtless about it. The common reason for this lack of active concern is that they keep worrying about their body or clothes being unclean or impure because of sickness or haunting doubt, or because they cannot make *wudu* or take a bath. Of course, the option of making *tayammum* is their, but they do not feel like doing it because it does not give them the ideal satisfaction. So, they would let their *Salah* go unperformed. This conscious *qada'* of *Salah* is an act of terrible ignorance. Once faced with scruples of this nature, the best course is to talk to an *'alim* and find out from him as to what should be done in that situation and then make the best use of leaves or concessions given by the Shari'ah of Islam. Missing *Salah* under such reasons is not permissible.

(Islah-i-Inqilab-i-Ummat, p. 224)

Some patients abandon their *Salah* on the excuse that their doctor has told them not to do it, although *Salah* is obligatory until such time that one is capable of performing it, even if it has to be by reducing regular movements to symbolic gestures. However, if there comes a time when one is incapable of making even such symbolic gestures, then, by all means, one can put off the *Salah* for another time and thus making up for the *Salah* so missed will be correct. Sickness is a messenger of death. One should be on guard when it comes and think of doing a little extra for whatever is in store for a person in the Hereafter. So, care, for caring is good for you.

(Islah-i-Inqilab-i-Ummat, v.1, p. 226)

Some patients are, no doubt, very punctual about their *Salah* but, because of the torpor of disease, or the onset of sleep, or too much weakness, eyes would close, stupor will prevail and they would not remain fully cognizant of the time of the due *Salah* to the limit that they would miss it, although they would never let this happen if they were alerted and told about the time of *Salah*. In such cases, what happens is that attendants who take care of the patient do not inform the patient about the time of his or her *Salah* just because they do not wish to disturb the patient and cause inconvenience to him. They would even go to the limit of stopping others from doing anything of the sort. If the patient was somehow alerted to make his *Salah,* they would not help him make his *wudu* or *tayammum* or change his clothes if needed or correct his orientation to the Qiblah. This simply makes them unwitting sinners. Doing so means doing no good to the patient and the attendant alike.

(Islah-i-Inqilab-i-Ummat, v.1, p. 226)

If a patient is unconscious, some people think that he is absolved of the obligation to perform *Salah.* This too is not correct because every state of unconsciousness does not absolve a person of his obligation to perform *Salah.* The state of unconsciousness in which a person is excused from making his *Salah* is the one in which he does not respond in spite of having been physically awakened and he remains in that state of unconsciousness continuously for a period in which six concurrent prayers could be offered as they become due on their time. If that be the condition, the person is totally excused of his obligation to make *Salah.* He is also not required to make up for this missed *Salah* later on by doing *qada.* However, if the state of such unconsciousness persists for a period less than that, for example, the time of four or five prayers elapses in that condition, then, the person is certainly not obligated to observe the percepts of the Shari'ah by offering his *Salah* simply because he is helpless in his state of unconsciousness; but once the person regains his consciousness, it becomes necessary that he makes up for the missed prayers by doing *qada'.* And in case, he delays in making up for his missed prayers, then it is necessary that he must, well before he dies, make a will to the effect that compensation *(fidya)* be paid for all such missed prayers.

(Islah-i-Inqilab-i-Ummat, v.1, p. 227)

The failure to observe what is obligatory in *Salah*

Some sick people make the mistake of making *tayammum* inspite of the fact that making a regular *wudu* would really not be that harmful for them. Sometimes their attendants or other well-wishers would stop them from making their *wudu* on the plea that the Islamic way favours convenience based on which one could get away with *tayammum,* the dry ablution. This approach is based on flat ignorance, for making *tayammum* is not permissible until such time that making a regular *wudu* is deemed to be decidedly harmful.

(Islah-i-Inqilab-i-Ummat, v.1, p. 227)

Some patients are quite capable of performing their *Salah* in its usual standing position, yet they would sit down and complete their *Salah* in that manner, although it is not permissible to perform *Salah* in a sitting position when one has the strength and ability to stand and offer *Salah* as due. Therefore, one should be very careful about *Salah* and try to go through it in its most complete form.

(Islah-i-Inqilab-i-Ummat, v.1, p. 227)

There are patients who can certainly control their moaning and groaning while in a state of *Salah,* yet one could hear their 'Ahs' and 'Oohs' and 'Ouches' all too clearly which shows that they have no concern about their *Salah* which may be seriously affected by such extra interjections. One must remember that introducing such 'pain-words', or their likes in *Salah*, in spite of having the capability to control such utterances, renders *Salah* invalid. *Salah* demands utmost care and concern. So, be thoughtful when you perform it.

(Islah-i-Inqilab-i-Ummat, v. 1, p. 227)

Not doing *tayammum* in spite of having an excuse admitted by the *Shari'ah*

Some patients act quite adamantly when they would brave all sorts of hardships, face the worsening of their disease, even risk their very lives, yet refuse to bend and do *tayammum* - their motto: *Wudu* or bust! This is a demonstration of rank excess in religion. In fact, this is a veiled rejection of the leave so graciously granted by Allah Almighty. *Wudu* is a command of Allah, so is *Tayammum*. Both are His commands. The job of a servant of Allah is to obey the command and not that he starts playing with the desire of his heart and electing as to which of the two satisfy his sense of cleanliness better. This is not servitude. Servitude means obeying the command as and when it comes, and doing it with all love and sacrifice at one's disposal.

(Ibid).

Seeing the *Satr* of the patient unnecessarily

Another incidence of carelessness common these days is that people are not particular about concealing the *Satr* of the patient (parts of the body the concealing of which is obligatory under the dictates of the Shari'ah). People tend not to notice the knee uncovered or the thigh showing up. May be the patient, under pain, cannot take care of himself, but those attending him must be vigilant and maintain the obligation and dignity of the patient as a matter of duty. Seeing the

Satr of the patient unnecessarily is not permissible.

(Islah-i-Inqilab-i-Ummat, v.1, p. 228)

Another incidence of neglect occurs when the patient has to be given an injection or has to be taken for an operation or dressing, or when it becomes necessary that the attending physician must see the ailing spot. On such occasions, no attention is paid to make sure that the body of the patient is opened no more than what must be clinically opened, and that it is opened only before those who are in charge of the treatment. What actually happens is that the body of the patient is summarily thrown open before everyone, physician or non-physician, although it is not permissible for those not connected with the medical treatment of the patient to see any part of the *Satr* of the patient. This requirement is taken very lightly to the point of common neglect. Please be very careful about it.

(Islah-i-Inqilab-i-Ummat, v.1, p. 228)

It is permissible for a physician to see the body of a patient, man or woman, within the limits of actual diagnostic need, but others present there are not permitted to see any part of the patient's *Satr*. For them, it is obligatory that they should move out from there, or close their eyes, or turn their face away.

(Ibid).

Using impure and unlawful medicine

Another very common failing is that people seem to have forgotten about making the necessary distinction between pure and impure and *halal* and *haram* medicines which they use in the treatment of their patient. Such is the proliferation of medicines from all corners of the world - the genuine, the fake and the advertised - that people just do not bother with the need to first check what is being used. Sometimes people fall victims to using medicines which are not needed really that acutely. What happens at the end of the pipeline is that the patient is given *haram* and impure medicines.

(Islah-i-Inqilab-i-Ummat, v.1, p. 229)

Paying no Need to the power of prayer

People would do anything to buy, the best possible treatment for their patient, procuring medicines, arranging medical advice and providing everything else needed to bring him back on his feet, no matter what amount of money it takes to do so. But, they do not even think about *du'a* or prayer. Making a sincere prayer is a far cry - although this act of prayer has been recommended as the greatest method in such situations by the Qur'an and Sunnah. Not being able to raise hands in prayer is a matter of terrible deprivation. Unfortunate are those who miss this *taufiq* of *du'a*. If possible, the patient should himself make the *du'a* (prayer), because *du'a* is accepted when its maker is sick. If the patient cannot do it, the attendants and relatives and friends should do it. Be very attentive, mindful and sincere when making *du'a*. Isn't it that the sickness of a member of the family and the distress of everyone in the household is by itself prompting that it is Allah Almighty to whom everyone has to turn. Then, this is also the very dictate of one's faith that he should focus his attention on his Creator and Master, turn to Him alone for help and succour, and supplicate to Him for the health and recovery and the well-being of the patient.

(Islah-i-Inqilab-i-Ummat, v.1, p.230)

The wrong method of making *du'a*

It is a mistake that some people would disregard the limits set for *du'a*. Unlike what has been determined by the Shari'ah, they would go about making prayers as one files a complaint. Some of these would sound like: 'O my God, what is going to happen now? I am all ruined. Where am I going to put these children of mine? Who is going to take care of them? O my God, just don't do that. If you do that, I am finished. Where do I go from here?' This complaint and advice, all jumbled together, is son of telling God what to do about it. May Allah forgive us: This is not adequate in the presence of your Lord, not certainly the proper way to approach the most exalted Creator of the universe. *Du'a* should always be made as if one is a helpless slave. Once this is done, let the ultimate decision rest with Allah. Then, be content and pleased with whatever it comes to be. This is obligatory.

(Islah-i-Inqilab-i-Ummat, p. 231)

Errors in acts of charity

One such error committed by the patient himself, or by his relatives, is that they would give *Sadaqah* by having meals prepared in the name of some deceased pious elder which is usually distributed among the poor, or is fed to them at the house. The 'belief' behind this activity is that this pious elder would be pleased with the offering and, may be, he somewhat jacks up the wishes of the host. This 'belief' is *shirk*, that is, it admits of the partnership of a mortal in the divinity of Allah Almighty. Some people, acting a little more cautiously, 'believe' in the efficacy of their *du'a* or prayer, while underlying their 'belief' is the 'certainty' that their prayer cannot be rejected. Nursing such a 'belief' is also against the dictates of the Shari'ah.

(Islaḥ-i-Inqilab-i-Ummat, v.1, p. 231)

Some people 'believe' in the principle, life for life, when offering *Sadaqah*. For example, they would have a goat or some such sacrificial animal, keep it overnight close by the patient; while others would have the patient touch the animal before it is given out in charity, or they would even slaughter the goat near about the patient and then give it out in charity. They think that the patient by touching the goat has all his troubles transferred to the animal. Then, the act of giving it in charity, further blows these troubles out of sight. As for acting on the principle, life for life, they surmise that the sacrifice of the animal would save the life of their patient. Let this be remembered well that such a 'belief' is against the percepts of the Shari'ah of Islam.

(Islah-i-Inqilab-i-Ummat, v.1, p. 231)

Some people keep food, wheat, flour and money near the patient and give it in charity by circulating it round the patient three or five or seven times and finally having the patient touch it before it is given out. Here too, the assumption is that by doing so the sickness of the patient and the misfortunes that surround him shall be transferred to that thing and its being given out in charity will make everything unpleasant go away. This 'belief' too is against the *Shar'*.

(Islah-i-Inqilab-i-Ummat, v.1, p. 231)

Some people have fixed particular things when making *Sadaqah*, for example, *maash* (black lentil, associated with casting of spells in India), oil and dark penny coins. The common denominator here seems to be something black. Perhaps, the visitation of evil in the form of disease and distress is supposed to be black and these seem to have been countered by the selection of equally dark objects. Frankly, these cock and bull tales have nothing to do with the Shari'ah of Islam. In fact, they are against it. As far as *Sadaqah* is concerned, specially in the absolute religious sense, it is a remover of misfortune, however, no particular thing, or colour, has been categorically fixed for it.

(Islah-i-Inqilab-i-Ummat, v.1, p. 232)

Charity being what it is, yet there are people who deem it necessary to feed common kites out of the sacrificial meat offered in Sadaqah. This too is patently wrong. The Shari'ah of Islam has itself determined the end-use of *Sadaqah*. Poor Muslims - not kites - are the best end-users for it.

(Islah-i-Inqilab-i-Ummat, v.1, p. 232)

Making a will contrary to the dictate of the Shari'ah

There are occasions when a patient makes a will to be executed after his death and it happens to be against the dictate of the Shari'ah, yet those around him fail to warn him against his error which might have helped him to retract his step and save himself from the sin of making an impermissible will, or may be, he then would have opted for making a legally valid will.

(Islah-i-Inqilab-i-Ummat, v.1, p. 233)

On some occasion, people around the patient advise him, even persuade him, to make wills which are not allowed by the Shari'ah, for example, they would tell him to make a will for more than one-third of his property, or make a will in favour of one of the heirs whose share in the inheritance already stands determined by the Shari'ah, or prevail on him to exclude a legitimate heir from the inheritance through his will, or push him to enter into his will the desire to have the third or tenth or the fortieth day after his death observed ceremoniously, or that a formal covenant in writing be placed in the grave along with his body. All this, and everything else similar, is against the dictates of the Shari'ah. In fact, it is not permissible to even persuade people to do so. Quite contrary to this, if the patient himself starts making such a will, others should tell him not to do so. If the patient does not correct himself in spite of that and goes ahead with his 'ill' wills, then, the rule is that such *anti-Shar'* wills do not have to be fulfilled of necessity. In fact, there are some which it is not permissible to execute. Details have already appeared earlier under 'WILLS'.

(Islah-i-Inqilab-i-Ummat, v.1, p. 233)

CUSTOMS AT THE TIME OF DEATH

The state of a person whose soul leaves the body is a state of great pain. This is known as being in the throes of death. The mark of this state of agony is that breath loses its momentum, moves faster, legs sag down unable to stand firm, the nose becomes awry and the temples sink.

When these or similar signs show up, be sure that the fated agony of death has arrived. May Allah make it easy on all of us. *Aameen.*

Unfortunately, even at a time like this, all sorts of mistakes are committed, more so by women. Some of these are indentified below. Please read carefully and do your best to see that such errors are not committed.

Mourning and rending of clothes

The need to maintain dignity in sorrow is seriously compromised when women, seeing a member of the family in the agony of death, forget all about the need to recite the *Kalamah* of Surah Yasin while praying that Allah make the agony of death easy on their departing relative and that his final going away ends in what is good for him, instead, they break into crying and wailing. If the person on his death-bed is conscious, he finds this emotional outburst nerve-racking which is frought with many evil effects. Frankly, the poor person who is already going through the excrutiating pangs of death hardly deserves that he be subjected to this sort of additional harassment. Let this be remembered well that crying and wailing aloud, mourning and lamenting plaintively, beating chests and rending clothes are all *haram*, forbidden, and acts of sin. But, there is certainly nothing wrong in shedding tears, if one feels like weeping, on condition that there be no crying and shouting.

(Islah-i-Inqilab-i-Ummat, v.1, p. 233)

Bringing wife and children before a dying person

Grossly unreasonable is the practice when some women in a closely-knit family bring forth the wife of the dying person to stand before him, or the wife takes the initiative and does it herself. In the first instance, people around ask the patient as to why was he leaving his wife all helpless in this wide world, or the wife would herself voice the complaint and inquire as to who would be her caretaker after him. Everyone almost corners the poor soul to come up with an answer. This is regrettable indeed. Here is a man breathing his last. This is a time when he must turn to his Lord, but right there you have some over-eager people who would still like to turn his attention towards His creation. This is rank injustice meted out to a helpless person on his death-bed. The most desirable approach at this juncture is to do everything to see that his attention is turned solely to his Lord-Creator, and definitely not that it turns to concerns of this mortal world, even if the dying person himself elects to do so without a valid reason or need admitted by the Shari'ah (such as making a will).

(Islah-i-Inqilab-i-Ummat, v.1, p. 234)

There are occasions when the children of the person on his death-bed are brought before him. Emotional scenes are created - 'Who is going to take care of these children? Kiss them goodbye. Give them a last pat on the head.' - the already harassed man gets more harassed. He is deprived of thinking of his Lord while making a negative use of the last moments of his life by being involved with mortal concerns. Then the children hardly get any relief out of this encounter, in fact, they are disappointed, hurt. On a time such as this, even if he himself were to pine for his children, he better be asked to keep his attention towards his Creator, towards where he was going.

Just in case, he insists on seeing his children, let them appear before him briefly so that this longing of his heart does not bother him anymore. But, should it be that he does not just think of his children, then, do not remind him of them. This sort of attitude is usually demonstrated by women, and even by some men with a flair for the feminine. Therefore, it is necessary that people who are sensible and religiously-observing stay near the dying person in agony. In case there are such women in the family, it is all right if they stay by the side of the person on his death-bed. So, whoever it may be, the purpose is to take all possible precautions in this serious matter.

(Islah-i-Inqilab-i-Ummat. v.1, p. 234)

Not reciting *Yasin* and staying away from the body of the deceased apprehending ill women

Some people find it difficult to reconcile with the idea of someone's impending death, so it is either to offset the ill omen, or simply because of a lack of regard for the power of their Faith, that they would demur from the reciting of the Surah Yasin at that crucial time, even cringe at the very thought of its being recited, and would neither recite the *Kalimah* themselves, nor would prompt the dying person to recite it while he is conscious and attentive. Instead of that, they either while away their time in wasteful conversation or get busy doing things the right time for which comes later. All these things are an exercise in ignorance. One must stay away from them.

(Islah-i-Inqilab-i-Ummat, v.1, p. 235)

There are places where the heirs of the deceased seem to be running around driven by the desire to take possession of his wealth, property and belongings. The ailing person is left all alone and that is how he breathes his last. This is a terrible lack of concern for the deceased which amounts to tyranny at its ugliest. More so, when the rule is that it is not permissible to grab the property of the deceased in that manner since nobody can become the 'owner' of whatever he can lay his hands on illegitimately - it is obligatory to distribute the entire inheritance of the deceased formally in accordance with the rules already set by the Shari'ah of Islam.

(Islah i-Inqilab-i-Ummat, v.1, p. 235)

Some people do not sit near the sick person for fear of catching his disease, although no disease can, unless Allah so wills, afflict somebody else. If it so happens somewhere, that too happens under the dictates of Allah's wisdom and will. Nothing happens without His will. Experience proves it when nothing of the sort comes to pass on most occasions. Therefore, shun this hard-heartedness. Never be superstitious. Do not leave the sick person alone and do nothing which breaks his heart.

(Islah-i-Inqilab-i-Ummat, v.1, p. 235)

Exceeding the limit when asking the dying person to say the, *Kalimah:*

Not rare are those who take it upon themselves to see that the last words the dying person says be the *Kalimah;* for this, they would virtually hound him back and forth. A little phase of unconsciousness or an intermission of silence would bring them back on their feet pushing him to restart the process of seeking forgiveness and saying the *Kalimah.* The sick person, with such people sitting on his head, might brave it, say it somehow, but they would hardly stop at that. If they could have their way, they would have him keep reciting it non-stop. This is ignorance. May Allah protect all of us from such conduct.

(Islah-i-Inqilab-i-Ummat, v.1, p. 236)

Incidentally, the correct method of prompting the dying person to say *Kalimah Tayyibah* as taught by the Holy Prophet صلى الله عليه وسلم has appeared earlier under Chapter 2. Please act accordingly.

Some people are really fond of acting excessively, even at times that least warrant such exercise. They would latch themselves on to the dying person and try to have him keep talking right to his last breath. The moment he regains his eversagging consciousness, they would come up with one or the other of their waking calls - 'Open your eyes. Look at me. See? Who am I ? How are you? Want to say something? Want to talk to someone? Like something? - there is no end to this wasteful jabbering which bothers the listener torn between two worlds, and is definitely incorrect. Nevertheless, if it is necessary to ask about something in the light of the Shari'ah, for example, asking about the place where the sick person has stored what he was given by someone to be kept in trust, or asking about a debt or some transaction the truth about which is not known to anyone else, or asking about any other unfulfilled right due against him. There is no hitch in asking about these, in fact, it is necessary that it be done, of course, subject to the sick person being in no unbearable pain while having to respond.

(Islah-i-Inqilab-i-Ummat, v.1, p. 236)

Then there are other ignorant people who carry the simple instruction of seeing that the deceased person is oriented towards the Qiblah. They would virtually sit holding the dead body in that position. In case, the dying person, under some involuntary convulsion of the body in the throes of death, betrays movement of the body or neck, they would hasten with their effort to twist and turn the body back into the Qiblah-oriented position. This too is a gross error, and very much a rash of ignorance. It must be kept in mind that turning the body of the patient towards the Qiblah means that it should be done when it is not hard and rough on the patient, or when he becomes totally still. Doing this forcibly by causing discomfort is not fair.

(Islah-i-Inqilab-i-Ummat, v.1, p. 237)

On seeing a non-*Mahram* male in the agony of death

Another incautious behaviour is demonstrated when non-*Mahram* women (those marriage with whom is permissible) come out to stand before a dying person under the impression that *hijab* or purdah is not necessary at a time like this. This again is exhibition of ignorance, because, in case the person in question is conscious enough to see and think, then, appearing before him and seeing him is not permissible; but, should it be that he is not conscious enough, he would at the most not see them, yet these women would have unnecessarily seen a non-*Mahram* male. This too has been prohibited in the *Hadith*. Therefore, non-*Mahram* women should not appear before the sick person in his throes of death. Similarly, there are men who would appear before non-*Mahram* women in an identical situation and start looking at them. For them too, doing this is not permissible.

(Islah-i-Inqilab-i-Ummat, v.1, p.237)

Applying henna on the hands of a dying woman

At certain places there is an evil custom that women would apply henna on the hands of a dying woman. They think it is a practice recommended by the Holy Prophet صلی اللہ علیہ وسلم. Let this be very clear that it is not, in fact, it is impermissible.

(Fatawa Darul-'Uloom, Deoband, v.5, p. 245)

Making a dying wife forgive her dower

This is common practice, and a bad one too. When a woman is about to die, incautious people around would ask her to forgive her dower (*mahr*), which she usually does. Now the husband takes this 'forgiveness' as sufficient to absolve him of his obligation to pay the debt of dower. He would even refuse to pay it to a legal heir if he demands that it be paid to him. To begin with, and let this be kept in mind, the act of making one's wife forgo and forgive her *mahr* in this manner and under such distressing circumstances is sheer hard-heartedness. Secondly, if the dying woman is fully conscious and forgives her dower willingly and cheerfully, the rule is that the *mahr* or dower will not be considered as forgiven. This we have already seen in the preceding chapter on *maradul-maut* where it was explained that such forgiveness during *maradul-maut* falls under the rule governing Wills, and no will can be made for the husband, because a will in favour of a legal heir is false. However, other heirs of the woman, who are sane and adult, can leave, out of their free will and choice, part of their respective share in the inheritance from this dower. But, the share of a heir who is either insane or minor will not be deemed as forgiven, even if permitted.

(Islah-i-Inqilab-i-Ummat, v.1, p. 238)

Sometimes, there are people who force the wife of a dying man to forgo and forgive her dower, if it has not been paid by him. This happens despite the fact that the wife is not willing to do so under any circumstances, yet she ultimately wilts under the pressure of people around her or finds the chains, of custom too hard to break and so forgoes her dower to avoid being put to shame. Let us remember that seeking to have the dower waived in this manner is not permissible. This is open tyranny.

CUSTOMS AFTER DEATH

Committing sins while expressing grief

There are occasions when women weep and cry

paying no heed to the need of being properly covered.

Then there are places which witness the strange practice of taking photographs of mourning men and women for actual publication in the media. This too is *haram*, and a great sin.

There are some homes where women, moved by intense grief, would weep bitterly embracing their non-*Mahram* relatives such as the brother of their husband or cousins from the father's or the mother's side. This is also *haram* because the injunctions of the Shari'ah are not suspended or eliminated under the state of grief.

Sometimes, visiting women would intentionally take a line of conversation which motivates contagious crying. Still others would fake weeping. All this is wrong, and forbidden.

(Thanavi, Islah-i-Rusum)

The practice elsewhere under which women of the house, including those visiting, would come out of the house wailing loudly and following the *janazah* of the deceased as it leaves the house. This action of theirs makes them *hijab*-less before non-*Mahram* males. Doing all this is impermissible and *haram*.

Post Mortem

Post Mortem performed on the bodies of homicide victims or those killed in accidents is very common these days. Operation is carried out on the bodies to determine the nature of death as proved through inside parts. Majority of situations are such as do, not need a post mortem, specially when it is done without a valid need as admitted by the Shari'ah. Situations where such legal need does exhist, in other words, where it becomes necessary to save the life of a persor. still alive, or to salvage the property of someone lest it goes waste - a situation in which it would still be necessary that the rules of the Shari'ah are observed fully by seeing that the *Satr* of the deceased in not exposed unnecessarily and that the dignity of the deceased is maintained at all times. It is also necessary that all parts of the body, once the post mortem is over, be buried.

(Imdadul-Fatawa, v.1, p. 508 & Kifayatul-Mufti, v.4, p.188)

Delaying the bathing shrouding and burial of the deceased

Not uncommon is the experience when the burial of the deceased is delayed for untenable reasons, such as, the inspection of property left by the deceased, or the preparation for the distribution of inheritance, or to wait for friends and relatives, or just to have a lot of people assemble for the *janazah* prayer. Sometimes, this delay is stretched for as long as two days. All these practices are impermissible and forbidden.

(Dalilul-Khairat)

At some places, there is a custom under which a recitation of *Kalimah Tayyibah*, a hundred thousand times (counted on pits or seeds) is considered necessary. Added to this is the practice of inviting people to come and share in the completion of the recitation. Whether they like it or not, people would still drag their feet to come to join in. A person who does not, or cannot come, skips his visit to condole, and to take part in the *janazah* as well, just because of his sense of shame on being a no-show person in the first 'function'. Being a source of several ills, and the reason for unnecessary delay in burial, this custom too deserves to be abandoned.

(Imdadul-Ahkam, v.1, p. 103)

A sewn pyjama and cap for the deceased

There are geographical areas where the deceased, man or woman, is attired in a pyjama and cap at the time of shrouding. This is not permissible.

(Fatawa Darul-Uloom, Deoband, v. 5, p. 271).

Saving cloth from the shroud of the deceased to make a prayer mat for the Imam of the prayer

A common custom is that a cloth piece about a yard in length is saved from the shroud of the deceased, or it is bought as extra to the standard shroud. This is supposed to be given to the Imam as his due after the *janazah* prayer is over. At some places, the sheet thrown over the *janazah* is also given to the Imam.

The truth of the matter is that the very act of making this extra prayer mat and sheet is all wrong. This has nothing to do with the legitimate expenses made on procuring the shroud. Then the Imam has just no claim on them. And lastly, giving these out in charity once they have come from the combined inheritance is also not permissible.

(Ahsanul-Fatawa, v.1, p. 379)

Writing the *Kalimah* on the chest and shroud of the deceased and placing there a *shajarah* (genealogical tree) and Covenant *(ahd-namah)*

There are places where the *Kalimah Tayyibah*, *Kalimah Shahadat*, *Ayat al-Kursi* and other prayers and verses of the Qur'an are written in ink, or some other fluid, on the chest or forehead of the deceased. This manner of writing these is not permissible because the rupturing of the body of the deceased will desecrate what is sacred. However, the act of writing something with the symbolic motion of a finger when no scribing fluid is used and no trace of writing is left, is permissible, subject to the condition that this too should not be taken as something practiced or recommended or considered necessary by the Holy Prophet صلى الله عليه وسلم otherwise, doing this will be ruled as an act of *Bid'ah* and which it will be obligatory to abandon.

(Ahsanul-Fatawa, v.1, p. 351)

Some people would place a written Covenant of allegiance *(Ahd-Namah)*, or a *Shajarah* (genealogical tree), or a copy of Surah Yasin on the chest of the deceased. As an alternate, these are scribed on a stone and placed in the grave. When the body ruptures inside the grave, these writings are desecrated, therefore, this practice must be abandoned wherever in force. As for things which the Shari'ah of Islam does not treat with that degree of sanctity such as the cloth-piece belonging to a pious elder in the line, could be - if it must be - placed in the grave.

(Islah-i-Inqilab-i-Ummat, v.1, p. 241)

Adding a turban along with the shroud of the deceased

At places, when handling the dead body of prominent leaders, an *'Alim* or a tribal chief, people would add a turban (*'amamah*) to the regular three cloth pieces which constitute the shroud of a deceased person. Showing respect in this manner by giving an

'Amamah is reprehensible *(makruh)*. The Holy Prophet صلى الله عليه وسلم himself was shrouded in three Yemenite sheets. There was no *'Amamah* in there. This fact has been very clearly mentioned in *ahadith*.

(Imdadul-Fatawa, v.1, p. 510; Fatawa Darul-Uloom, Deoband, v.4, p. 259)

Beautifying eyes and styling the hair of the deceased

In some rural areas of the East, people line the eyes of the deceased with black *kohl* or *surma* (powdered galena - not 'antimony' which is an ingredient of bombs!). Some comb hair on the head, clip nails and trim hair. All this is impermissible.

(Fatawa Darul-Uloom, Deoband, v.5, p. 248)

A letter from the Imam for the shrouded deceased

There are people who would shroud the deceased formally and then put in his hands a letter of recommendation from their Imam. This too is baseless and grossly absurd.

(Fatawa Darul-Uloom, Deoband, v.5, p. 256)

Supplicating in congregation before and after the *Salah* of *Janazah*

At some places there is a custom that people would shroud the deceased, make the *janazah* all set to be moved, then, everyone present would jointly recite the *Fatiha* and make *Du'a*. Somewhere else this *Du'a* or supplication involving the whole congregation is made after the *Salah* of *Janazah*, has been performed.

Here is something all of us should remember. The

salah of *Janazah* is a *Du'a* or supplication by itself. It has been prescribed by the Shari'ah of Islam for the deceased. This supplication which is recited in congregation and which we know as the *Salah* of *Janazah* is a wonderful prayer for the deceased as well as for all Muslims, very comprehensive and very effective, a prayer which we cannot better even if we were to spend a life-time thinking about ways to do it. The truth is that there is no proof in the Shari'ah which could support the making of an additional *Du'a* in congregation, before or after the *Salah* of *Janazah*, or reciting the *Fatiha* in that manner. Therefore, this is impermissible, and is an act of *Bid'ah*.

May be, at this point, someone may doubt: 'prayer for Muslims, living or dead, is certainly permissible at all times, why would this become reprehensible at this particular occasion?' The answer is that Muslim jurists, God bless them all, did not prohibit people from making such prayers individually. This could be done at the time of the death of the person they knew, even earlier as well when they went to visit the deceased during his life-time. That they did it individually is proved by relevant material available in *ahadith* and in the books of *Fiqh*. Every Muslim has the right, in fact, it is better that he prays for the patient he goes to visit; also, that he prays for his forgiveness by Allah when he dies. He can go on doing this right through the time the deceased is buried, and for that matter, he can continue praying for him all his life by reciting the Holy Qur'an and by other acts of worship involving his physical or financial sacrifices, the reward for which would, hopefully, keep reaching the deceased by the grace and will of Allah. All these are situations in which there is no hitch in praying individually for the deceased and in doing things the reward for which is most likely to reach him.

However, the binding condition is that one should not invent anything on his own which goes against the Shari'ah and that one should not superimpose conditions or restrictions of his choosing, conditions and restrictions which were simply not imposed by the Shari'ah.

Our most merciful master, may Allah bless him for ever and ever, has prescribed for a deceased Muslim, the one and only method of praying for his soul in a congregation, and this method is known as the *Salah* of *Janazah*. On a personal basis, every individual can raise his hands of prayer anywhere, anytime. But, assembling in a congregation and making a prayer is proved as valid only within the *Salah* of *Janazah*. The practice of assembling people for making *Du'a* on particularized occasions, before or after it, is what people have invented for themselves. This sort of assembly or congregation is exactly what the jurists of Islam rule as reprehensible *(makruh)* because it is an innovation in established religion.

(Dalilul-Khairat, pp. 51-53; Imdadul-Mufti'in p. 444)

Things do not seem to stop at persistence with a malpractice. Ironically enough, one who does not take part in this *Bid'ah* is made a target of criticism. May Allah keep us safe against all sorts of baseless innovations in our Faith, and from attitudes of ignorance and error, and may He bless us with the *taufiq* of living while upholding the *sunnah* of our Prophet صلى الله عليه وسلم, and dying while doing just that. *Amin*.

Throwing a flower-spread on the *Janazah* or the grave

A counterpart of the wreath, a commonly noticed

custom which has gained currency these days is that people would throw a sheet-like spread made of threaded flowers over the *Janazah* and the grave. This is taken to be something good while bringing the body of the deceased for burial. Added to this is the burning of incense on the grave site, although there is no proof for any of these three practices from the authority of the Qur'an and Sunnah or from the noble Companions and the *mujtahid* Imams. So, this too is *Bid'ah* and impermissible.

(Imdadul-Ahkam, v.1, p. 92 & by Concensus of Scholars)

Shifting the *janazah* from one city to the other

Another custom becoming common is that a person who dies in a city, or country, other than his own, is not buried right there. Instead of that, making arrangements to shift his body to his home country and burying him there is considered necessary, even if it comes to bearing the heavy cost of air transportation to achieve this purpose. This too is an act of transgression from the legal limits set by the Shari'ah of Islam. The recommended *(mustahabb)* method is to bury a person wherever he dies. Taking his body from one country to the other or from one city to another for the purpose of burial is contrary to the preferred method *(khilaf aula)*, subject to the condition that this other place not be more than one or two miles. If it is farther than that, then, taking the body of the deceased to another place is simply not permissible Incidentally, exhuming a body after it has been buried once and then taking it away for this purpose is impermissible under all conditions.

(Bahishti Gauhar, p. 92)

Offering *Janazah Salah* in Absentia

According to the Hanafi juristic ruling, the condition for a valid *Salatul-Janazah* is that the body of the deceased for whom it is being offered should be present in front. Without it, the *Salatul-Janazah* is not correct. But, these days the custom of offering *Salatul-Janazah* in absentia is gaining currency (for reasons not necessarily religious). Since there is no provision for this in Hanafi *Fiqh*, those who follow it do not have justification for their participation in it.

(Imdadul-Ahkam, v.1, p.742)

Offering *Salatul-Janazah* repeatedly

Yet another error is being committed when *Salatul-Janazah* for the deceased is performed several times which is generally done at the time of shifting the body of the deceased from one city to another, in which case, *Salatul-Janazah* is performed in both cities. Performing *Salatul-Janazah* repeatedly is a *Bid'ah* and is classed as reprehensible in the degree of prohibition *(makruh at-tahrimi)*. However, if the case be that others have performed the *Salatul-Janazah* without the permission of the *wali* (acknowledged guardian or successor of the deceased) and the *wali* himself has not performed this *Salah* with them, then, he has the right to do it all over again.

(Imdadul-Ahkam, v.1, p. 735)

Publishing photographs of *Salatul-Janazah*

Contemporary times are not free of their curses, one of them being the publication of photographs of *Salatul-Janazah* in newspapers where prominent personalities are made to appear distinct, although this picturization is *haram*.

Performing *Salatul-Janazah* with shoes on

As part of a general lack of awareness about rules, it is observed that people would offer *Salatul-Janazah* in shoes they usually wear, or they would simply take their feet out of the shoes and stand on top of them, without first checking if the shoes are really clean, although offering this *Salah* with shoes on requires that the ground-surface and the sides in and under should both be clean. Otherwise, the *Salah* will just not take place. And if feet have been taken out of the shoes and placed on the upper part, then, it is necessary that this upper part of the shoes which touches the feet must be clean, even though the sole may be unclean. If this upper part of the shoes is also unclean, performing *Salah* with feet on it will not be correct.

(Imdadul Ahkam, v.1, p. 740)

Taking photographs of the deceased

When the *Janazah Salah* is over, some people would open the face of the deceased and take photographs, or have others do it, usually to keep them as memento of the departed person. Please remember that photography or the making of pictures (despite its currency) is forbidden in the absolute sense, and thus, taking photographs of a deceased person is also forbidden. The end product is that both the photographer and the photographed commit a major sin by doing it.

(Mufti Muhammad Shafi, *Taswir kay Shar'i Ahkam*)

***Making the niyyah* of *Janazah Salah* in a loud voice**

At places it is observed that people form the intention *(niyyah)* for the *Janazah Salah* in a loud voice.

This too has no basis. However, if the Imam was to demonstrate the way of forming an intention once in a while by way of teaching people how to do it, then, there is nothing wrong with it. This is correct as such, but making a routine out of it and giving it there is of something necessary is *Bid'ah*.

(By consensus of scholars)

Reciting the *Kalimah* of *Shahadah* in a loud voice while Walking with the *Janazah*

Customs have a strange way of creeping in. One such custom becoming common is that some people, one individual or more than one in unison, while raising the *Janazah* over their shoulders, or on the way to the graveyard, would give out sort of a caution in a loud voice - *'Kalimah Shahadat'* - and all those walking with the *Janazah* recite it loudly, although reciting *Kalimah Shahadat* and *Kalimah Tayyibah* or any other sanctified word of *Dhikr* in a loud voice while walking with the *Janazah* is not the *Sunnah* of the Holy Prophet صلى الله عليه وسلم He used to remain silent at this time as you may have already read in the chapter dealing with the raising of *Janazah*. So, this custom too is contrary to *Sunnah* and is a clear *Bid'ah*.

(Imdadul-Mufti'in, p. 176)

Sending eatables or money with the *Janazah*

At certain places, food grains or fruits or cash is sent ahead of the *Janazah* and these are distributed in the graveyard. An act of charity with the intention that its reward reaches the deceased is certainly something good, but doing this in a self-designed form has no supporting evidence anywhere in the annals of Islamic religious practice. So, based on more than one reason, this is *Bid'ah*, and hence, impermissible.

(Dalilul-Khairat)

Showing lack of concern for the etiquette associated with graveyards

A common failing observed in a graveyard is that people do not stop talking about the mundane after having reached where thin ground separates the living from the dead, a place to shudder and become instantly chastened, with thoughts of what would happen beyond the stage of interment, how long shall the wait be until comes the fateful hour of the last Day and the sorrows of the Judgment, and what would become of the one thus worried while still living ?

Islam has its way of greeting the living. It also has recommended a way of greeting the inmates of the graves as soon as one enters the graveyard. There are particular words authentically reported for this purpose. Unfortunately, most people miss this act of grace just because of heedlessness.

It is also observed that many people would bypass the normal passage of entry into the graveyard, recklessly leapfroging over graves just to reach the grave of the deceased. Once in a while they would end up standing on top of the graves. It should be kept in mind that doing this is forbidden. One should walk into the graveyard taking the known and set pathway, even if it takes a little longer to cover.

Then there are people who, once they are in the graveyard, would sit glued around the body of the deceased. The purpose is to witness the proceedings of the actual burial. But, this assemblage of people so close to the grave causes great inconvenience to the family members of the deceased and to those preparing the grave. Not only that, such crowding brings acute discomfort to everyone present there. When people mill around in this manner, many would be heartlessly trampling over graves close by. Let us remember that watching the proceedings of the burial is not something religiously obligatory or necessary, but causing pain to other people by our action is *haram* or forbidden. Then, trampling over graves is also not permissible. These are sins, therefore, stay away from them. Let only those working on the grave stay near it so that they can finish their job peacefully and swiftly. When the time comes to fill earth in the grave, that is the time to go near the grave and throw in one's share of three handfuls of earth into the grave. Some people act very haste-fully while moving in to throw earth in the grave. They would push, mob or crane over each other in that effort, causing acute discomfort. This too is impermissible.

Showing the face of the deceased to his grave

Some people think it is necessary to show the face of the deceased to the grave by opening the shroud once the body has been placed inside. This has no basis in the Shari'ah.

(Islah-i-Inqilab-i-Ummat, p. 241)

Turning only the face of the deceased towards the Qiblah

It is noticed that some people place the body of the deceased in the grave flat on its back and turn just the face of the deceased towards the Qiblah. The rest of the body is not turned on its side. This too is against clear juristic rulings. The correct method is to carefully turn the entire body of the deceased oriented towards the Qiblah.

(Islah-i-Inqilab-i-Ummat, p. 240)

Burying as trust (*Amanat*)

There are places where people would place the body of a person who died elsewhere in a coffin and bury it saying that they were doing it for the time being as a matter of trust. Then, on some other occasion, they would take the coffin out and then carry it to their native land for reburial. Let this be clear that once the body has been buried, whether buried as a trust or without it, it cannot be taken out as it is impermissible. As for burying as *amanat* or trust, there is no basis for it in the Shari'ah.

('Azizul-Fatawa, v.1, p. 342)

Placing self-proposed things on or inside the grave

Some people would place pebbles on which they have recited the *Quls* on the grave by the side where rests the head of the deceased (*Qul* stands for the four Surahs towards the end of the Qur'an which begin with the word, *qul*, that is, Surahs al-Kafirun, al-Ikhlas, al-Falaq and an-Naas). Having no proof in the Shari'ah, this act is *Bid'ah* and must be abandoned. So is the incidence of leaving any food items there, or that of placing the deceased on some sort of mattress spread on the floor of the grave. These too are baseless and must be abandoned.

(By a concensus of scholars)

Telling the deceased how to answer questions posed by angels, *Munkir* and *Nakir*, who visit the grave after the burial

There are people who, after they have buried the deceased, put their finger on the grave and start a dialogue with the deceased - 'Now, if some angel asks you as to who is your Lord, you say: My Lord is Allah and my Prophet is Muhammad صلى الله عليه وسلم and my religion is Islam' - which incidentally is the way of the *Rawafid* and obviously not free from its ill offshoots, Therefore, such prompting is unrealistic and should be avoided.

(Imdadul-Ahkam, v.1, pp. 115-119)

Reciting Surah al-Muzzammil and calling *Adhan* after the burial

There are places where people would sit in a circle and deem it necessary to recite Surah al-Muzzammil or to raise hands of prayer collectively. Also, the incidence of calling *Adhan* on the grave after the burial in a certain part of Pakistan is quite common. None of these practices have any proof in the Qur'an and Sunnah, nor in the practice and teaching of the Companions, their Successors, the *mujtahid* Imams and the most revered elders of the community. This custom is, therefore, a *Bid'ah*.

(By a concensus of scholars)

Fortifying the grave

The custom of making reinforced graves has become very common. Some people would do it using the traditional ingredients of lime and sand. Others use cement-concrete blocks. There are still others who would give their dear ones a marble structure on the grave. Doing anything of the sort is impermissible. *Ahadith* clearly forbid these.

(Fatawa Darul-Uloom Deoband, v.5, p. 377)

Putting domes on the grave and railings around it

Some people let part of the top portion of the grave keep showing its earth-filled surface, but go ahead and put up a reinforced structure covering the sides and the front and the back of the grave, using bricks, blocks or RCC work, adding trellises around, or even a marble fence, or a railing in some other material. Then there are those who would go further ahead and mount a dome, a cupola or an arch over the grave. All this is impermissible and is an act of *Bid'ah*. *Ahadith* forbid it.

(Fatawa Darul-Uloom, v. 5, p. 395)

Lighting lamps on the grave: *morte et lumiere*

The custom of putting the traditional oil lamps or candles on the graves is common sight. Regular effort is made to do this on special nights of *Jumu'ah, Mi'raj, Bara'ah* and that of *Qadr,* with displays of spots, neons, colour series and other sorts of decorative lights. All this is impermissible, and is *Bid'ah* (a 'shining' example of that, indeed!).

(Sunnah and Bid'ah, p. 82-83)

Organizing *Khatm* gatherings for *Isal* of *Thawab*

When people return from the graveyard, they would get together, either the same day or the second or the third day, and sit down to recite the Holy Qur'an or the well-known *Ayah Karimah* or the *Kalimah Tayyibah.* If thirty parts of the Holy Qur'an are recited jointly, it amounts to a complete recitation of the whole Qur'an popularly known as *Khatm* which literally means 'to finish'. When a group of people finish the later, usually completing a pre-designated number which reaches several thousands, that too is referred to as the *Khatm.* In this matter the incongruity of things has reached the limits when such gatherings are advertised in newspapers! Then comes the supplementary activity of praying in group for the peace of the deceased and the bequeathal of whatever reward accrues from this recitation to him. This is followed by serving specially cooked food for everyone present. At some places the feast is replaced by a distribution of individual shares of sweets.

To begin with, this manner of getting together in a special way and observing the custom of doing *Khatm* and the *Isal* of *Thawab* for the benefit of the deceased has no proof in the Shari'ah anywhere, for which reason, this is *Bid'ah.* Then there are additional evils which lurk behind such practices. For example, friends and relatives would normally go along, show up for the day, but it is usually to ward off any complaints later. The actual *'Isal* of *Thawab* is rarely the primary objective. In case a relative was to recite the entire Qur'an all by himself while sitting at his home and let the reward be bequeathed to the deceased in all earnestness, the immediate family circle of the deceased would still not find it good enough, for they would continue complaining about the physical absence of that relative. Conversely, if he was to come there for a short while, sit down a little and excuse himself out shortly after, he would be spared of that complaint. Any act coupled with such absurd ways hardly deserves any reward, from which it follows that a reciter who himself remains deprived of the reward for his recital, what in the world is he going to bequeath to the deceased? As for the poor and needy, the truth of the matter is that, not one of them will show up just in case they found out that they are not going to get anything where they were going except a long session of dry recitation. This tells us that they come there in the hope that they would get something out of it. So, when the motive of their recitation is worldly gain, they are not going to get any reward for it. What, then, are they doing to bequeath to the deceased? In addition to that, when people make the recitation of the Holy Qur'an a means of affluence and influence, they earn a sin which keeps hanging on their head. Let us remember that the way it is not permissible to take something in return for the recitation of the Holy Qur'an, so it is with giving anything in return which is equally impermissible. It has been repeatedly emphasized earlier that praying for the deceased is something very good, but the Shari'ah has not restricted it to an assembly of people, or a particular day or date or time. Everyone can, when and where he wants, hope to bequeath the reward of any of his acts of worship, and make all supplications he wants to do for the deceased. The act of proposing and imposing ever-new restrictions, conditions and compulsions from one's own side is what constitutes *Bid'ah* and is, therefore, impermissible.

(Thanavi Islahur-Rusum, p. 172)

The feast hosted by the family of the deceased

As the custom goes, the family of the deceased invites, following the burial, its clan or family circle to a feast on a given day. Let us keep in mind that the invitation to the feast as well as its acceptance are both prohibited. Remaining always impermissible, this is an evil custom and everyone must stay away from it. 'Allama Shami says: "There is no doubt in its being forbidden." He has also mentioned the consensus of the Hanafiyyah and the Shafi'iyyah regarding its impermissibility. Furthermore, he reports from the Musnad of Ahmad and *Sunnan* Ibn Majah that this feast was considered impermissible even during the blessed times of the noble Companions.

(Imdadul Ahkam, v.1, p. 115)

Giving clothes worn by the deceased in charity

Following another custom, people give away sets of clothes belonging to the deceased, specially those he used to wear, although everything owned by the deceased, big or small, forms an integral part of the inheritance left by him which it is obligatory to distribute among heirs in accordance with rules prescribed by the Shari'ah. Then there are minors among heirs whose rights are compromised if things are given away summarily. So, it is important that nothing should be given in charity before the formal distribution of the inheritance. However, if all heirs are adults, and present on the spot, and they all agree to give something out in charity cheerfully, then, this act of charity is permissible. But, taking this to be something obligatory or necessary still remains an act of *Bid'ah*.

The gathering of women at the home of the deceased

Women are prone to assemble at the home of the deceased several times, although it is reprehensible to go back to offer condolences after it has already been done once. Obviously, they come to provide solace to the berieved family, but what actually happens there is something far from giving them comfort and strength in their hour of trial. They would rather remind the grieved family of the great loss while crying and making others cry. There will be other women sitting there talking about everything under the sun, preying on the hospitality of the berieved family and showing off their apparel, coiffure and ornamentation. Besides lack of propriety, this practice carries other ill effects and should, therefore, be avoided.

(Islah ur-Rusum, p. 174)

A visit to the grave of the deceased on the third day

There are places where people make special arrangements for a group visit to the grave of the deceased on the third day following the burial. It begins by a *Fatiha* ceremony at the house of the deceased which is repeated in the mosque of the locality, then it is done on the grave of the deceased. When the group returns from the graveyard, it stops after having covered a distance equal to forty steps, recites *Fatiha* there and finally, when they reach the house of the deceased, *Fatiha* is offered all over again. All these customs and self-appointed restrictions are nothing else but *Bid'ah* and must be abandoned.

Observing post-death days like the third, tenth, twentieth and the fortieth

Observing these or any other fixed days after the death of a person with the belief that doing so was necessary and with the attitude that anyone not doing so deserved censure is a patent act of *Bid'ah* and is impermissible.

(By concensus of scholars)

Celebrating the fourteenth of Sha'ban as the day of the dead

Some people celebrate the fourteenth of Sha'ban as the day of *Eid* for the deceased. Special foods, *halawa*, sherbet and their likes are prepared and given to poor people with the intention that the reward for this act of charity reaches the soul of the deceased. Sending a spiritual gift for the deceased is certainly a desirable act, but this is something for which the Shari'ah of Islam has not fixed a day or date or menu. In absence of any such restriction there, when people add up these restrictions on their own, they commit nothing but *Bid'ah*. So, there is no basis for such celebration in Islam, which is simply impermissible.

(By consensus of scholars)

Sending food to the family of the deceased: Wrong customs

Relatives send food for the family of the deceased. This is very good, very much in line with the practice of the Holy Prophet صلى الله عليه وسلم. Unfortunately, people have contaminated an otherwise desirable practice with too many evils, something which should be corrected. For example, there are places where families think of receiving things on a standard that they had maintained on some other occasion, or the sending of food by a distant relative despite there being a close one around is considered blameworthy. The poor but near relatives would, even though short of the means, send good food as if necessary, not minding incurring a debt in that effort. All such customs are against the dictates of the Shari'ah. When sending food, being simple and informal is all that is needed. Let a relative who has the ability and the convenience send food without being burdened with any of the considerations mentioned above, and definitely without bothering about relations being near or distant. The sooner we can correct these practices, the better it is for all of us.

(Islahur-Rusum, p. 177)

Observing anniversaries and memorial days

According to contemporary custom, the day a man of authority or excellence dies becomes the day when every next year it is celebrated with memorial gatherings, meetings and processions. There are receptions and feasts and a great amount of effort is put in to make the whole affair successful. There is no proof of such celebrations in the texts of the Qur'an and Sunnah nor in the words and deeds of the Companions and their Successors, the Imams of religious schools and the pious elders who followed them. Therefore, it is necessary that this practice must be abandoned.

(Imdadul-Mufti'in, pp. 157-161)

Celebrating *Urs*

In vast parts of South Asia, special annual celebrations are held at the grave sites or *mazars* of revered Muslim elders during fixed days of a year. These are known as *'Urs*. This is a kind of oblation or homage supposedly paid to the great spiritual qualities of the deceased elder held in high esteem. A great number of people take part in these celebrations and regard such participation as a source of blessings and rewards from Allah. In this connection, it is important to remember that visiting the grave sites of revered elders who were staunch followers of the *Sunnah* of the Holy Prophet صلى الله عليه وسلم is certainly a source of blessings, but the problem is that considering the restriction of a fixed date or time as necessary, or believing it to be worthy of *thawab* (reward), or to turn the celebration into a fun-fair is *Bid'ah*. More so, since custom has forced its way into some of these *Urs* spectacles with singing parties, exposure of women and many other modes of conduct which are forbidden in Islam. May Allah Almighty give us the ability and the courage to stay safe from all such acts of *Bid'ah*, and sins that latch on to us in their wake. *Amin.*

Laying ceremonial sheet-covers on the graves and making vows

Also very common is the practice of laying a ceremonial sheet on such oft-visited graves as a respectful offering. Equally common, specially among women, is the practice of making vows, or *mannat*, in popular parlance, in the name of the honoured occupant of the grave. Both these acts are against the percepts of the Shari'ah of Islam and are absolutely forbidden.

(Sunnah and Bid'ah, p. 76)

Making an offering on the grave and then taking it as having become something sacred

There are many occasions, such as, the nights of *Juma'ah* and *Bara'ah (Lailatul-Bara'ah* or *Shab-i-Bara'at)*, when all sorts of fancy foods, drinks, fruits and sweets are offered on sanctified graves to seek the pleasure of the occupant. Things like these are also placed there after the maker of a wish on the site being under a vow is pleased with the outcome. This is known as the fulfilment of a wish, vow, *nadhr* or *mannat*. These offerings are later removed from the grave and distributed among keepers of the site, as well as, among those present. This is regarded as a *tabarruk* (sanctified or blessed share from the offerings) from the haloed occupant of the grave.

Please remember that this offering is *haram* (forbidden) because an act of worship oriented towards anybody else is not permissible, and taking it to be *halal* (lawful), and a *tabarruk* (a blessed partaking) lands one into the hazardous environs of *Kufr* (disbelief). Refuge with Allah against all deviations from the straight path!

(Sunnah and Bid'ah, p.76)

Making rounds of the grave offering prostration

People are seen busy making *tawaf* (making rounds; also - circumambulation - an earlier tongue-twister for *tawaf*) of the four corners of the grave, as well as, making *sajdah* (the Muslim way of prostration as different from the Christian, or animist) before the occupant of the grave. That this is absolutely *haram* (forbidden) is an open fact of Muslim religious belief. Moreover, if this is done with the intention of an act of worship, it would then be a loud and clear act of *Kufr* (disbelief). In case this *tawaf* and *sajdah* are supposed to show only respect, and are not intended as acts of worship, even then, there is no doubt about their being *haram*, and very much a major sin. Refuge with Allah!

(Sunnah and Bid'ah, p. 77)

Becoming keepers or attendants of grave

There are people who disengage themselves from normal social living, seemingly by renouncing worldly life, who end up at known grave sites and shrines. They are known as *Mujawirs*, which literally means, neighbour, but it has come to refer to keepers, attendants or servers of grave sites, *mazars* or shrines. They virtually live off what is offered at these *mazars*. Many among them, quite contrary to being free from worldly temptations, are known to indulge in marijuana and similar other forbidden intoxicants. So, the setting up of residence at *mazars* in this manner is totally prohibited. It is also impermissible to help them keep promoting and sustaining this false custom.

(Sunnah and Bid'ah, p. 71)

The case of women visiting graveyards

These days, the frequency of visits made by women to the graveyards specially to known *mazars* of pious elders, has increased alarmingly. One should know that women can visit graves, but there are condition to it. For instance, such visiting woman should be old, not young. She goes there modestly covered. Then, she indulges in no *Shirk* there, that is, does nothing which would amount to ascribing partners to the pristine divinity of Allah. She must conduct herself following the *Sunnah* method of visiting graveyards, avoiding all activities which are against it and are classed as *Bid'ah* - offer no flowers and sheetcovers for the grave, nor ask the occupant of the grave to give her something, nor take a row and promise offering in return, nor Wail or mourn, in short, do nothing against the etiquette of visiting graveyards as prescribed by the Shari'ah. A woman who can fulfil these conditions is free to go to the graveyard. A woman who cannot fulfil these conditions, for her it is *haram* (unlawful) to go to the graveyard or to the *mazars* of pious elders. Observation and experience prove that women just do not observe their commitment to these conditions, specially on occasions of unguarded *Urs* celebrations which have become a mixture of forbidden practices, innovations in the fair name of religion and a breeding ground of many moral ills. Therefore, the visit of women, in particular, to these places is, no doubt, *haram*, and impermissible. In *Hadith*, such women have been cursed.

(Imdadul-Ahkam, v.1, p. 720)

Having the Qur'an recited on payment of wages for the *Isal* of *Thawab*

With rampant commercialism operating in almost everything one does in contemporary society, some people find it more convenient to hire a fluent reciter of the Holy Qur'an on wages and appoint him to recite it on a daily basis at the grave of a deceased family member. This reciter, in his estimation, thinks that he is transferring the reward of his recitation to the soul of the deceased. Let this be very clear that reciting the Holy Qur'an against payment of wages and for bequeathing its reward to the deceased, or having it recited by somebody else for this purpose, is *haram.* As for the recitation of *Ayah Karimah* and *Kalimah Tayyibah* and the arrangements made to have them completed in a pre-determined number of times for the purpose of bequeathing its reward to the soul of the deceased, the Shari'ah rules this too as *haram*, if done on payment of wages.

(Ahsanul-Fatawa, v. 1, p. 375)

CHAPTER IX

Post-Death States Of A True Muslim

Even death is a blessing for a true Muslim

Allah Almighty says in the Holy Qur'an:

كُلُّ نَفْسٍ ذَائِقَةُ الْمَوْتِ وَإِنَّمَا تُوَفَّوْنَ أُجُورَكُمْ يَوْمَ الْقِيَامَةِ فَمَنْ زُحْزِحَ عَنِ
النَّارِ وَأُدْخِلَ الْجَنَّةَ فَقَدْ فَازَ، وَمَا الْحَيٰوةُ الدُّنْيَا إِلَّا مَتَاعُ الْغُرُورِ

The verse quoted above, as well as several other verses of the Holy Qur'an, prove that the way life is, both materially and spiritually, a wonderful blessing of Allah Almighty, so it is with death which, both materially and spiritually, is also a great blessing, specially the kind of death which comes in peace, with a touch of Divine mercy, and which is blessed with a sense of security in this world and in the one-to-come and, not any lesser in importance, with the ever-live gift of unflinching faith present in one's heart. The reason is very simple. Life is temporary. It is going to end. After that begins another world. Death leads to what is beyond death. Whoever thinks about the post-death scenario while still alive in the present world and leads a life of obedience to his Creator, he is a lucky man for he has found the secret of his appearance in this mortal world and when he walks into the laps of death he is a winner having attained what he desired. The Holy Qur'an has described these states very clearly at several places, and in great detail, which is a treasure-house of good counsel of those who care to accept it. As for those who elect to stay deprived, for them there is not much left to keep except a recurring sense of loss and the ever-present pinch of remorse.

This is why the Holy Prophet صلی اللہ علیہ وسلم has said that wise is the man who understands the purpose of his life and is aware of the reason which brings him into this world, then remembers death abundantly and consistently, keeps preparing for what is after death, doing everything he could do for the life-to-come, and finally leaves this world having lived in it like a traveller. Poignant are the words he used to say this:

كُنْ فِي الدُّنْيَا كَاَنَّكَ غَرِيْبٌ اَوْعَابِرُ سَبِيْلٍ

Be in the world as if you are a traveller (away from home), or some wayfarer.

It has been narrated from Sayyidah 'A'ishah رضی اللہ عنہا that the Holy Prophet صلی اللہ علیہ وسلم said: "A true Muslim will be recompensed for everything (unpleasant), even for the vomit under agony, and for the spasm of choked breath too."

(Nurus-Sudur, p. 24)

Also narrated Sayyidna 'Ubaid ibn 'Umar that he (all of a sudden) asked Sayyidah 'A'ishah رضی اللہ عنہا about death: 'Should it be hated?' She replied: 'Why? Why should it be hated? When I asked the Holy Prophet صلی اللہ علیہ وسلم about it, he said: Death is nothing but peace for a true Muslim, but for evil-doers it is, not doubt, nothing but remorse.'

(Nurus-Sudur, p. 25)

For a true Muslim there is nothing in death but honour, welcome and visions of coming happiness

It has been narrated from Sayyidna Bara' ibn 'Azib رضی اللہ عنہ that the Holy Prophet صلی اللہ علیہ وسلم said: 'When a true Muslim is in between the state of his departure from the mortal world and the state of his arrival into what lies beyond called *Akhirah*, angels from the heavens come to him. Their faces radiant like the sun, they have the shroud and the perfume of Paradise with them. Then they seem to sit by the farthest limit of human sight. Then the angel of death descends close down by his head and says: 'O soul at peace with the command of thy Lord, return to thy Lord, towards His forgiveness and pleasure.' So, the spirit comes out (easy) like some drop (of water) sliding down a leather waterbag, even though you may see it (outwardly) otherwise (since the excruciating pain of the disengagement of the spirit from the mortal body is visible on the body everyone can see, but the spirit itself finds it comfortable). In short, once the angels have drawn this spirit out, they do not leave it in the hands of the angel of death even for a wink, rather take it and put it in the shroud and perfume they brought from Paradise. This releases a unique scent, somewhat like the strongest fragrance of must we could smell in the mortal world. Then the angels, spirit in hand, ascend upwards and when they pass by one or the other group of angels, they ask: 'Whose blessed spirit is this?' They tell him the best of his names he was known with in the world he left, his name and the name of his father, until they reach the firmament closest to the world in that state, from where they take him towards the seventh heaven (passing through the rest of heavens). Now Allah Almighty says: 'Enter his deeds in the '*Illiyyin* and take him back to earth (to answer questions asked in the grave).' The spirit is then returned to the body (corresponding to the conditions of the state of *Barzakh* which is a state in between, not like the world of our experience). Then two angels come to him, make him sit and put two questions to him: 'Who is your Lord and what is your religion?' He says:

'My Lord is Allah and my religion is Islam.'

'Who was this man (meaning, Muhammad صلى الله عليه وسلم) sent to you from among you? He says: 'He is the messenger of Allah'. They say: 'How do you know?' He says" 'I read the Qur'an and I believed in it and I attested to its veracity.' Then there comes a voice, a proclaimer proclaiming (the word of Allah): 'The answer given by My servant is correct. Lay the floor of Paradise for him. Dress him in the apparel of Paradise and open for him a door facing Paradise.' So, the breeze and the fragrance of Paradise reach out to him and the space in his grave extends all around him as far as he can see. Then a person, elegantly dressed and perfume-anointed, comes and speaks to him: 'Congratulations to you for this is the (blessed) day you were promised all the time.' He asks: 'Who are you? Your very face seems to be making that promise good.' He says: 'I am your good deed.' The deceased says again and again (all excited): 'O my Lord, let the Doom come so that I can go and see my family (then).'

(Shauq-i-Watan, p. 17-20, with reference to Abu Dawud, Ahmad and Hakim)

Post-Death Meeting with the Dead

Sayyidna Abu Ayyub al-Ansari رضى الله عنه narrates that the Holy Prophet صلى الله عليه وسلم said: 'When the spirit of a true Muslim is taken out in full, the servants of Allah already dead reach out and meet him very much like people of this world who go forward and greet some harbinger of good news. Then, (some of them) say: 'Give him respite for a while because he was in great pain (in the physical world).' Then, they start asking him about a certain person - How is he? Is he single? Is he married? - and if they happen to ask him about a person who had died before this one, who announces the fact of his death earlier than him, then they recite إِنَّا لِلّٰهِ وَإِنَّا إِلَيْهِ رَاجِعُوْنَ (To Allah we belong and to Him we are to return) and say: 'That is it, He has been taken to his abode, meaning the Hell). That is an evil place to go and an evil place to live.'

The deeds of the living are presented before their deceased relatives

Towards the end of this very *hadith,* the Holy Prophet صلى الله عليه وسلم is reported to have said: 'Your deeds are presented before those of your relatives and family members who are in the Hereafter (meaning - in the intermediary state of *Barzakh).* If the deed is good, they are delighted, saying: 'This is Your grace and mercy. Let these blessings of Yours cover him all the way through his life and then, let him meet his death in that very state.' Also presented before them is the deed of the sinner when they say: 'O Allah, let there be good in his heart, good that becomes the pathway to Your pleasure and nearness.'

(Shauq-i-Watan, p. 24-25, with reference to Sharh as-Sadr at-Tibrani and Ibn Abi ad-Dunya)

The angels, *Munkir* and *Nakir,* and the grave itself, are soft on a true Muslim

Sayyidah 'A'ishah رضى الله عنها said: *"Ya Rasul Allah* صلى الله عليه وسلم since the day you have frightened me by talking about the voices of *Munkir* and *Nakir* and the bear-hug of the grave, I do not seem to like anything." "He said: O 'A'ishah, the voice of *Munkir* and *Nakir* will feel as nice and soft into the ears of a true Muslim as the applying of *kohl* into the eyes, and the bear-hug of the grave will be, in the case of a true Muslim, something like a loving mother applying a tender hold on the head of her child when he complains of a headache. But, O 'A'ishah, woe be to him who used to have doubts about Allah. He will be ground in the grave like an egg being ground with a heavy grind-stone."

(Nurus-Sudur, p. 64)

The spirit watches its bathing, shrouding and burial

Sayyidna 'Amru bin Dinar رضی الله عنه narrates: 'The Spirit of a person who dies rests in the hand of an angel. It sees its body, how it is bathed, how it is shrouded and how it is raised and carried off to the burial place. The angels around tell him while the abandoned body is still lying on the bathing board: 'Listen to the good words people are saying about you (initial glad tidings pointing to forthcoming blessings).'

(Shauq-i-Watan, p. 26, with reference to Abu Nu'aim)

Who will go to Paradise?

Sayyidna Ibn Mas'ud رضی الله عنه narrates that the Holy Prophet صلی الله علیه وسلم said: 'One who dies towards the end of the month of Ramadan will be a *Jannati* (*Jannat:* Paradise; *Jannati:* One who will go to Paradise); and one who dies on the day of *'Arafah,* that is, in the later part of the day on the 9th of Dhil-Hijjah, will be a *Jannati;* and the person who dies after having given *sadaqah* (charity in the way of Allah) will be a *Jannati.*'

(Nurus-Sudur, p. 148)

Sayyidna Hudhaifah رضی الله عنه narrates that the Holy Prophet صلی الله علیه وسلم said: 'Whoever says (There is no god except Allah) at the time of his death, intending and meaning it most sincerely, will be a *Jannati;* and whoever kept a fast in obedience to Allah and for Him alone and died in that very state, he will be a *Jannati:* and whoever gives *sadaqah,* intending it truly and honestly, and then dies, will be a *Jannati.*'

(Nurus-Sudur, p.148)

Sayyidna Ibn 'Abbas رضی اللہ عنہ narrates that the Holy Prophet صلی اللہ علیہ وسلم said: 'Whoever keeps reciting *Ayat al-Kursi* after every *Fard salah,* Allah Almighty will bless him with the heart of the Grateful and the deed of the Truthful and the reward of the prophets and will shower His mercy on him - and it is (only) death which stops him from entering Paradise (which means that he will enter Paradise soon after death).'

(Nurus-Sudur, p. 147)

Sayyidna Ibn 'Umar رضی اللہ عنہ narrates that the Holy Prophet صلی اللہ علیہ وسلم said: 'A true Muslim who dies during the day or night of *Jumu'ah* will be delivered by Allah Almighty from the punishment of the grave.' And Sayyidna 'Ata' ibn Yasar narrates that the Holy Prophet صلی اللہ علیہ وسلم said: 'A Muslim, man or woman, who dies during the day or night of Jumu'ah, will be safe from the punishment of the grave and the questioning of the two angels, *Munkir* and *Nakir;* and he will not have to account for his deeds on the Day of Judgment; and his deeds will bear witness to his being a *Jannati.*'

(Nurus-Sudur, 77)

The punishment of the grave

The celebrated Imam al-Bukhari narrates from Sayyidna Abu Hurairah رضی اللہ عنہ that the Holy Prophet

صلى الله عليه وسلم used to recite the following *Du'a* (to educate his community):

اَللّٰهُمَّ اِنِّیْ اَعُوْذُبِكَ مِنْ عَذَابِ الْقَبْرِ

O Allah, I seek refuge in Thee from the punishment of the grave.

(Nurus-Sudur, p. 82)

Sayyidah 'A'ishah رضی الله عنها narrates that the Holy Prophet صلى الله عليه وسلم said: 'The punishment of the grave is *haqq* (true, real and fitting for the deserving) for men (not having repented from sins) punished in the grave, and all living creatures (except human beings and the Jinn) hear (sounds of) the punishment of the grave.' (Nurus-Sudur, p. 82)

Good deeds defend the deceased in his grave

It has been narrated from Sayyidna Ka'b رضی الله عنه that soon after a righteous servant of Allah has been buried in his grave, his good deeds - *salah, sawm, hajj, jihad, sadaqah*-come to him. Then come the angels of death from the side where his legs are. *Salah* says: 'Stay away from him. No way you can go through here. With these feet, he has gone to the *masjid* and on these he has stood to offer his *salah.*' Then they come from the side where his head is, when *Sawm* says: 'No way you can go through here. He has braved the hardship of hunger and thirst in the world for the pleasure of Allah.' Then they come from the sides, when *Hajj* and *Jihad* say: 'Stay away from him. He has endured extreme hardships on himself. He has carried out *Hajj* and *Jihad* for Allah. No way you can go through here.' Then they come from the side where his hands are, when *Sadaqah* says: 'You stay away from him. With these hands, he has given *sadaqah*. No way you can go through here.' Then, from the Unseen comes the Voice: 'Congratulations to you. You were good in life and good you are after death.' The angels of mercy bring a floor-covering from Paradise and lay it in his grave. The space in the grave is widened as far as he can see, and they bring a filigreed candelabrum of light *(qindil)* from the Paradise and place it in his grave, a source of light which keeps his grave illuminated right through the Day of Doom.' And another narration says that for him in the grave a door is opened, a door towards the Paradise. He sees Paradise and admires its aroma, when his good deeds tell him: 'You have certainly endured a lot of hardships for us in your life in the world. This day we shall be with you right through the time we take you to Paradise.' (Nurus-Sudur, p. 139)

The Benefit of *'Isal Thawab*[1] and *Sadaqah Jariyah*[2]

Sayyidna Anas narrates رضی الله عنه that he heard the Holy Prophet صلی الله علیه وسلم say: 'When anyone dies in a family, people in the family give *sadaqah* on his behalf. Sayyidna Jibra'il علیه السلام , the noble angel of Allah carries the reward *(thawab)* for this act of charity *(sadaqah)* on a tray of light all the way to his grave, stands there and says: 'O inmate of the grave, this is a gift sent to you by your family. Please accept it. 'So,

1. *'Isal Thawab* (literally, the transmittal of the accrued reward). When, after the death of a person, his relatives and friends give *sadaqah* on behalf of the deceased or engage in the recitation of the Holy Qur'an or pray for the departed soul believing sincerely that Allah Almighty will accept these acts of worship and that the reward in their hour of trial for having submitted in this manner to Him alone will reach the deceased.

2. *Sadaqah* is a charitable gift in the way of Allah, the recognition and reward of which comes from Him. *Sadaqah Jariyah* is a *sadaqah* the consequential benefits of which continue for a long time for the donee and the donor both.

the person in the grave is delighted and passes on the good news to his neighbour who like others who have not received such gift from anyone sulks under a sense of deprivation.

(Nurus-Sudur, p. 138)

Performing Hajj on behalf of parents

Sayyidna 'Abdullah ibn 'Umar رضى الله عنه narrates that the Holy Prophet صلى الله عليه وسلم said: To anyone who, after the death of his parents, performs Hajj on their behalf, Allah Almighty grants freedom from the fire of Hell and both of them are blessed with the real and full reward of a regular Hajj, without any reduction.'

(Nurus-Sudur, p. 138)

Deceased parents benefit when their sons and daughters pray for their forgiveness

Sayyidna Abu Hurairah رضى الله عنه narrates: 'Allah Almighty will confer on His righteous servant a great rank in Paradise. All surprised, he would say: 'O my Lord, whence did I get this rank?' Allah Almighty would say: 'From the *barakah* and benediction of what your son did - he prayed and sought forgiveness for you.'

(Nurus-Sudur, p.140)

Seven things the reward for which keeps reaching the deceased

Sayyidna Abu Hurairah رضى الله عنه narrates that the Holy Prophet صلى الله عليه وسلم said: 'When a true Muslim dies, his time to act is all over, but there are seven things the reward for which reaches him even after his death:

1. Whoever imparts the knowledge of Faith to anyone gets its reward continuously as long as his knowledge continues circulating in the world.
2. Having good children who keep praying for him.
3. Leaving the Holy Qur'an behind (a copy which people would read).
4. Making a Masjid.
5. Making a rest-house for the comfort of travellers.
6. Making a well or canal available for public use.
7. The giving of *Sadaqah* in one's life-time.

So, the reward for all these things shall continue reaching the deceased as long as they remain.'

(Nurus-Sudur, p. 140)

Two Other forms of *Sadaqah Jariyah*

Sayyidna Abu Sa'id al-Khudri رضی اللہ عنہ narrates that the Holy Prophet صلی اللہ علیہ وسلم said: 'Whoever teaches anyone some of the Holy Qur'an, or explains a religious question, Allah Almighty keeps increasing his reward right through the Day of Doom, until it becomes like a hill.'

(Nurus-Sudur, p.104)

The dead answer greetings

Sayyidna Abu Razin رضی اللہ عنہ asked: *'Ya Rasul* Allah صلی اللہ علیہ وسلم do the dead hear our *salam?'* He said: "Yes, they do - and respond, but you cannot hear.'

(Nurus-Sudur, p.103)

Four ways of doing a favour to the deceased

Sayyidna Abu Usayd رضی اللہ عنہ narrates that a man came to the Holy Prophet صلی اللہ علیہ وسلم and said: *'Ya Rasul* صلی اللہ علیہ وسلم Allah my parents have died. Is there a way I can do some favour to my father and mother?' He said: 'Yes, there are four ways in which you can still be good to them:

1. Pray for them.
2. Stay on the good counsel they gave to you, or any will they made.
3. Respect their friends.
4. Love and maintain cordial relations with the relative specially close to them.

(Nurus-Sudur, p.136)

Say nothing but good about the deceased

Sayyidna Ibn 'Umar رضی اللہ عنہ narrates that the Holy Prophet صلی اللہ علیہ وسلم said: "Talk about the virtues of the deceased and keep your tongue tied on vices."

(Nurus-Sudur, p.136)

THE PLACE WHERE SPIRITS LIVE

As for the place where spirits live, narrations differ - though, they are all correct. Then, there are positions taken by scholars about it. They vary too, but deeper investigation reveals that these narrations have no contradiction in reality. All narrations are correct as they are in their respective setting. 'Allama Ibn Qaiyyim demonstrates an excellent understanding of the subject and presents it with the support of sound research which brings forth the veracity of relevant narrations in proper perspective.

It is good to know that there is another state of being in between the present life and the life-to-come. This is known as *Barzakh*. This 'world' is the place where spirits live. *Barzakh* is larger than the world of our experience, but much smaller than the world-to-come, the *Akhirah*. *Barzakh* has many ranks and levels, and spirits too have different ranks in terms of deeds. These spirits will live with these ranks and levels in accordance with their respective deeds.

(Nurus-Sudur, p.13)

The relationship of the spirit with the body: The five types

We should know that the spirit is related to the body in five ways:

1. The first connection: The womb of the mother, though weak

2. The second connection: From birth to the rest of life. This is stronger than the first.

3. The third connection: In the state of sleep. This connection is very weak because, in a dream, the spirit gets connected with the world of *Barzakh* which weakens its connection with the body. Then, there is the (true) dream one sees. This is an outcome of the outing one has in the world of *Barzakh*.

4. The fourth connection: This is the *Barzakh* connection activated after death. Here, the spirit though leaves the body because of death, yet the spirit and the body do not get separated totally, rather the spirit retains a kind of connection and linkage with the body, and as such, the spirit takes practically no time to shuttle between one place and the other or one world

and the other. It comes and goes just like that. Think of a man asleep. He sees a dream, when in a flash of time, his spirit finishes its excursion of the universe of the physical world of our sense. It would even go for an outing all the way upto the seventh heaven, see wonders and return within the spell of a breath. It was for this connection that the visiting of graves became a practice as recommended by the Holy Prophet صلى الله عليه وسلم. The spirit hears the *salam* of those who visit the grave, and responds. This connection remains there right through the Day of Doom.

5. The fifth connection: This relates to the Day of Doom, when the dead would be resurrected from their graves. This connection is so strong and perfect that it can neither weaken nor be lost. Connections mentioned earlier have just no bearing or impact on this one for the simple reason that the body is not going to decompose, nor there is any sleep or death now.

(Nurus-Sudur, p. 114)

The four kinds of spirits

We should know that there are four kinds of spirits: the spirits of blessed prophets, the spirits of righteous Muslims, the spirits of evil-doing Muslims and the spirits of disbelievers and polytheists.

We should also realize that the place where the spirits live after death is a place nobody knows about except the Holy Prophet صلى الله عليه وسلم, nor can anyone describe it. The Holy Prophet صلى الله عليه وسلم went by the two worlds on the night of Ascent (*Mi'raj*), met spirits, and Allah Almighty let him become aware of so many things. Therefore, whatever the Holy Prophet has described in this matter is what is the truth. As for whatever has been described by the noble Companions, may Allah bless them all, they have described whatever they have heard from the Holy Prophet صلى الله عليه وسلم. They have not allowed their personal opinion to affect their reports.

Now, that the spirit is not like anything of this mortal world, nor can it be seen, so it is a gross error to speculate on its nature using the analogy of anything in the world of our experience. This would be like somebody trying to draw analogous conclusions by comparing hunger and thirst with wood and stone, or happiness and sorrow with tree and mountain, which in turn, would be regarded as no more than an unnecessary exercise in ignorance.

Once we know this much, let us open our minds to the proposition that the spirit of man is consigned to a category of its own which is in accord with the kind of deeds he has come up with during his life in the mortal world. Good spirits are in the superior category and live in what the Qur'an calls, *'Illiyin.* These are the spirits of the prophets. The Holy Prophet صلى الله عليه وسلم has met them on the night of Ascent *(Mi'raj).* Some spirits are placed into the pouches of green birds. They live in Paradise and go wherever they wish. These are martyrs who met their *shahadah* in *Jihad*-subject to their being free of debt. Those who have not fulfilled the legitimate right of somebody will stay deprived of entry into the Paradise.

(Nurus-Sudur. p.115)

Sayyidna Muhammad Ibn 'Abdullah رضی الله عنه narrates that a man came to the Holy Prophet صلى الله عليه وسلم and said: *'Ya Rasul* Allah صلى الله عليه وسلم if I were to lay down my life as a *shaheed* in the way of Allah, would I be getting something in return?' He said: 'Paradise.'

When the man rose and started walking back, he called him back and said: 'On condition that you owe no debt to anyone. This is what Jibra'il has told me just now.'

(Nurus-Sudur, p. 115)

Some spirits will live by the gate of Paradise. Some will be confined to their graves and keep facing whatever reward or punishment must come to them. Some spirits will be confined way down seven strata under active punishment. These will be the spirits of the disbelievers and the polytheists. Some spirits will be punished in chambers of heat and others in streams of blood. The prophets and the martyrs live in Paradise and go where they wish, by the leave of Allah. Spirits of people other than these live in *Barzakh;* their connection with the grave remains operative; they get reward or they get punishment. This is what is called the reward of the grave or the punishment of the grave.

(Nurus-Sudur, p. 115)

Spirits and the different states of their being

The spirits of true Muslims live in different states of being. Some live like birds on the trees of Paradise and some inside green birds and some inside white birds and some in the filigreed candelabrums hanging below the Throne and some in the form of the Paradisiacal man and some in newer forms matching their good deeds. Some spirits go on an excursion of the moral world, even come into their body while some others go about meeting the spirits of the dead elsewhere. Some spirits live in the charge of angel, Mika'il and some others in the charge of Sayyidna Adam عليه السلام. There are many more *ahadith* and reports from Companions regarding the place where spirits live, but we shall conclude our presentation by quoting one more *hadith* as follows:

Sayyidna Ibn 'Abbas رضى الله عنه narrates that the Holy Prophet صلى الله عليه وسلم said: 'The spirits of martyrs live in green birds. They go to streams of water and savor fruits and retire into gold candela-brums hanging below the Throne.'

Some scholars have interpreted living in green birds to mean that they would move atop green birds going around and seeing things. Some scholars say that their form is transformed in the world of *Barzakh* appearing beautiful like green birds. This is similar to when, at times, angels appear in the image of man. But, on the Last Day - the *Akhirah,* those spirits will be recast into the human form. A similar narration has been reported from the Companions, Sayyidna Ibn Mas'ud, Ibn 'Umar and *Ka'b* رضى الله عنهم اجمعين

(Nurus-Sudur, p.116)